D1008079

Costa Rican
Spanish
PHRASEBOOK & DICTIONARY

Acknowledgments
Associate Publisher Mina Patria
Managing Editor Angela Tinson
Editor Branislava Vladisavljevic
Series Designer Mark Adams
Managing Layout Designer Chris Girdler
Layout Designer Frank Deim
Language Writer Thomas Kohnstamm
Cover Image Researcher Naomi Parker

Thanks
Ruth Cosgrove, Carol Jackson, Wayne Murphy, Tony Wheeler

Published by Lonely Planet Publications Pty Ltd
ABN 36 005 607 983

4th Edition – October 2013
ISBN 978 1 74321 438 1
Text © Lonely Planet 2013
Cover Image Waterfall at Rara Avis, Costa Rica
Michael & Pactricia Fogden / Getty Images
Printed in China 10 9 8 7 6 5 4

Contact lonelyplanet.com/contact

MIX
Paper from
responsible sources
FSC™ C021741

Anyone can speak another language! It's all about confidence. Don't worry if you can't remember your school language lessons or if you've never learnt a language before. Even if you learn the very basics (on the inside covers of this book), your travel experience will be the better for it. You have nothing to lose and everything to gain when the locals hear you making an effort.

finding things in this book

For easy navigation, this book is in sections. The Basics chapters are the ones you'll thumb through time and again. The Practical section covers basic travel situations like catching transport and finding a bed. The Social section gives you conversational phrases, pick-up lines, the ability to express opinions – so you can get to know people. Food has a section all of its own: gourmets and vegetarians are covered and local dishes feature. Safe Travel equips you with health and police phrases, just in case. Remember the colours of each section and you'll find everything easily; or use the comprehensive Index. Otherwise, check the two-way traveller's Dictionary for the word you need.

being understood

Throughout this book you'll see coloured phrases on each page. They're phonetic guides to help you pronounce the language. You don't even need to look at the language itself, but you'll get used to the way we've represented particular sounds. The pronunciation chapter in Basics will explain more, but you can feel confident that if you read the coloured phrase slowly, you'll be understood.

communication tips

Body language, ways of doing things, sense of humour – all have a role to play in every culture. 'Local talk' boxes show you common ways of saying things, or everyday language to drop into conversation. 'Listen for …' boxes supply the phrases you may hear. They start with the language (so local people can point out what they want to say to you) and then lead in to the pronunciation guide and the English translation.

introduction 8

basics 11

practical 41

CONTENTS

5

social 97

CONTENTS

7

costa rican spanish

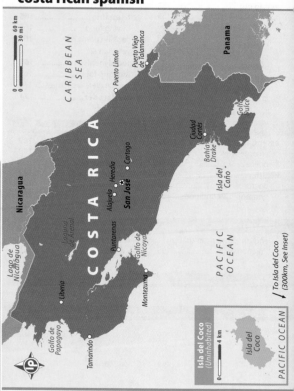

official language

For more details, see the **introduction**.

Costa Rican Spanish lounges under the beach umbrella of Latin American Spanish – the term given to the many varieties of Spanish that have evolved in the Americas after the Spanish conquests in the 16th century. The language that originally emerged as one of the branches of vulgar Latin successfully took root and spread in the New World and now has official status in 20 countries of Latin America.

Not only did the Spanish language successfully transplant itself, it also hybridised with the indigenous languages and became a colourful array of different varieties of Spanish. Among them, Costa Rican stands out as a unique linguistic entity with its own intriguing quirks of both grammar and vocabulary.

The main grammatical peculiarity is *voseo* vo·se·o – the use of *vos* (meaning 'you') as the second-person singular pronoun, which is considered an archaism in Spain. This is a feature that Costa Rican shares with varieties of Spanish found in other Latin American countries, particularly Argentina, Uruguay, Paraguay, Guatemala, Honduras, Nicaragua and El Salvador. In vocabulary, the abundance of diminutives formed by adding *-tico* ·tee·ko and *-tica* ·tee·ka to the ends of masculine and feminine words respectively – a cutesy way of saying 'small' or expressing affection – has earned Costa Ricans the nickname *Ticos*.

Perhaps what gives Costa Rican Spanish its most distinctive flavour is the rich store of slang expressions commonly known as *tiquismos* tee·kees·mos.

at a glance ...

language name:
Costa Rican Spanish

name in language:
español (costarricense)
es·pa·nyol
(kos·ta·ree·*sen*·se),
castellano kas·te·ya·no

language family: Romance

approximate number of speakers: over 3 million

close relatives:
Castilian Spanish,
Latin American Spanish,
Italian, French,
Portuguese

introduction

9

This phrasebook contains many of these unique turns of phrase to get you talking like a Tico or a Tica and blending in with the crowd. Take it with you and you'll learn exactly why the expression *pura vida* poo·ra vee·da embodies the friendly, unhurried approach to life in Costa Rica. You'll also learn a lot about other key elements of Costa Rican culture expressed in the language.

Though it's a distinct variety of Spanish, Costa Rican does share many similarities with its Latin American siblings which set it apart from the mother language, Castilian Spanish. Costa Rican was influenced by the southern Spanish dialect of Andalucia, from where the first Spanish conquistadors sailed to the New World. The most noticeable trait that sets Costa Rican pronunciation apart from Castilian Spanish is common for the entire continent – *seseo* se·se·o, or the absence of the lisping consonants *c* and *z*, as in *cerveza* ser·ve·sa (beer).

By learning some Costa Rican Spanish, you're opening the door to a world of over 350 million speakers – and be reassured, while it's a distinct variety with its own beautiful individualities, Costa Rican Spanish will be understood by speakers all over Latin America – and even in Spain.

This book gives you the practical phrases you need to get by, as well as the fun, social phrases that lead to a better understanding of Costa Rica and its people. It will also ensure that you can pronounce them like a true *Tico* or *Tica*. To help you get the most out of your travels in beautiful Costa Rica with its many natural wonders, this phrasebook also provides you with an ecotourism section listing the names of flora, fauna and natural features in both Spanish and English.

The contacts you make through speaking Costa Rican Spanish will make your travel experience unique. Local knowledge, new relationships and a sense of satisfaction are on the tip of your tongue – so don't just stand there, say something!

abbreviations used in this book

a	adjective	n	noun
adv	adverb	pl	plural
f	feminine	pol	polite
inf	informal	sg	singular
m	masculine	v	verb

Costa Rican Spanish pronunciation isn't hard, as most of the sounds are also found in English. The best way to learn the correct pronunciation is to listen to the people around you.

Costa Rican Spanish pronunciation differs from the Castilian Spanish spoken in Spain. The most obvious difference is the lack of the lisping 'th' sound. With a little practice you'll soon get the basics and even if you can't roll your r's or hiss out your j's like a Tico or a Tica, your efforts are certain to be rewarded.

vowel sounds

Vowels are generally short and clear. In a number of cases, however, two vowels can be very closely combined (so-called 'diphthongs').

symbol	english equivalent	spanish example	transliteration
a	run	*agua*	a·gwa
ai	aisle	*baile*	bai·le
ay	say	*seis*	says
e	bed	*edad*	e·dad
ee	bee	*idioma, y*	ee·dyo·ma, ee
o	not	*ojo*	o·kho
oo	good	*uva*	oo·va
ow	cow	*autobús*	ow·to·boos
oy	boy	*hoy*	oy
ya	yard	*viaje*	vya·khe
ye	yes	*tiempo*	tyem·po

consonant sounds

symbol	english equivalent	spanish example	transliteration
b	big	*barco*	*bar·*ko
ch	chat	*chico*	*chee·*ko
d	dog	*dedo*	*de·*do
f	friend	*falso*	*fal·*so
g	get	*gato*	*ga·*to
k	kick	*cabeza, quitar*	ka·*be·*sa, kee·*tar*
kh	as in the Scottish 'loch' (a harsh, breathy sound from the back of your throat)	*gente, jamón*	*khen·*te, kha·*mon*
l	let	*lado*	*la·*do
m	man	*manto*	*man·*to
n	not	*nada*	*na·*da
ny	canyon	*riñón*	ree·*nyon*
p	pig	*padre*	*pa·*dre
r	right (lightly rolled, but at the start of a word and in words with *rr* strongly rolled)	*pero, roto, carro*	*pe·*ro, *ro·*to, *ka·*ro
s	so	*celos, sábado, zeta*	*se·*los, *sa·*ba·do, *se·*ta
t	top	*tiempo*	*tyem·*po
v	a soft 'b', half way between a 'v' and a 'b'	*vago*	*va·*go
w	wet	*puedo*	*pwe·*do
y	yes	*ya, llamada*	ya, ya·*ma·*da

word stress

Words in Spanish have stress, which means that you emphasise one syllable over another. Rule of thumb: when a word ends in -n, -s or a vowel, the stress falls on the second-last syllable. Otherwise, the last syllable is stressed. If you see an accent mark over a syllable, it cancels out these rules and you just stress that syllable instead. Don't worry if you can't remember these rules – in our coloured pronounciation guides, the stressed syllable is always in italics.

reading & writing

The Spanish alphabet is presented in the following table. For spelling purposes (eg when you need to spell your name to book into a hotel), the pronunciation of each letter is provided. The order shown below is used in the **menu decoder** and the **costa rican spanish–english dictionary**.

spanish alphabet				
A, a a	*B, b* be *lar*·ga	*C, c* se	*Ch, ch** che	*D, d* de
E, e e	*F, f* e·fe	*G, g* khe	*H, h* a·che	*I, i* ee
J, j kho·ta	*K, k* ka	*L, l* e·le	*Ll, ll** do·ble e·le	*M, m* e·me
N, n e·ne	*Ñ, ñ* e·nye	*O, o* o	*P, p* pe	*Q, q* koo
R, r er	*Rr, rr** e·re	*S, s* e·se	*T, t* te	*U, u* oo
V, v be *kor*·ta	*W, w* do·ble be	*X, x* e·kees	*Y, y* ee *grye*·ga	*Z, z* se·ta

* The letters *ch*, *ll* and *rr* are no longer officially considered separate letters, but they're still sounds in their own right.

The relationship between Spanish sounds and their spelling is quite straightforward and consistent. The rules given in the table below will help you read any written Costa Rican Spanish that you may come across outside this phrasebook.

letter	pronunciation	example	transliteration
c	before *e* or *i* pronounced as an 's'	*cerveza, cinco*	ser·*ve*·sa, *seen*·ko
	before *a, o* and *u* pronounced as a 'k'	*carro, corto, cubo*	*ka*·ro, *kor*·to, *koo*·bo
g	before *e* or *i* pronounced as the 'ch' in 'loch'	*gente, gigante*	*khen*·te, khee·*gan*·te
	before *a, o* and *u* pronounced as the 'g' in 'go'	*gato, gordo, guante*	*ga*·to, *gor*·do, *gwan*·te
gu	pronounced as the 'g' in 'go' (the *u* is not pronounced unless there are two dots over the *u*)	*guerra, güiski*	*ge*·ra, *gwees*·kee
h	never pronounced (silent)	*haber, huevo*	a·*ber*, *we*·vo
j	as the 'ch' in 'loch'	*jardín*	khar·*deen*
ll	pronounced as the 'y' in 'yes'	*llave*	*ya*·ve
ñ	pronounced as the 'ny' in 'canyon'	*niño*	*nee*·nyo
qu	pronounced as a 'k' (the *u* is not pronounced)	*quince*	*keen*·se
z	pronounced as an 's'	*zorro*	*so*·ro

contents

The index below shows which grammatical structures you can use to say what you want. Look under each function – listed in alphabetical order – for information on how to build your own sentences. For example, to tell the taxi driver where your hotel is, look for **giving instructions** and you'll be directed to information on **demonstratives** and **prepositions**. A **glossary** of grammatical terms is included at the end of this chapter to help you.

a–z phrasebuilder

adjectives & adverbs

describing people/things • doing things

When using an adjective to describe a noun, you need to use the appropriate ending depending on whether the noun is masculine or feminine, and singular or plural (see **gender** and **plurals**). Most adjectives have four forms and the endings are easy to remember:

masculine	sg	*un sombrero blanco* oon som·bre·ro blan·ko	a white hat
	pl	*unos sombreros blancos* oo·nos som·bre·ros blan·kos	some white hats
feminine	sg	*una camisa blanca* oo·na ka·mee·sa blan·ka	a white shirt
	pl	*unas camisas blancas* oo·nas ka·mee·sas blan·kas	some white shirts

As you can see above, unlike English adjectives, Spanish adjectives almost always come after the noun. However, 'adjectives' of quantity (such as 'much', 'a lot', 'a little/a few', 'too much'), numbers, and words expressing possession ('my' and 'your') always precede the noun.

many cars	*muchos carros* m pl (lit: many cars)	moo·chos ka·ros
first class	*primera clase* f sg (lit: first class)	pree·me·ra kla·se
my passport	*mi pasaporte* m sg (lit: my passport)	mee pa·sa·por·te

Adverbs are formed by adding the ending *-mente* to the singular form of an adjective (in the feminine form if there is one). If the adjective has an accent marked in writing, the stress remains on that syllable with the additional stress in pronunciation on *-mente*. Adverbs generally follow the verb they modify.

She has a fantastic voice.

 Ella tiene una voz
 fantástica.
 (lit: she has a voice fantastic)

e·ya tye·ne oo·na vos
fan·tas·tee·ka

She sings fantastically.

 Ella canta
 fantásticamente.
 (lit: she sings fantastically)

e·ya kan·ta
fan·tas·tee·ka·men·te

articles

describing people/things • naming people/things •
pointing things out

The articles *el* and *la* both mean 'the'. Whether you use *el* or
la depends on the gender of the noun talked about, which in
Spanish will always be either masculine or feminine. *El* is used
with masculine nouns while *la* is used with feminine nouns.
When talking about plural nouns you use *los* instead of *el* and
las instead of *la*. See also **gender** and **plurals**.

	singular		plural	
masculine	*el carro* el ka·ro	the car	*los carros* los ka·ros	the cars
feminine	*la tienda* la tyen·da	the shop	*las tiendas* las tyen·das	the shops

Spanish also has masculine and feminine articles meaning
'a/an': *un* and *una*. Again, the gender of the noun determines
which one you use. *Un* and *una* also have plural forms: *unos*
and *unas*, meaning 'some'.

	singular		plural	
masculine	*un huevo* oon we·vo	an egg	*unos huevos* oo·nos we·vos	some eggs
feminine	*una tortuga* oo·na tor·too·ga	a turtle	*unas tortugas* oo·nas tor·too·gas	some turtles

be

Spanish has two words for the verb 'be' – *ser* and *estar*. These two verbs have slightly different functions which are outlined below:

use *ser* to express	examples	
permanent characteristics of people/things	*Ángel es muy amable.* an·khel es mooy a·ma·ble	Ángel is very nice.
occupations or nationalities	*Pablo es de Costa Rica.* pa·blo es de kos·ta ree·ka	Pablo is from Costa Rica.
the time & location of events	*Son las tres.* son las tres	It's 3 o'clock.
possession	*¿De quién es esta mochila?* de kyen es es·ta mo·chee·la	Whose backpack is this?

use *estar* to express	examples	
temporary characteristics of people/things	*La comida está fría.* la ko·mee·da es·ta free·a	The meal is cold.
the time & location of people/things	*Estamos en San José.* es·ta·mos en san kho·se	We're in San José.
the mood of a person	*Estoy contento/a.* m/f es·toy kon·ten·to/a	I'm happy.

The forms of both verbs are given on the next page.

forms of *ser*

I	am	*yo*	yo	*soy*	soy
you	are	*tú/vos* *	too/vos	*eres/sos* *	e·res/sos
you	are	*usted*	oos·*ted*	*es*	es
he/she	is	*él/ella*	el/*e*·ya	*es*	es
we	are	*nosotros/as* m/f	no·*so*·tros/as	*somos*	*so*·mos
you	are	*ustedes*	oos·*te*·des	*son*	son
they	are	*ellos/as* m/f	*e*·yos/as	*son*	son

forms of *estar*

I	am	*yo*	yo	*estoy*	es·*toy*
you	are	*tú/vos* *	too/vos	*estás*	es·*tas*
you	are	*usted*	oos·*ted*	*está*	es·*ta*
he/she	is	*él/ella*	el/*e*·ya	*está*	es·*ta*
we	are	*nosotros/as* m/f	no·*so*·tros/as	*estamos*	es·*ta*·mos
you	are	*ustedes*	oos·*te*·des	*estan*	es·*tan*
they	are	*ellos/as* m/f	*e*·yos/as	*estan*	es·*tan*

* For an explanation on the alternate forms, see **personal pronouns**.

demonstratives

**giving instructions • indicating location •
naming people/things • pointing things out**

To refer to or point at a person or thing, use one of the words
from the table below, depending on whether someone or
something is close (this/these), away from you (that/those) or
even further away in time or distance (that/those over there).

Demonstratives can be used on their own or with a noun.
They go before the noun they accompany and agree in gender
and number with it (see **gender** and **plurals**). They're written
without an accent mark when used with a noun. If they're used
on their own, an accent mark is added in writing.

masculine	singular		plural	
close (this/these)	*éste*	es·te	*éstos*	es·tos
away (that/those)	*ése*	e·se	*ésos*	e·sos
further away (that/those over there)	*aquél*	a·kel	*aquéllos*	a·ke·yos
feminine	singular		plural	
close (this/these)	*ésta*	es·ta	*éstas*	es·tas
away (that/those)	*ésa*	e·sa	*ésas*	e·sas
further away (that/those over there)	*aquélla*	a·ke·ya	*aquéllas*	a·ke·yas

this plant	*esta mata* f sg (lit: this plant)	es·ta *ma*·ta
those animals	*esos animales* m pl (lit: those animals)	e·sos a·nee·*ma*·les

a–z phrasebuilder

21

gender

In Spanish, all nouns are either masculine or feminine. The gender of a noun is not really concerned with the sex of something – the word for turtle, *tortuga* tor·*too*·ga, is a feminine noun, even if the animal is male! There's no rule as to why, say, the sun (*el sol* el sol) is masculine but a cloud (*la nube* la *noo*·be) is feminine. The gender is often arbitrary, but here are some handy tips to help you determine gender:

- gender is masculine when talking about a man and feminine when talking about a woman
- words ending in *-o* are usually masculine
- words ending in *-a* are usually feminine
- words ending in *-d*, *-z* or *-ión* are usually feminine

All nouns in the **dictionaries**, the **menu decoder** and the word lists in this phrasebook have their gender marked with the abbreviations m and f for masculine and feminine respectively. For more information, see the box **masculine or feminine?** in **feelings & opinions**, page 115.

Remember that the gender of nouns also determines the endings on any articles, adjectives and demonstratives you use to describe them. See also **articles**, **adjectives & adverbs**, **demonstratives**, **plurals** and **possessives**.

have

The easiest way of expressing possession in Spanish is by using the verb *tener* (have). The present tense forms of this verb are shown in the table on the following page.

I have two brothers.

> *Tengo dos hermanos.*   *ten*·go dos er·*ma*·nos
> (lit: I-have two brothers)

forms of *tener*					
I	have	*yo*	yo	*tengo*	ten·go
you sg inf	have	*tú/vos* *	too/vos	*tienes/ tenés* *	tye·nes/ te·nes
you sg pol	have	*usted*	oos·ted	*tiene*	tye·ne
he/she	has	*él/ella*	el/e·ya	*tiene*	tye·ne
we	have	*nosotros/ as* m/f	no·so·tros/ as	*tenemos*	te·ne·mos
you pl	have	*ustedes*	oos·te·des	*tienen*	tye·nen
they	have	*ellos/as* m/f	e·yos/as	*tienen*	tye·nen

* For an explanation on the alternate forms, see **personal pronouns**.

Ownership can also be expressed with possessive pronouns – for more information, see **possessives**.

negatives

negating

To make a sentence negative, just add the word *no* (no) before the main verb:

I (don't) live with my family.
   (No) Vivo con mi familia.   (no) vee·vo kon mee fa·mee·ya
   (lit: (no) I-live with my family)

personal pronouns

making statements • naming people/things

Costa Rican Spanish has three forms for the singular 'you'. The polite form of 'you' singular (*usted*) is used when you're meeting someone for the first time, talking to someone older than you or when you're in a formal situation (eg talking to the police, customs officers etc). When talking to someone familiar to you or younger than you, use the informal forms *tú* or *vos*, rather than the polite form *usted*. *Tú* and *vos* are used more or less interchangeably though *vos* is more common.

All phrases in this book use the form of 'you' that's appropriate for the situation. Where you see the symbols **pol** (polite) and **inf** (informal) you're given a choice as either form might be appropriate depending upon the situation. For 'you' plural there's no informal/formal distinction – you just use *ustedes*.

I	yo	yo
you sg inf	*tú/vos*	too/vos
you sg pol	*usted*	oos·*ted*
he	*él*	el
she	*ella*	e·ya
it	*ello*	e·yo
we	*nosotros/as* m/f	no·*so*·tros/as
you pl	*ustedes*	oos·*te*·des
they	*ellos/as* m/f	e·yos/as

Personal pronouns are often left out in Spanish because the endings on verbs tell you who is the doer of the action (subject) – you only need to use them if you want to emphasise who or what is doing the action. You may also notice that *tú* verb forms differ slightly from *vos* verb forms – eg *tienes* ('you have' – *tú* form) versus *tenés* ('you have' – *vos* form).

You don't need to worry about this feature of Costa Rican Spanish because all phrases in this book use the appropriate verb forms. If you do want to try your hand at concocting your own phrases, Costa Ricans will understand if you just stick to *tú* rather than trying your hand at the relatively idiosyncratic *vos*. This feature is called *voseo* vo·*se*·o and is limited to only a few varieties of Central American Spanish and the Spanish spoken in Argentina, Paraguay and Uruguay.

See also **be**, **have**, **verbs** and **word order**.

plurals

describing people/things • naming people/things

In general, if the noun ends in a vowel, you add -s for plural. If the noun ends in a consonant, you add -es:

singular			plural		
bed	*cama*	ka·ma	beds	*camas*	ka·mas
woman	*mujer*	moo·kher	women	*mujeres*	moo·khe·res

See also **articles**, **adjectives & adverbs**, **demonstratives**, **gender** and **possessives**.

possessives

naming people/things • possessing

There are a number of words for 'my', 'your' etc in Spanish. Choose the correct form according to the gender and number of the noun – ie the thing owned, not the owner.

	with singular noun		with plural noun	
my	*mi*	mee	*mis*	mees
your sg inf	*tu*	too	*tus*	toos
your sg pol	*su*	soo	*sus*	soos
his/her/its	*su*	soo	*sus*	soos
our	*nuestro/a* m/f	nwes·tro/a	*nuestros/as* m/f	nwes·tros/as
your pl	*su*	soo	*sus*	soos
their	*su*	soo	*sus*	soos

Ownership can also be expressed with the word *de* (of) or by using the verb *tener* (have).

This is my friend's tent.
Esta es la carpa de mi   *es·*ta es la *kar·*pa de mee
amiga.   a·*mee·*ga
(lit: this is the tent of my friend)

We have two dogs.
Tenemos dos perros.   te·*ne·*mos dos *pe·*ros
(lit: we-have two dogs)

See also **gender**, **have** and **plurals**.

prepositions

giving instructions • indicating location

Prepositions are used to show the relationship between words in a sentence, just like in English. They're placed before the word they accompany. These are the most useful ones:

at (place)	*en*	en	on (place)	*en*	en
at (time)	*a*	a	on (time)	*a*	a
for (purpose)	*para*	*pa·*ra	outside	*fuera de*	*fwe·*ra de
for (time)	*durante*	doo·*ran·*te	since	*desde*	*des·*de
from (time)	*desde*	*des·*de	to (place)	*a*	a
in (place)	*en*	en	until	*hasta*	*as·*ta
in (time)	*en*	en	with	*con*	kon
inside	*dentro de*	*den·*tro de	without	*sin*	seen

Let's meet at eight o'clock at the entrance.
Veámonos a las ocho   ve·*a·*mo·nos a las *o·*cho
en la entrada.   en la en·*tra·*da
(lit: let-see-us at the eight at the entrance)

questions

To ask a question, simply make a statement, but raise your intonation towards the end of the sentence, as you would in English. The inverted question mark written at the start of a sentence prompts you to do this.

Do you have a car?

¿Tienes un carro?	tye·nes oon ka·ro
(lit: you-have a car)	

You can also place the following question words at the beginning of a phrase:

How?	*¿Cómo?*	ko·mo
How many?	*¿Cuántos/as?* m/f pl	kwan·tos/as
How much?	*¿Cuánto?*	kwan·to
What?	*¿Qué?*	ke
When?	*¿Cuándo?*	kwan·do
Where?	*¿Dónde?*	don·de
Which?	*¿Cuál/Cuáles?* sg/pl	kwal/kwa·les
Who?	*¿Quién/Quiénes?* sg/pl	kyen/kye·nes
Why?	*¿Por qué?*	por ke

When does the bus arrive?

¿Cuándo llega	kwan·do ye·ga
el autobús?	el ow·to·boos
(lit: when arrives the bus)	

Where can I buy tickets?

¿Dónde puedo	don·de pwe·do
comprar tiquetes?	kom·prar tee·ke·tes
(lit: where I-can buy tickets)	

It's not impolite to answer questions with a simple *sí* (yes) or *no* (no) in Spanish. Unlike in English, there's no direct way in Spanish to say 'Yes, it is/does', or 'No, it isn't/doesn't'.

requests

A polite and easy way to make a request is by starting with the word *¿Podría …?* (equivalent to 'Could you …?') followed by the infinitive (dictionary form) of the main verb:

Please help me.
   ¿Podría ayudarme?   po·*dree*·a a·yoo·*dar*·me
   (lit: could-you help-me)

See also **questions** and **verbs**.

there is/are

indicating location • pointing things out

To say 'there is/are' in Spanish, use the word *hay* (lit: it-has). Add *no* before it to say 'there isn't/aren't'.

Do you have any rooms?
   ¿Hay habitaciones?   ai a·bee·ta·*syo*·nes
   (lit: it-has rooms)

There aren't any.
   No hay.   no ai
   (lit: no it-has)

See also **negatives**.

verbs

doing things • making statements

There are three groups of verbs in Spanish – those ending in -*ar* (eg *hablar* 'speak'), -*er* (eg *comer* 'eat') and -*ir* (eg *vivir* 'live'). Tenses are formed by adding different endings for each person to the verb stem (part of the verb that remains after you take off -ar, -er and -ir). These endings vary according to which one of the three groups the verb belongs to. The present tense endings for each person are given in the table below.

present tense						
	hablar		*comer*		*vivir*	
I	-o	-o	-o	-o	-o	-o
you (*tú*)	-as	-as	-es	-es	-es	-es
you (*vos*)	-ás	-as	-és	-es	-ís	-ees
you	-a	-a	-e	-e	-e	-e
he/she	-a	-a	-e	-e	-e	-e
we	-amos	-a·mos	-emos	-e·mos	-imos	-ee·mos
you	-an	-an	-en	-en	-en	-en
they	-an	-an	-en	-en	-en	-en

As in any language, some verbs are irregular. The most important ones are *ser* (be), *estar* (be) and *tener* (have). For more details, see **be** and **have**.

word order

asking questions • making statements • negating

Sentences in Spanish have a basic word order of subject–verb–object, just as English does.

I study business.

    Yo estudio comercio.   yo es·*too*·dyo ko·*mer*·syo
    (lit: I study-I business)

However, the subject pronoun is often omitted – '*Estudio comercio*' is enough. Generally, you only use a subject pronoun if you wish to emphasise who is the 'doer' of an action. See also **negatives** and **questions**.

glossary

adjective	word that describes something – '**active** volcanoes are widespread'
adverb	word that explains how an action is done – 'jaguars are **rarely** seen'
article	the words 'a', 'an' and 'the'
demonstrative	word that means 'this' or 'that'
direct object	thing or person in the sentence that has the action directed to it – 'national parks protect the **wildlife**'
gender	grouping of *nouns* into classes (like masculine and feminine), requiring other words (eg *adjectives*) to belong to the same class
indirect object	person or thing in the sentence that is the recipient of the action – 'birds are the main attraction for **nature lovers**'
infinitive	dictionary form of a *verb* – 'monkeys are the easiest to **observe** in the wild'
noun	thing, person or idea – 'the **environment**'
number	whether a word is singular or plural – 'there are deadly poisonous **snakes**'
personal pronoun	word that means 'I', 'you', etc
possessive pronoun	word that means 'mine', 'yours', etc
preposition	word like 'for' or 'before' in English
subject	person or thing in the sentence that does the action – '**sea turtles** are dying out'
tense	form of a *verb* that tells you whether the action is in the present, past or future – eg 'eat' (present), 'ate' (past), 'will eat' (future)
verb	word that tells you what action happened – 'ecotourism **is growing**'
verb ending	ending added to the *verb stem* to indicate the *tense* and/or the *subject* in the sentence
verb stem	part of a *verb* which does not change – 'surf' in '**surf**ing' and '**surf**ed'

BASICS

30

language difficulties
dificultades con el lenguaje

Do you speak (English)?
¿Habla (inglés)?   a·bla (een·gles)

Does anyone speak (English)?
¿Alguien habla (inglés)?   al·gyen a·bla (een·gles)

Do you understand (me)?
¿(Me) Entiende?   (me) en·tyen·de

Yes, I understand.
Sí, entiendo.   see en·tyen·do

No, I don't understand.
No, no entiendo.   no no en·tyen·do

---

talking like a *tico*

If you know any Spanish at all, you're bound to expand your repertoire of slang expressions no end while in Costa Rica. The following colourful turns of phrase are typical Costa Rican slang and colloquialisms (known as *tiquismos* tee·kees·mos).

agüevado/a m/f	a·gwe·va·do/a	bored/boring
buena nota f	bwe·na no·ta	all right
chapulín m	cha·poo·leen	young thief
chunche m	choon·che	thingumajig
guavero/a m/f	gwa·ve·ro/a	lucky
macho/a m/f	ma·cho/a	blonde person
sabanero m	sa·ba·ne·ro	cowboy
salado m	sa·la·do	bad luck

For other *tiquismos*, see the box **talking *tiquismos***, page 134.

language difficulties

31

I speak (English).
Hablo (inglés).   *a*·blo (een·*gles*)

I don't speak (Spanish).
No hablo (español).   no *a*·blo (es·pa·*nyol*)

I speak a little.
Hablo un poquito.   *a*·blo oon po·*kee*·to

I'd like to practise (Spanish).
Quisiera practicar   kee·*sye*·ra prak·tee·*kar*
(español).   (es·pa·*nyol*)

Let's speak (Spanish).
Hablemos (español).   a·*ble*·mos (es·pa·*nyol*)

Pardon?
¿Perdón?   per·*don*

What does (*pura vida*) mean?
¿Que significa (pura vida)?   ke seeg·nee·*fee*·ka (*poo*·ra *vee*·da)

How do you …?	¿Cómo …?	*ko*·mo …
pronounce	*se pronuncia*	se pro·*noon*·sya
this	*esto*	*es*·to
write	*se escribe*	se es·*kree*·be
(*pura vida*)	(*pura vida*)	(*poo*·ra *vee*·da)

Could you please …?	¿Podría …?	po·*dree*·a …
repeat that	*repetir eso*	re·pe·*teer e*·so
speak more	*hablar más*	a·*blar* mas
slowly	*despacio*	des·*pa*·syo
write it down	*escribirlo*	es·kree·*beer*·lo

---

rev it up

When you see the letter *r* at the beginning of a Spanish word, or when you see a double *rr*, remember to trill the 'r' sound. It's a case of blowing air past your tongue so that it produces a sound like a cat purring. It may help to visualise yourself sitting astride a powerful motorbike revving on the throttle as you do so. Try practising on the word *Costarricense(s)* **sg/pl** kos·ta·ree·*sen*·se(s), the official name for the Costa Rican people.

cardinal numbers

números cardinales

0	*cero*	*se·ro*	6	*seis*	says
1	*uno*	*oo·no*	7	*siete*	*sye·*te
2	*dos*	dos	8	*ocho*	*o·*cho
3	*tres*	tres	9	*nueve*	*nwe·*ve
4	*cuatro*	*kwa·*tro	10	*diez*	dyes
5	*cinco*	*seen·*ko			

11	*once*	*on·*se
12	*doce*	*do·*se
13	*trece*	*tre·*se
14	*catorce*	ka·*tor·*se
15	*quince*	*keen·*se
16	*dieciséis*	dye·see·*says*
17	*diecisiete*	dye·see·*sye·*te
18	*dieciocho*	dye·see·*o·*cho
19	*diecinueve*	dye·see·*nwe·*ve
20	*veinte*	*vayn·*te
21	*veintiuno*	vayn·tee·*oo·*no
22	*veintidós*	vayn·tee·*dos*
30	*treinta*	*trayn·*ta
40	*cuarenta*	kwa·*ren·*ta
50	*cincuenta*	seen·*kwen·*ta
60	*sesenta*	se·*sen·*ta
70	*setenta*	se·*ten·*ta
80	*ochenta*	o·*chen·*ta
90	*noventa*	no·*ven·*ta
100	*cien*	syen
200	*doscientos*	do·*syen·*tos
1000	*mil*	meel
2000	*dos mil*	dos meel
1,000,000	*un millón*	oon mee·*yon*

ordinal numbers

Ordinal numbers are written with a degree sign – 1st is written '1º', 2nd is '2º', and so on.

1st	*primero/a* m/f	pree·*me*·ro/a
2nd	*segundo/a* m/f	se·*goon*·do/a
3rd	*tercero/a* m/f	ter·*se*·ro/a
4th	*cuarto/a* m/f	*kwar*·to/a
5th	*quinto/a* m/f	*keen*·to/a

fractions

fracciones

a quarter	*un cuarto*	oon *kwar*·to
a third	*un tercio*	oon *ter*·syo
a half	*un medio*	oon *me*·dyo
three-quarters	*tres cuartos*	tres *kwar*·tos
all	*todos/as* m/f pl	*to*·dos/as
none	*ninguno/a* m/f	neen·*goo*·no/a

useful amounts

cantidades útiles

How much?	*¿Cuánto/a?* m/f	*kwan*·to/a
How many?	*¿Cuántos/as?* m/f pl	*kwan*·tos/as
Please give me ...	*Por favor deme ...*	por fa·*vor de*·me ...
(just) a little	*un poquitito*	oon po·kee·*tee*·to
a lot	*mucho/a* m/f	*moo*·cho/a
many	*muchos/as* m/f pl	*moo*·chos/as
some	*unos/as* m/f pl	*oo*·nos/as

For more amounts, see **self-catering**, page 165.

BASICS

34

telling the time

diciendo la hora

Time is expressed by the phrase *Son las ...* (It is ...) followed by a number. Times past the hour are expressed using *y* (and) while times before the hour take *para* (to). The words *medianoche* me·dya·*no*·che (midnight) and *mediodía* me·dyo·*dee*·a (midday) are used instead of 12am and 12pm.

Costa Ricans refer to a 12-hour clock. The terms 'am' and 'pm', however, are used only in writing. When speaking, time is designated by the part of the day. The day is roughly broken up into four time periods. To specify whether a time is am or pm, just state the hour and link it to the time of the day using the phrase *de la* (lit: of the).

What time is it?	¿Qué hora es?	ke *o*·ra es
It's one o'clock.	Es la una.	es la *oo*·na
It's (ten) o'clock.	Son las (diez).	son las (dyes)
Five past (ten).	(Diez) y cinco.	(dyes) ee *seen*·ko
Quarter past (ten).	(Diez) y cuarto.	(dyes) ee *kwar*·to
Half past (ten).	(Diez) y media.	(dyes) ee *me*·dya
Quarter to (eleven).	Cuarto para las (once).	*kwar*·to *pa*·ra las (*on*·se)
am (dawn)	de la madrugada	de la ma·droo·*ga*·da
am (morning)	de la mañana	de la ma·*nya*·na
pm (afternoon)	de la tarde	de la *tar*·de
pm (evening)	de la noche	de la *no*·che
At what time ...?	¿A qué hora ...?	a ke *o*·ra ...
At (five).	A las (cinco).	a las (*seen*·ko)
At (7.57pm).	A las (siete y cincuenta y siete de la noche).	a las (*sye*·te ee seen·*kwen*·ta ee *sye*·te de la *no*·che)

the calendar

days

Monday	*lunes*	*loo*·nes
Tuesday	*martes*	*mar*·tes
Wednesday	*miércoles*	*myer*·ko·les
Thursday	*jueves*	*hwe*·ves
Friday	*viernes*	*vyer*·nes
Saturday	*sábado*	*sa*·ba·do
Sunday	*domingo*	do·*meen*·go

months

January	*enero*	e·*ne*·ro
February	*febrero*	fe·*bre*·ro
March	*marzo*	*mar*·so
April	*abril*	a·*breel*
May	*mayo*	*ma*·yo
June	*junio*	*khoo*·nyo
July	*julio*	*khoo*·lyo
August	*agosto*	a·*gos*·to
September	*septiembre*	se·*tyem*·bre
October	*octubre*	ok·*too*·bre
November	*noviembre*	no·*vyem*·bre
December	*diciembre*	dee·*syem*·bre

dates

Dates are expressed using cardinal numbers. The exception to this rule is the first day of the month which uses the ordinal number – eg *el primero de octubre* el pree·*me*·ro de ok·*too*·bre (lit: the first of October).

What date is it today?
  ¿Qué fecha es hoy?   ke *fe*·cha es oy

It's (18 October).
  Es (el dieciocho   es (el dye·see·o·cho
  de octubre).   de ok·*too*·bre)

seasons

dry season	*estación seca* f	es·ta·*syon* se·ka
wet season	*estación lluviosa* f	es·ta·*syon* yoo·*vyo*·sa
spring	*primavera* f	pree·ma·*ve*·ra
summer	*verano* m	ve·*ra*·no
autumn	*otoño* m	o·*to*·nyo
winter	*invierno* m	een·*vyer*·no

present

el presente

now	*ahora*	a·*o*·ra
today	*hoy*	oy
tonight	*hoy en la noche*	oy en la *no*·che
this morning	*hoy en la mañana*	oy en la ma·*nya*·na
this afternoon	*hoy en la tarde*	oy en la *tar*·de
this week	*esta semana*	*es*·ta se·*ma*·na
this month	*este mes*	*es*·te mes
this year	*este año*	*es*·te *a*·nyo

past

el pasado

yesterday	*ayer*	a·*yer*
day before yesterday	*anteayer*	an·te·a·*yer*
(three days) ago	*hace (tres días)*	*a*·se (tres *dee*·as)
since (May)	*desde (mayo)*	*des*·de (*ma*·yo)
last night	*anoche*	a·*no*·che
last week	*la semana pasada*	la se·*ma*·na pa·*sa*·da
last month	*el mes pasado*	el mes pa·*sa*·do
last year	*el año pasado*	el *a*·nyo pa·*sa*·do

yesterday …	*ayer …*	a·*yer* …
morning	*en la mañana*	en la ma·*nya*·na
afternoon	*en la tarde*	en la *tar*·de
evening	*en la noche*	en la *no*·che

future

el futuro

tomorrow	*mañana*	ma·*nya*·na
day after tomorrow	*pasado mañana*	pa·*sa*·do ma·*nya*·na
in (two days)	*dentro de (dos días)*	*den*·tro de (dos *dee*·as)
until (June)	*hasta (junio)*	*as*·ta (*khoo*·nyo)
next …	*… entrante*	… en·*tran*·te
week	*la semana*	la se·*ma*·na
month	*el mes*	el mes
year	*el año*	el *a*·nyo
tomorrow …	*mañana …*	ma·*nya*·na …
morning	*en la mañana*	en la ma·*nya*·na
afternoon	*en la tarde*	en la *tar*·de
evening	*en la noche*	en la *no*·che

during the day

durante el día

afternoon	*tarde* f	*tar*·de
dawn	*madrugada* f	ma·droo·*ga*·da
day	*día* m	*dee*·a
evening	*noche* f	*no*·che
midday	*mediodía* m	me·dyo·*dee*·a
midnight	*medianoche* f	me·dya·*no*·che
morning	*mañana* f	ma·*nya*·na
night	*noche* f	*no*·che
sunrise	*amanecer* m	a·ma·ne·*ser*
sunset	*atardecer* m	a·tar·de·*ser*

How much is it?
¿Cuánto es? — kwan·to es

Can you write down the price?
¿Podría escribir el precio? — po·dree·a es·kree·beer el pre·syo

What's the exchange rate?
¿A cómo está el tipo de cambio? — a ko·mo es·ta el tee·po de kam·byo

What's the charge?
¿Cuánto me cobrás? — kwan·to me ko·bras

I'd like to ...	*Quiero ...*	kye·ro ...
cash a cheque	*cambiar un cheque*	kam·byar oon che·ke
change a travellers cheque	*cambiar un cheque de viajero*	kam·byar oon che·ke de vya·khe·ro
change money into *colones*	*cambiar dinero a colones*	kam·byar dee·ne·ro a ko·lo·nes
change money/ dollars	*cambiar plata/ dólares*	kam·byar pla·ta/ do·la·res
get a cash advance	*que me den un adelanto en efectivo*	ke me den oon a·de·lan·to en e·fek·tee·vo
withdraw money	*sacar plata*	sa·kar pla·ta

Do you accept ...?	*¿Acepta ...?*	a·sep·ta ...
credit cards	*tarjetas de crédito*	tar·khe·tas de kre·dee·to
debit cards	*tarjetas de débito*	tar·khe·tas de de·bee·to
travellers cheques	*cheques de viajero*	che·kes de vya·khe·ro

I'd like …, please.	Quiero …, por favor.	kye·ro … por fa·vor
a receipt	un recibo	oon re·see·bo
a refund	un reintegro	oon re·een·te·gro
my change	mi vuelto	mee vwel·to
to return this	devolver ésto	de·vol·ver es·to

Where's a/an …?	¿Dónde hay …?	don·de ai …
automated teller machine	un cajero automático	oon ka·khe·ro ow·to·ma·tee·ko
foreign exchange office	una casa de cambio	oo·na ka·sa de kam·byo

How much is it per …?	¿Cuánto es por …?	kwan·to es por …
day	día	dee·a
hour	hora	o·ra
night	noche	no·che
person	persona	per·so·na
visit	visita	vee·see·ta

the colour of money

The Costa Rican currency is the *colón* ko·lon, named after the explorer Christopher Columbus (whose name in Spanish is *Cristóbal Colón* krees·to·bal ko·lon). One *colón* comprises 100 *centavos* sen·ta·vos (cents). The plural of *colón* is *colones* ko·lo·nes. In practice though, *pesos* pe·sos – the slang term for money – is often used. In addition, you may come across the following colourful terms for individual amounts:

media teja f   me·dya te·kha   50 *colón* coin
  (lit: half tile)

teja f   te·kha   100 *colón* coin
  (lit: tile)

rojo m   ro·kho   1000 *colón* bill
  'red' – refers to the red colour of the bill. Also known as
  pargo par·go 'red snapper' (type of fish).

tucán m   too·kan   5000 *colón* bill
  'toucan' – depicts one of Costa Rica's avian emblems

getting around

para transportarse

Which ... goes to (Quepos)?	¿Cuál ... va para (Quepos)?	kwal ... va pa·ra (ke·pos)
4WD	cuatro por cuatro	kwa·tro por kwa·tro
boat	barco	bar·ko
bus	bus	boos
jeep	jeep	yeep
train	tren	tren

Is this the ... to (Limón)?	Este es el ... que va para (Limón)?	es·te es el ... ke va pa·ra (lee·mon)
boat	barco	bar·ko
bus	bus	boos
train	tren	tren

When's the ... (bus)?	¿A qué hora sale el ... (bus)?	a ke o·ra sa·le el ... (boos)
first	primer	pree·mer
last	último	ool·tee·mo
next	próximo	prok·see·mo

What time does it leave?
¿A qué hora sale?　　　　a ke o·ra sa·le

What time does it get to (San José)?
¿A qué hora llega a (San José)?　a ke o·ra ye·ga a (san kho·se)

How long will it be delayed?
¿Cuánto se va a atrasar?　　kwan·to se va a a·tra·sar

Is this seat taken?
¿Está ocupado?   es·ta o·koo·*pa*·do

That's my seat.
Este es mi asiento.   es·te es mee a·*syen*·to

Please tell me when we get to (Alajuela).
Por favor, avíseme cuando   por fa·*vor* a·*vee*·se·me *kwan*·do
lleguemos a (Alajuela).   ye·*ge*·mos a (a·la·*khwe*·la)

Please stop here.
Puede parar aquí, por favor.   pwe·de pa·*rar* a·*kee* por fa·*vor*

How long do we stop here?
¿Cuánto tiempo vamos   *kwan*·to *tyem*·po *va*·mos
a parar aquí?   a pa·*rar* a·*kee*

tickets

Transportation in Costa Rica is mainly on cheap and cheerful (and often crowded) buses. Seating on buses isn't divided up into separate classes. The only time you may need to specify which class you wish to travel is on international flights in and out of San José.

Where do I buy a ticket?
¿Dónde puedo comprar   *don*·de *pwe*·do kom·*prar*
un pasaje?   oon pa·*sa*·khe

Do I need to book (well in advance)?
¿Necesito reservar el   ne·se·*see*·to re·ser·*var* el
tiquete (muy por   tee·*ke*·te (mooy por
adelantado)?   a·de·lan·*ta*·do)

A ... ticket (to Monteverde).	Un pasaje ... para (Monteverde).	oon pa·*sa*·khe ... *pa*·ra (mon·te·*ver*·de)
child's	para niño	*pa*·ra *nee*·nyo
one-way	solo de ida	*so*·lo de *ee*·da
return	de ida y vuelta	de *ee*·da ee *vwel*·ta
student	de estudiante	de es·too·*dyan*·te

I'd like a/an ... seat.	Quiero un asiento en ...	kye·ro oon a·syen·to en ...
aisle	el pasillo	el pa·see·yo
nonsmoking	el área de no fumado	el a·re·a de no foo·ma·do
smoking	el área de fumado	el a·re·a de foo·ma·do
window	la ventana	la ven·ta·na

Is there a ...?	¿Tiene ...?	tye·ne ...
blanket	una cobija	oo·na ko·bee·kha
sick bag	una bolsa para vomitar	oo·na bol·sa pa·ra vo·mee·tar
toilet	un baño	oon ba·nyo

Is there air conditioning?
¿Tiene aire acondicionado?   tye·ne ai·re a·kon·dee·syo·na·do

How long does the trip take?
¿Cuánto dura el viaje?   kwan·to doo·ra el vya·khe

Is it a direct route?
¿Es un viaje directo?   es oon vya·khe dee·rek·to

How much is it?
¿Cuánto cuesta?   kwan·to kwes·ta

Can I get a stand-by ticket?
¿Puedo comprar un tiquete de stand-by?   pwe·do kom·prar oon tee·ke·te de sten·bai

What time should I check in?
¿A qué hora debo hacer el chequeo?   a ke o·ra de·bo a·ser el che·ke·o

I'd like to ... my ticket, please.	Quisiera ... mi tiquete, por favor.	kee·sye·ra ... mee tee·ke·te por fa·vor
cancel	cancelar	kan·se·lar
change	cambiar	kam·byar
confirm	confirmar	kon·feer·mar

agente de viajes m&f	a·*khen*·te de vee·*a*·khes	**travel agent**
atrasado/a m/f	a·tra·*sa*·do/a	**delayed**
cancelado/a m/f	kan·se·*la*·do/a	**cancelled**
huelga f	*wel*·ga	**strike** n
itinerario m	ee·tee·ne·*ra*·ryo	**timetable**
lleno/a m/f	*ye*·no/a	**full**
plataforma f	pla·ta·*for*·ma	**platform**
ventanilla f	ven·ta·*nee*·ya	**ticket window**

luggage

equipaje

Where's (a/the) ...?	*¿Dónde está el ...?*	*don*·de es·*ta* el ...
baggage claim	*reclamo de equipaje*	re·*kla*·mo de e·kee·*pa*·khe
left-luggage office	*cuarto para guardar equipaje*	*kwar*·to *pa*·ra gwar·*dar* e·kee·*pa*·khe
luggage locker	*lócker para equipaje*	*lo*·ker *pa*·ra e·kee·*pa*·khe
trolley	*carrito para equipaje*	ka·*ree*·to *pa*·ra e·kee·*pa*·khe

Can I have some coins/tokens?
¿Me puede dar monedas/fichas?
me *pwe*·de dar mo·*ne*·das/*fee*·chas

My luggage has been damaged.
Me dañaron el equipaje.
me da·*nya*·ron el e·kee·*pa*·khe

My luggage has been lost.
Se perdieron mis maletas.
se per·*dye*·ron mees ma·*le*·tas

My luggage has been stolen.
Se robaron mis maletas.
se ro·*ba*·ron mees ma·*le*·tas

That's (not) mine.
Eso (no) es mío.
e·so (no) es *mee*·o

plane

avión

Where does flight (CO52) arrive/depart?

¿Dónde llega/sale   *don·*de *ye·*ga/*sa·*le
el vuelo (CO52)?   el *vwe·*lo (se o seen·*kwen·*ta dos)

A (1st-class) ticket to (New York).

Un pasaje (en primera   oon pa·*sa·*khe (en pree·*me·*ra
clase) para (Nueva York).   *kla·*se) *pa·*ra (*nwe·*va york)

Where's (the) …?	*¿Dónde está …?*	*don·*de es·*ta* …
airport shuttle	*la buseta del aeropuerto*	la boo·*se·*ta del a·e·ro·*pwer·*to
arrivals hall	*el área de llegadas*	el *a·*re·a de ye·*ga·*das
departures hall	*el área de salidas*	el *a·*re·a de sa·*lee·*das
duty-free shop	*el duty-free*	el *dyoo·*tee·free
gate (7)	*la puerta (siete)*	la *pwer·*ta (*sye·*te)

bus

bus

There are two main types of buses in Costa Rica – *directos* dee·*rek·*tos and *colectivos* ko·lek·*tee·*vos. The term *directos* is a bit of a misnomer because they still stop frequently. Not as frequently, however, as the *colectivos*, which require a Latin American patience to endure. *Buses de turistas* boo·ses de too·*rees·*tas are privately owned and used only for tours.

transport

Is this a bus stop?
¿Esta es una parada de bus?   es·ta es oo·na pa·ra·da de boos

How often do buses come?
¿Cada cuánto pasa el bus?   ka·da kwan·to pa·sa el boos

Does it stop at (Puerto Viejo)?
¿Hace parada en   a·se pa·ra·da en
(Puerto Viejo)?   (pwer·to vye·kho)

What's the next stop?
¿Cuál es la próxima   kwal es la prok·see·ma
parada?   pa·ra·da

I'd like to get off at (San Pedro).
Quiero bajarme en   kye·ro ba·khar·me en
(San Pedro).   (san pe·dro)

bus station	*estación de buses* f	es·ta·syon de boo·ses
bus terminal	*terminal de buses* f	ter·mee·nal de boo·ses
departure bay	*área de salida* m	a·re·a de sa·lee·da
local bus station	*estación de buses locales* f	es·ta·syon de boo·ses lo·ka·les
minibus	*microbús* m	mee·kro·boos
shuttle bus	*buseta* f	boo·se·ta
timetable display	*pizarra con itinerario* f	pee·sa·ra kon ee·tee·ne·ra·ryo

listen for ...

equipaje de mano m	e·ke·pa·khe de ma·no	**carry-on baggage**
exceso de equipaje m	ek·se·so de e·kee·pa·khe	**excess baggage**
ficha f	fee·cha	**token**

Travelling by bus can be a chaotic affair in Costa Rica. In San José there's no central terminal of the kind that you might be used to – just an area called 'the Coca Cola' in honour of a bottling plant that used to occupy the site. Other terminals and offices are scattered all over the city.

Brightly painted timetables on station walls may not have been updated … ever. Always ask at the ticket office about departure times. If there isn't one, try your luck with the women who clean the restrooms. These phrases might help:

Where's the bus terminal?

| ¿Dónde está la terminal de buses? | don·de es·ta la ter·mee·nal de boo·ses |

What time does bus number (five) leave?

| ¿A qué hora sale el bus número (cinco)? | a ke o·ra sa·le el boos noo·me·ro (seen·ko) |

boat

barco

What's the lake/sea like today?

| ¿Cómo está el lago/ mar hoy? | ko·mo es·ta el la·go/ mar oy |

What island/beach is this?

| ¿Cuál isla/playa es esta? | kwa ees·la/pla·ya es es·ta |

I feel seasick.

| Me siento mareado/a. m/f | me syen·to ma·re·a·do/a |

Are there life jackets?

| ¿Hay chalecos salvavidas? | ai cha·le·kos sal·va·vee·das |

Can I dine at the captain's table?

| ¿Podría cenar con el capitán? | po·dree·a se·nar kon el ka·pee·tan |

boat (general)	*barco* m	*bar·ko*
boat (small)	*bote* m	*bo·te*
cabin	*cabina* f	ka·*bee*·na
captain	*capitán* m	ka·pee·*tan*
car deck	*plataforma para*	pla·ta·*for*·ma *pa*·ra
	carros f	*ka*·ros
deck	*cubierta* f	koo·*byer*·ta
ferry	*ferry* m	*fe*·ree
hammock	*hamaca* f	a·*ma*·ka
lifeboat	*bote*	*bo*·te
	salvavidas m	sal·va·*vee*·das
life jacket	*chaleco*	cha·*le*·ko
	salvavidas m	sal·va·*vee*·das
yacht	*yate* m	*ya*·te

taxi

taxi

I'd like a	*Quiero un taxi*	*kye*·ro oon *tak*·see
(shared) taxi …	*(compartido) …*	(kom·par·*tee*·do) …
at (9am)	*para las (nueve*	*pa*·ra las (*nwe*·ve
	de la mañana)	de la ma·*nya*·na)
for a full day	*para un*	*pa*·ra oon
	día entero	*dee*·a en·*te*·ro
for a half day	*para medio*	*pa*·ra *me*·dyo
	día	*dee*·a
for (two) hours	*para (dos) horas*	*pa*·ra (dos) *o*·ras
now	*para ahora*	*pa*·ra a·*o*·ra
tomorrow	*para mañana*	*pa*·ra ma·*nya*·na

PRACTICAL

48

Where's the taxi stand?

¿Dónde está la   *don*·de es·*ta* la
parada de taxis?   pa·*ra*·da de *tak*·sees

Is there a taxi available?

¿Hay un taxi disponible?   ai oon *tak*·see dees·po·*nee*·ble

Please take me to (this address).

Por favor, lléveme a   por fa·*vor ye*·ve·me a
(esta dirección).   (*es*·ta dee·rek·*syon*)

How much is it to (San Isidro)?

¿Cuánto es hasta   *kwan*·to es *as*·ta
(San Isidro)?   (san ee·*see*·dro)

How much is the (initial) charge?

¿Cuánto es la tarifa   *kwan*·to es la ta·*ree*·fa
(básica)?   (*ba*·see·ka)

Please put the meter on.

Por favor, ponga la maría.   por fa·*vor pon*·ga la ma·*ree*·a

I don't want to pay a flat fare.

No quiero pagar   no *kye*·ro pa·*gar*
una tarifa fija.   *oo*·na ta·*ree*·fa *fee*·kha

Please ...	*Por favor, ...*	por fa·*vor* ...
come back at (10pm)	*vuelva a las (diez de la noche)*	*vwel*·va a las (dyes de la *no*·che)
slow down	*baje la velocidad*	*ba*·khe la ve·lo·see·*dad*
stop here	*pare aquí*	*pa*·re a·*kee*
wait here	*espéreme aquí*	es·*pe*·re·me a·*kee*

For other useful phrases, see **directions**, page 57, and **money**, page 39.

---

all the way to Chepe

Both the man's name *José* kho·*se* and the capital city *San José* san kho·*se* carry the nickname *Chepe* *che*·pe. Rumour has it that if you ask a taxi driver to take you from the airport to *Chepe*, rather than to *San José*, you'll get a better deal on the taxi fare.

car & motorbike hire

I'd like to hire a/an …	*Quiero alquilar …*	kye·ro al·kee·*lar* …
4WD	*un cuatro por cuatro*	oon *kwa*·tro por *kwa*·tro
automatic	*un carro automático*	oon *ka*·ro ow·to·*ma*·tee·ko
car	*un carro*	oon *ka*·ro
manual	*un carro de marchas*	oon *ka*·ro de *mar*·chas
motorbike	*una motocicleta*	*oo*·na mo·to·see·*kle*·ta
with …	*con …*	kon …
air conditioning	*aire acondicionado*	*ai*·re a·kon·dee·syo·na·do
a driver	*un chofer*	oon cho·*fer*

How much for daily/weekly hire?
¿Cuánto cuesta el alquiler por día/semana?
kwan·to kwes·ta el al·kee·*ler* por *dee*·a/se·*ma*·na

Does that include insurance/mileage?
¿Incluye seguro/ kilometraje?
een·*kloo*·ye se·*goo*·ro/ kee·lo·me·*tra*·khe

Do you have a guide to the road rules (in English)?
¿Tiene un manual de tránsito (en inglés)?
tye·ne oon ma·*nwal* de tran·see·to (en een·*gles*)

Do you have a road map?
¿Tiene un mapa de carreteras?
tye·ne oon *ma*·pa de ka·re·*te*·ras

on the road

What's the speed limit?
¿Cuál es el límite
de velocidad?

kwal es el *lee*·mee·te
de ve·lo·see·*dad*

Is this the road to (Tamarindo)?
¿Por aquí se va a
(Tamarindo)?

por a·*kee* se va a
(ta·ma·*reen*·do)

Where's a petrol station?
¿Dónde hay una bomba?

don·de ai *oo*·na *bom*·ba

Please fill it up.
Lleno, por favor.

ye·no por fa·*vor*

I'd like (25) litres.
Échele (veinticinco) litros,
por favor.

e·che·le (*vayn*·tee·*seen*·ko)
lee·tros por fa·*vor*

diesel	*diesel* m	dee·*sel*
premium	*súper* m	*soo*·per
regular	*regular* m	re·goo·*lar*

Can you	*¿Le revisa …,*	le ree·*vee*·sa …
check the …?	*por favor?*	por fa·*vor*
oil	*el aceite*	el a·*say*·te
tyre pressure	*las llantas*	las *yan*·tas
water	*el agua*	el *a*·gwa

(How long) Can I park here?
¿(Cuánto tiempo) (*kwan*·to *tyem*·po)
Puedo parquear aquí? *pwe*·do par·ke·*ar* a·*kee*

Do I have to pay?
¿Tengo que pagar? *ten*·go ke pa·*gar*

signs		
Alto	*al*·to	**Stop**
Ceda	*se*·da	**Give Way**
Desvío	des·*vee*·o	**Detour**
Entrada	en·*tra*·da	**Entrance**
No Hay Paso	no ai *pa*·so	**No Entry**
Peaje	pe·*a*·khe	**Toll**
Peligro	pe·*lee*·gro	**Danger**
Salida	sa·*lee*·da	**Exit**
Una Vía	*oo*·na *vee*·a	**One Way**

problems

I need a mechanic.
Necesito un mecánico. ne·se·*see*·to oon me·*ka*·nee·ko

I've had an accident.
Tuve un accidente. *too*·ve oon ak·see·*den*·te

The car has broken down (at Golfito).
El carro se varó (en Golfito). el *ka*·ro se va·*ro* (en gol·*fee*·to)

The motorbike has broken down (at Golfito).
La moto se varó (en Golfito). la *mo*·to se va·*ro* (en gol·*fee*·to)

PRACTICAL

52

The car won't start.
El carro no arranca.   el *ka*·ro no a·*ran*·ka

The motorbike won't start.
La moto no arranca.   la *mo*·to no a·*ran*·ka

I have a flat tyre.
Se me estalló una llanta.   se me es·ta·*yo* oo·na *yan*·ta

I've lost my car keys.
Se me perdieron   se me per·*dye*·ron
las llaves del carro.   las *ya*·ves del *ka*·ro

I've locked the keys inside.
Dejé las llaves adentro.   de·*khe* las *ya*·ves a·*den*·tro

I've run out of petrol.
Me quedé sin gasolina.   me ke·*de* seen ga·so·*lee*·na

Can you fix it (today)?
¿Lo puede arreglar (hoy)?   lo *pwe*·de a·reg·*lar* (oy)

How long will it take?
¿Cuánto va a durar?   *kwan*·to va a doo·*rar*

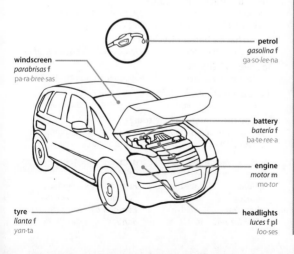

petrol
gasolina f
ga·so·*lee*·na

windscreen
parabrisas f
pa·ra·*bree*·sas

battery
batería f
ba·te·*ree*·a

engine
motor m
mo·*tor*

tyre
llanta f
yan·ta

headlights
luces f pl
loo·ses

bicycle

bicicleta

I'd like ...	*Quiero ...*	*kye·ro ...*
my bicycle repaired	*que me arreglen la bicicleta*	ke me a·re·glen la bee·see·kle·ta
to buy	*comprar*	kom·prar
a bicycle	*una bicicleta*	oo·na bee·see·kle·ta
to hire a bicycle	*alquilar una bicicleta*	al·kee·lar oo·na bee·see·kle·ta

I'd like a ... bike.	*Quiero una bicicleta ...*	*kye·ro oo·na bee·see·kle·ta ...*
mountain	*montañera*	mon·ta·nye·ra
racing	*de carreras*	de ka·re·ras
second-hand	*de segunda mano*	de se·goon·da ma·no

How much is it per day/hour?
¿Cuánto cuesta por día/hora? kwan·to kwes·ta por dee·a/o·ra

Do you have a better bicycle?
¿Tiene una bici mejor? tye·ne oo·na bee·see me·khor

Do I need a helmet?
¿Necesito un casco? ne·se·see·to oon kas·ko

I have a puncture.
Se me estalló una llanta. se me es·ta·yo oo·na yan·ta

Can you recommend a bike tour?
¿Me podría recomendar un tur de bici? me po·dree·a re·ko·men·dar oon toor de bee·see

costa rican place names

Alajuela	a·la·khwe·la	**Puerto**	pwer·to
Cartago	kar·ta·go	**Limón**	lee·mon
Heredia	e·re·dya	**Puntarenas**	poon·ta·re·nas
Montezuma	mon·te·soo·ma	**San José**	san kho·se

border crossing
cruzando la frontera

border crossing

cruzando la frontera

I'm …	Estoy …	es·toy …
in transit	de paso	de pa·so
on business	de negocios	de ne·go·syos
on holiday	de vacaciones	de va·ka·syo·nes

I'm here for …	Voy a estar aquí por …	voy a es·tar a·kee por …
(10) days	(diez) días	(dyes) dee·as
(three) weeks	(tres) semanas	(tres) se·ma·nas
(two) months	(dos) meses	(dos) me·ses

I'm going to (Jacó).
Voy para (Jacó). voy pa·ra (kha·ko)

I'm staying at (the Hotel Tropical).
Estoy hospedado es·toy o·spe·da·do
en (el Hotel Tropical). en (el o·tel tro·pee·kal)

listen for …

familia f	fa·mee·lya	**family**
grupo m	groo·po	**group**
impuesto	eem·pwes·to	**departure**
de salida m	de sa·lee·da	**tax**
pasaporte m	pa·sa·por·te	**passport**
solo/a m/f	so·lo/a	**alone**
visa f	vee·sa	**visa**

border crossing

55

at customs

I have nothing to declare.
No tengo nada que declarar.
no *ten*·go *na*·da ke de·kla·*rar*

I have something to declare.
Tengo algo para declarar.
ten·go *al*·go *pa*·ra de·kla·*rar*

Do I have to declare this?
¿Tengo que declarar esto?
ten·go ke de·kla·*rar es*·to

That's (not) mine.
Eso (no) es mío.
e·so (no) es *mee*·o

I didn't know I had to declare it.
Yo no sabía que tenía que declararlo.
yo no sa·*bee*·a ke te·*nee*·a ke de·kla·*rar*·lo

Do you have this form in (English)?
¿Tiene este formulario en (inglés)?
tye·ne *es*·te for·moo·*la*·ryo en (een·*gles*)

Could I please have an (English) interpreter?
¿Podría conseguirme un intérprete (en inglés), por favor?
po·*dree*·a kon·se·*geer*·me oon een·*ter*·pre·te (en een·*gles*) por fa·*vor*

For phrases on payments and receipts, see **money**, page 39.

signs		
Aduana	a·*dwa*·na	**Customs**
Control de Pasaporte	kon·*trol* de pa·sa·*por*·te	**Passport Control**
Cuarentena	kwa·ren·*te*·na	**Quarantine**
Duty-Free	*dyoo*·tee·free	**Duty-Free**
Migración	mee·gra·*syon*	**Immigration**

PRACTICAL

56

Where's (the bank)?
¿Dónde está (el banco)?   *don*·de es·*ta* (el *ban*·ko)

What's the address?
¿Cuál es la dirección?   kwal es la dee·rek·*syon*

How do I get there?
¿Cómo llego ahí?   *ko*·mo *ye*·go a·*ee*

How far is it?
¿Qué tan largo está?   ke tan *lar*·go es·*ta*

Can you show me (on the map)?
¿Me puede enseñar   me *pwe*·de en·se·*nyar*
(en el mapa)?   (en el *ma*·pa)

What ... is this?	*¿Cuál ... es este/a?* m/f	kwal ... es *es*·te/a
square	*plaza* f	*pla*·sa
street	*calle* f	*ka*·ye
village	*pueblo* m	*pwe*·blo

It's ...	*Está ...*	es·*ta* ...
behind ...	*detrás de ...*	de·*tras* de ...
close	*cerrado*	se·*ra*·do
here	*aquí*	a·*kee*
in front of ...	*en frente de ...*	en *fren*·te de ...
near ...	*cerca de ...*	*ser*·ka de...
next to ...	*a la par de ...*	a la par de ...
opposite ...	*opuesto a ...*	o·*pwes*·to a ...
straight ahead	*aquí directo*	a·*kee* dee·*rek*·to
there	*ahí*	a·*ee*

---

just around the corner

Costa Ricans will often give directions using the phrase *cien metros* syen *me*·tros (100 metres). This is really shorthand for 'one city block', known locally as *una cuadra* oo·na *kwa*·dra.

Turn ...	*Doble ...*	do·ble ...
at the corner	*en la esquina*	en la es·kee·na
at the traffic lights	*en el semáforo*	en el se·ma·fo·ro
left	*a la izquierda*	a la ees·kyer·da
right	*a la derecha*	a la de·re·cha
north	*norte*	nor·te
south	*sur*	soor
east	*este*	es·te
west	*oeste*	o·es·te
by bus	*por bus*	por boos
by taxi	*por taxi*	por tak·see
by train	*por tren*	por tren
on foot	*por a pie*	a pye

For information on Costa Rican addresses, see the box **return to sender**, page 82.

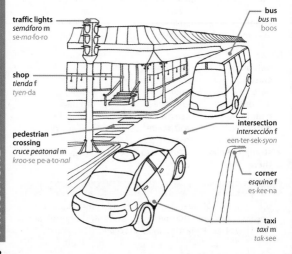

traffic lights
semáforo m
se·ma·fo·ro

shop
tienda f
tyen·da

pedestrian crossing
cruce peatonal m
kroo·se pe·a·to·nal

bus
bus m
boos

intersection
intersección f
een·ter·sek·syon

corner
esquina f
es·kee·na

taxi
taxi m
tak·see

accommodation
hospedaje

finding accommodation

encontrando un lugar para hospedarse

An *apartotel* is basically a hotel room equipped with a kitchen to allow for self-catering. The word *cabina* is loosely used to cover cheap to mid-range accommodation. Both the words *pensión* pen·*syon* and *casa de huéspedes* are used for 'guesthouse'. Bed and breakfasts are an increasingly popular accommodation option and the English term is used.

Where's a/an ...?	¿Dónde hay ...?	*don*·de ai ...
apartotel	un apartotel	oon a·par·to·*tel*
cabina	una cabina	oo·na ka·*bee*·na
camping	una área para	oo·na *a*·re·a *pa*·ra
ground	acampar	a·kam·*par*
ecolodge	un ecolodge	oon e·ko·loj
guesthouse	una casa de	oo·na *ka*·sa de
	huéspedes	*wes*·pe·des
hostel	un hospedaje	oon os·pe·*da*·khe
hotel	un hotel	oon o·*tel*
youth hostel	un albergue	oon al·*ber*·ge
	juvenil	khoo·ve·*neel*

Can you	¿Me podría	me po·*dree*·a
recommend	recomendar	re·ko·men·*dar*
somewhere ...?	algún lugar ...?	al·*goon* loo·*gar* ...
cheap	barato	ba·*ra*·to
good	bueno	*bwe*·no
luxurious	lujoso	loo·*kho*·so
nearby	cerca de aquí	*ser*·ka de a·*kee*
romantic	romántico	ro·*man*·tee·ko
safe for women	que sea seguro	ke *se*·a se·*goo*·ro
travellers	para mujeres	*pa*·ra moo·*khe*·res

accommodation

59

I want something	Quiero algo que	kye·ro al·go ke
near the …	esté cerca …	es·te ser·ka …
beach	de la playa	de la pla·ya
bus stop	de la parada	de la pa·ra·da
	de buses	de boo·ses
city centre	del centro	del sen·tro
shops	de las tiendas	de las tyen·das
What's the	¿Cuál es la	kwal es la
address?	dirección?	dee·rek·syon

For responses, see **directions**, page 57.

For responses, see **directions**, page 57.

local talk

dive n	chinchorro m	cheen·cho·ro
roach motel	cucarachero m	koo·ka·ra·che·ro
top spot	lugar pura vida m	loo·gar poo·ra vee·da

booking ahead & checking in

haciendo una reservación y llegando

I'd like to book a room, please.
Quiero reservar una
habitación, por favor.
kye·ro re·ser·var oo·na
a·bee·ta·syon por fa·vor

I have a reservation.
Tengo una reservación.
ten·go oo·na re·ser·va·syon

My name's …
Mi nombre es …
mee nom·bre es …

For (three) nights/weeks.
Por (tres) noches/semanas.
por (tres) no·ches/se·ma·nas

From (2 July) to (6 July).
Del (dos de julio)
al (seis de julio).
del (dos de khoo·lyo)
al (says de khoo·lyo)

Do I need to pay upfront?
¿Necesito pagar
por adelantado?
ne·se·see·to pa·gar
por a·de·lan·ta·do

¿Cuántas noches?	kwan·tas no·ches	**How many nights?**
llave f	ya·ve	**key**
lleno/a m/f	ye·no/a	**full**
pasaporte m	pa·sa·por·te	**passport**
recepción f	re·sep·syon	**reception**

Do you have a ... room?	¿Tiene una habitación ...?	tye·ne oo·na a·bee·ta·syon ...
single	sencilla	sen·see·ya
double	doble	do·ble
twin	con dos camas sencillas	kon dos ka·mas sen·see·yas

How much is it per ...?	¿Cuánto es por ...?	kwan·to es por ...
night	noche	no·che
person	persona	per·so·na
week	semana	se·ma·na

Can I pay by ...?	¿Puedo pagar con ...?	pwe·do pa·gar kon ...
credit card	tarjeta de crédito	tar·khe·ta de kre·dee·to
debit card	tarjeta de débito	tar·khe·ta de de·bee·to
travellers cheque	cheque de viajero	che·ke de vya·khe·ro

Can I see it?	¿Puedo verla?	pwe·do ver·la
I'll take it.	Sí, la quiero.	see la kye·ro

signs

Baño	ba·nyo	**Bathroom**
Espacio Disponible	es·pa·syo dees·po·nee·ble	**Vacancy**
Lavandería	la·van·de·ree·a	**Laundry**
No Hay Espacio	no ai es·pa·syo	**No Vacancy**

accommodation

61

requests & queries

Is breakfast included?
¿Incluye el desayuno? een·*kloo*·ye el de·sa·*yoo*·no

When/Where is breakfast served?
¿Cuándo/Dónde kwan·do/*don*·de
sirven el desayuno? *seer*·ven el de·sa·*yoo*·no

Is there hot water all day?
¿Hay agua caliente ai *a*·gwa ka·*lyen*·te
todo el día? *to*·do el *dee*·a

Please wake me at (seven).
Por favor, despiérteme por fa·*vor* des·*pyer*·te·me
a las (siete). a las (*sye*·te)

Do you have a/an …?	*¿Tienen …?*	*tye*·nen …
elevator	*ascensor*	a·sen·*sor*
laundry service	*servicio de lavandería*	ser·*vee*·syos de la·van·de·*ree*·a
message board	*pizarra de mensajes*	pee·*sa*·ra de men·*sa*·khes
safe	*caja fuerte*	*ka*·kha *fwer*·te
swimming pool	*piscina*	pee·*see*·na
Can I use the …?	*¿Podría usar …?*	po·*dree*·a oo·*sar* …
kitchen	*la cocina*	la ko·*see*·na
laundry	*la lavandería*	la la·van·de·*ree*·a
telephone	*el teléfono*	el te·*le*·fo·no

Who is it?	¿Quién es?	kyen es
Just a moment.	Un momento.	oon mo·men·to
Come in.	Pase.	pa·se
Come back later, please.	Vuelva más tarde, por favor.	vwel·va mas tar·de por fa·vor

Could I have (a) ..., please?	¿Me podría dar ..., por favor?	me po·dree·a dar ... por fa·vor
mosquito net	un mosquitero	oon mos·kee·te·ro
my key	la llave	la ya·ve
receipt	una factura	oo·na fak·too·ra

Do you ... here?	¿Aquí ...?	a·kee ...
arrange tours	organizan tours	or·ga·nee·san toors
change money	cambian dinero	kam·byan dee·ne·ro

Is there a message for me?
¿Tengo algún mensaje? ten·go al·goon men·sa·khe

Can I leave a message for someone?
¿Le puedo dejar un le pwe·do de·khar oon
mensaje a alguien? men·sa·khe a al·gyen

I'm locked out of my room.
No puedo entrar al cuarto. no pwe·do en·trar al kwar·to

complaints

quejas

It's too ...	Está demasiado ...	es·ta de·ma·sya·do ...
bright	claro	kla·ro
cold	frío	free·o
dark	oscuro	os·koo·ro
expensive	caro	ka·ro
hot	caliente	ka·lyen·te
noisy	ruidoso	rwee·do·so
small	pequeño	pe·ke·nyo

The ... doesn't work.   *El ... no sirve.*   el ... no *seer*·ve

   air conditioner   *aire acondicionado*   *ai*·re a·kon·dee·syo·*na*·do

   fan   *ventilador*   ven·tee·la·*dor*

   toilet   *baño*   *ba*·nyo

Can I get (another blanket)?
   ¿Me podría dar (otra cobija)?   me po·*dree*·a dar (*o*·tra ko·*bee*·kha)

This ... isn't clean.
   Este/a ... está sucio/a. m/f   es·te/a ... es·*ta soo*·syo/a

There's no hot water.
   No hay agua caliente.   no ai *a*·gwa ka·*lyen*·te

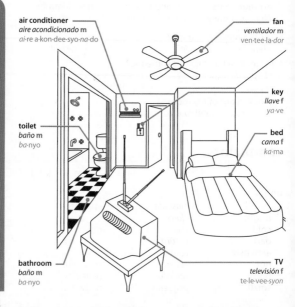

air conditioner
aire acondicionado m
ai·re a·kon·dee·syo·*na*·do

fan
ventilador m
ven·tee·la·*dor*

key
llave f
ya·ve

toilet
baño m
ba·nyo

bed
cama f
ka·ma

bathroom
baño m
ba·nyo

TV
televisión f
te·le·vee·*syon*

checking out

What time is checkout?
¿A qué hora es la salida?　　a ke *o*·ra es la sa·*lee*·da

Can I have a late checkout?
¿Puedo salir más tarde?　　*pwe*·do sa·*leer* mas *tar*·de

Can you call a taxi for me (for 11 o'clock)?
¿Usted me podría llamar　　oos·*ted* me po·*dree*·a ya·*mar*
un taxi (para las once)?　　oon *tak*·see (*pa*·ra las *on*·se)

I'm leaving now.
Ya me voy.　　ya me voy

Can I leave my bags here?
¿Puedo dejar mis　　*pwe*·do de·*khar* mees
maletas aquí?　　ma·*le*·tas a·*kee*

There's a mistake in the bill.
Hay un error en la cuenta.　　ai oon e·*ror* en la *kwen*·ta

I had a great stay, thanks.
La pasé muy bien,　　la pa·*se* mooy byen
muchas gracias.　　*moo*·chas *gra*·syas

I'll recommend it to my friends.
Voy a recomendar　　voy a re·ko·men·*dar*
a mis amigos.　　a mees a·*mee*·gos

Could I have my ..., please?	*¿Me puede dar ..., por favor?*	me *pwe*·de dar ... por fa·*vor*
deposit	*mi depósito*	mee de·*po*·see·to
passport	*mi pasaporte*	mee pa·sa·*por*·te
valuables	*mis valores*	mees va·*lo*·res

I'll be back ...	*Voy a volver ...*	voy a vol·*ver* ...
in (three) days	*en (tres) días*	en (tres) *dee*·as
on (Tuesday)	*el (martes)*	el (*mar*·tes)

accommodation

65

camping

acampar

Can I ...?	¿Puedo ...?	pwe·do ...
camp here	acampar aquí	a·kam·par a·kee
park next to my tent	parquearme a la par de la tienda	par·ke·ar·me a la par de la tyen·da

How much is it per ...?	¿Cuánto cuesta por ...?	kwan·to kwes·ta por ...
person	persona	per·so·na
tent	tienda de campaña	tyen·da de kam·pa·nya
vehicle	carro	ka·ro

Do you have (a) ...?	¿Tiene ...?	tye·ne ...
electricity	electricidad	e·lek·tree·see·dad
laundry service	servicio de lavandería	ser·vee·syos de la·van·de·ree·a
shower facilities	duchas	doo·chas
site	un espacio	oon es·pa·syo
tents for hire	tiendas de campaña para alquilar	tyen·das de kam·pa·nya pa·ra al·kee·lar
toilets	baños	ba·nyos

Who do I ask to stay here?
¿A quién le pregunto para quedarme aquí?   a kyen le pre·goon·to pa·ra ke·dar·me a·kee

Is it coin-operated?
¿Es de monedas?   es de mo·ne·das

Is the water drinkable?
¿Se puede beber el agua?   se pwe·de be·ber el a·gwa

Could I borrow ...?
¿Podría prestarme ...?   po·dree·a pres·tar·me ...

For cooking utensils, see **self-catering,** page 166.

renting

I'm here about the ... for rent.	*Vengo por el/la ... que está alquilando.* m/f	*ven*·go por el/la ... ke es·*ta* al·kee·*lan*·do
Do you have a/an ... for rent?	*¿Tiene un/una ... para alquilar?* m/f	*tye*·ne oon/*oo*·na ... *pa*·ra al·kee·*lar*
apartment	*apartamento* m	a·par·ta·*men*·to
cabina	*cabina* f	ka·*bee*·na
house	*casa* f	*ka*·sa
room	*cuarto* m	*kwar*·to
villa	*villa* f	*vee*·ya
(partly) furnished	*(parcialmente) amueblado*	(par·syal·*men*·te) a·mwe·*bla*·do
unfurnished	*sin amueblar*	seen a·mwe·*blar*

Is there a deposit?
¿Hay que dejar depósito?   ai ke de·*khar* de·*po*·see·to

Are utilities included?
¿Incluye los servicios de luz y agua?   een·*kloo*·ye los ser·*vee*·syos de loos ee *a*·gwa

staying with locals

If you're invited to stay with a local family, make sure you not only bring a small gift (such as food or a souvenir), but also offer to help with the housework. You may need to insist on helping out, as your offer will usually be declined on first attempt.

Can I stay at your place?
¿Puedo quedarme en su casa?   *pwe*·do ke·*dar*·me en soo *ka*·sa

accommodation

67

I have my own …	Yo tengo mi propio/a … m/f	yo ten·go mee pro·pyo/a …
sleeping bag	saco de dormir m	sa·ko de dor·meer
sleeping mat	colchoneta f	kol·cho·ne·ta

Is there anything I can do to help?
¿En que le puedo ayudar?   en ke le pwe·do a·yoo·dar

Can I bring anything for the meal?
¿Le traigo algo   le trai·go al·go
para la comida?   pa·ra la ko·mee·da

Can I set/clear the table?
¿Pongo/Quito la mesa?   pon·go/kee·to la me·sa

Can I take out the rubbish?
¿Saco la basura?   sa·ko la ba·soo·ra

Thanks for your hospitality.
Muchas gracias   moo·chas gra·syas
por hospedarme.   por os·pe·dar·me

---

the host with the most

If you're invited to share a meal in a Costa Rican home, your solicitous hosts will ply you with food and drink. Remember that politeness is highly valued in their culture, so be sure to extoll the virtues of your hosts' cooking. This phrase should do the trick:

La comida está muy rica!
la ko·mee·da es·ta mooy ree·ka   **The food is very good!**

For more dining-related phrases, see **eating out**, page 153.

looking for ...

Are shops open (on Independence Day)?
¿El comercio abre (el día   el ko·*mer*·syo *a*·bre (el *dee*·a
de la independencia)?   de la een·de·pen·*den*·sya)

What hours are shops open?
¿Cuál es el horario   kwal es el o·*ra*·ryo
de las tiendas?   de las *tyen*·das

Where can I buy (a padlock)?
¿Dónde puedo   *don*·de *pwe*·do
comprar (un candado)?   kom·*prar* (oon kan·*da*·do)

Where's (a/the) ...?	*¿Dónde hay ...?*	*don*·de ai ...
department store	*una tienda*	*oo*·na *tyen*·da
kiosk	*un quiosco*	oon *kyos*·ko
mall	*un mall*	oon mol
neighbourhood store	*una pulpería*	*oo*·na pool·pe·*ree*·a
market	*un mercado*	oon mer·*ka*·do

For more items and shopping locations, see the **dictionary**.

making a purchase

I'm just looking.
Sólo estoy viendo.   *so*·lo es·*toy* vyen·do

I'd like to buy (an adaptor plug).
Quiero (un adaptador).   *kye*·ro (oon a·dap·ta·*dor*)

How much is it?
¿Cuánto cuesta? kwan·to kwes·ta

Can you write down the price?
¿Podría escribir el precio? po·dree·a es·kree·beer el pre·syo

Can I look at it?
¿Lo/la puedo ver? m/f lo/la pwe·do ver

Do you have any others?
¿Tiene más? tye·ne mas

Is this (240) volts?
¿Éste es de (doscientos es·te es de (do·syen·tos
cuarenta) voltios? kwa·ren·ta) vol·tee·os

Do you accept …?	¿Acepta …?	a·sep·ta …
credit cards	tarjetas de crédito	tar·khe·tas de kre·dee·to
debit cards	tarjetas de débito	tar·khe·tas de de·bee·to
travellers cheques	cheque de viajero	che·ke de vya·khe·ro

Could I have a …, please?	¿Me da …, por favor?	me da … por fa·vor
bag	una bolsa	oo·na bol·sa
receipt	un recibo	oon re·see·bo

I don't need a bag, thanks.
No necesito bolsa, gracias. no ne·se·see·to bol·sa gra·syas

Could I have it wrapped?
¿Me lo puede me lo pwe·de
envolver, por favor? en·vol·ver por fa·vor

Does it have a guarantee?
¿Tiene garantía? tye·ne ga·ran·tee·a

Can I have it sent abroad?
¿Lo puedo mandar lo pwe·do man·dar
al extranjero? al eks·tran·khe·ro

Can you order it for me?
¿Usted me lo podría pedir? oos·ted me lo po·dree·a pe·deer

Can I pick it up later?
¿Puedo pasar a   pwe·do pa·sar a
recogerlo después?   re·ko·kher·lo des·pwes

The quality isn't good.
No es de buena calidad.   no es de bwe·na ka·lee·dad

It doesn't work.
No funciona.   no foon·see·o·na

It's broken/damaged.
Está roto/dañado.   es·ta ro·to/da·nya·do

It's dirty/stained.
Está sucio/manchado.   es·ta soo·syo/man·cha·do

I'd like to return this.
Quiero devolver ésto.   kye·ro de·vol·ver es·to

I'd like (a) …, please.	*Me da …, por favor.*	me da … por fa·vor
my change	*el vuelto*	el vwel·to
receipt	*un recibo*	oon re·see·bo
refund	*un reintegro*	oon re·een·te·gro

local talk

bargain n	*ganga* f	gan·ga
rip-off	*robo* m	ro·bo
sale	*promoción* f	pro·mo·syon

bargaining

el regateo

That's too expensive.
Está muy caro.   es·ta mooy ka·ro

Can you lower the price?
¿Podría bajarle el precio?   po·dree·a ba·khar·le el pre·syo

Do you have something cheaper?
¿Tiene algo más barato?   tye·ne al·go mas ba·ra·to

What's your final price?
¿Entonces, cuál — en·*ton*·ses kwal
es el precio final? — es el *pre*·syo fee·*nal*

I'll give you (1000 *colones*).
Le doy (mil colones). — le doy (meel ko·*lo*·nes)

listen for ...		
¿Algo más?	*al*·go mas	**Anything else?**
¿Le puedo ayudar	le *pwe*·do a·yoo·*dar*	**Can I help you?**
en algo?	en *al*·go	
No tenemos.	no te·*ne*·mos	**We don't have any.**

books & reading

libros y lectura

Can you recommend a book to me?
¿Me podría — me po·*dree*·a
recomendar un libro? — re·ko·men·*dar* oon *lee*·bro

Do you have ...?	*¿Tiene ...?*	tye·ne ...
a book by	un libro de	oon *lee*·bro de
(Carmen Lyra)	(Carmen Lyra)	(*kar*·men *lee*·ra)
an entertainment	una guía de	*oo*·na *gee*·a de
guide	entretenimientos	en·tre·te·nee·*myen*·tos

Is there an English-	*¿Hay alguna ...*	ai al·*goo*·na ...
language ...?	*de (inglés)?*	de (een·*gles*)
bookshop	librería	lee·bre·*ree*·a
section	sección	sek·*syon*

I'd like a ...	*Quiero ...*	*kye*·ro ...
dictionary	un diccionario	oon deek·syo·*na*·ryo
newspaper	un periódico	oon pe·*ryo*·dee·ko
(in English)	(en inglés)	(en een·*gles*)

Do you have ...?	*¿Tiene ...?*	tye·ne ...
guidebooks	guías	*gee*·as
phrasebooks	libros de frases	*lee*·bros de *fra*·ses

clothes

ropa

My size is …	Mi talla es …	mee ta·ya es …
small	pequeño	pe·ke·nyo
medium	mediano	me·dya·no
large	grande	gran·de

Can I try it on?
¿Me lo puedo probar?   me lo pwe·do pro·bar

It doesn't fit.
No me queda.   no me ke·da

hairdressing

peluquería

I'd like (a) …	Quiero …	kye·ro …
colour	un tinte	oon teen·te
my beard	que me recorten	ke me re·kor·ten
trimmed	la barba	la bar·ba
my hair	que me laven/	ke me la·ven/
washed/dried	sequen el pelo	se·ken el pe·lo
shave	que me afeiten	ke me a·fay·ten
streaks	hacerme unos	a·ser·me oo·nos
	rayitos	ra·yee·tos
trim	que me recorten	ke me re·kor·ten
	el pelo	el pe·lo

Don't cut it too short.
No me lo corte   no me lo kor·te
demasiado corto.   de·ma·sya·do kor·to

Please use a new blade.
Por favor, use   por fa·vor oo·se
una navajilla nueva.   oo·na na·va·khee·ya nwe·va

Shave it all off!
Córtemelo todo.   kor·te·me·lo to·do

music

I'd like a ...	Quiero un ...	kye·ro oon ...
blank tape	cassette	ka·se·te
	en blanco	en blan·ko
CD/DVD	CD/DVD	se de/de ve de
video	vídeo	vee·de·o

I'm looking for something by (Editus).
Estoy buscando   es·toy boos·kan·do
algo de (Editus).   al·go de (e·dee·toos)

Can I listen to this?
¿Lo puedo escuchar?   lo pwe·do es·koo·char

Will this work on any DVD player?
¿Este servirá en   es·te ser·vee·ra en
cualquier DVD?   kwal·kyer de ve de

Is this for a (PAL/NTSC) system?
¿Es para un sistema   es pa·ra oon sees·te·ma
(PAL/NTSC)?   (pe a e·le/e·ne te e·se se)

photography

Can you ...?	¿Puede ...?	pwe·de ...
develop digital photos	revelar fotos digitales	re·ve·lar fo·tos dee·khee·ta·les
develop this film	revelar este rollo	re·ve·lar es·te ro·yo
load my film	ponerme este rollo en la cámara	po·ner·me es·te ro·yo en la ka·ma·ra
recharge the battery for my digital camera	recargar la batería de mi cámara digital	re·kar·gar la ba·te·ree·a de mee ka·ma·ra dee·khee·tal
transfer photos from my camera to CD	pasar las fotos de mi cámara digital a un CD	pa·sar las fo·tos de mee ka·ma·ra dee·khee·tal a oon se de

I need a/an ... film for this camera.	Necesito un rollo ... para esta cámara.	ne·se·see·to oon ro·yo ... pa·ra es·ta ka·ma·ra
APS	APS	a pe e·se
B&W	blanco y negro	blan·ko ee ne·gro
colour	a color	a ko·lor
slide	para diapositivas	pa·ra dee·a·po·see·tee·vas
(200) speed	asa (doscientos)	a·sa (do·syen·tos)

Do you have a ... for this camera?	¿Tiene un ... para esta cámara?	tye·ne oon ... pa·ra es·ta ka·ma·ra
flash	flash	flash
light meter	medidor de luz	me·dee·dor de loos
telephoto lens	teleobjetivo	te·le·ob·khe·tee·vo
zoom lens	zoom	soom

Do you have ... for this camera?	¿Tiene ... para esta cámara?	tye·ne ... pa·ra es·ta ka·ma·ra
batteries	baterías	ba·te·ree·as
memory cards	memorias	me·mo·ree·as

... camera	... cámara	... ka·ma·ra
digital	digital	dee·khee·tal
disposable	desechable	de·se·cha·ble
underwater	sumergible	soo·mer·khee·ble
video	de vídeo	de vee·de·o

I need a cable to connect my camera to a computer.

Necesito un cable para conectar mi cámara a la computadora.

ne·se·see·to oon ka·ble pa·ra ko·nek·tar mee ka·ma·ra a la kom·poo·ta·do·ra

I need a cable to recharge this battery.

Necesito un cable para recargar esta batería.

ne·se·see·to oon ka·ble pa·ra re·kar·gar es·ta ba·te·ree·a

I need a video cassette for this camera.
Necesito un cassette ne·se·*see*·to oon ka·*se*·te
para esta cámara de vídeo. *pa*·ra *es*·ta *ka*·ma·ra de *vee*·de·o

I need a passport photo taken.
Necesito tomarme una ne·se·*see*·to to·*mar*·me *oo*·na
foto tamaño pasaporte. *fo*·to ta·*ma*·nyo pa·sa·*por*·te

I'm not happy with these photos.
No me gusta la no me *goos*·ta la
calidad de estas fotos. ka·lee·*dad* de *es*·tas *fo*·tos

I don't want to pay the full price.
No quiero pagarle el no *kye*·ro pa·*gar*·le el
precio completo. *pre*·syo kom·*ple*·to

repairs

reparaciones

Can I have my	¿Me pueden	me *pwe*·den
... repaired here?	arreglar ... aquí?	a·reg·*lar* ... a·*kee*
backpack	mi mochila	mee mo·*chee*·la
bag	mi bolso	mee *bol*·so
(video) camera	mi cámara	mee *ka*·ma·ra
	(de vídeo)	(de *vee*·de·o)
(sun)glasses	mis anteojos	mees an·te·*o*·khos
	(oscuros)	(os·*koo*·ros)
shoes	mis zapatos	mees sa·*pa*·tos

When will it be ready?
¿Cuándo va a estar listo? *kwan*·do va a es·*tar lees*·to

souvenirs

ceramics	cerámica f	se·*ra*·mee·ka
hammock	hamaca f	a·*ma* ka
handicraft	artesanías f pl	ar·te·sa·*nee*·as
jewellery	joyas f pl	*kho*·yas
painted miniature ox carts	carretas f pl	ka·*re*·tas

the internet

internet

Where's the local Internet café?
    ¿Dónde hay un   *don·*de ai oon
    café internet?   ka·*fe* een·ter·*net*

I'd like to …	*Quiero …*	*kye·*ro …
burn a CD	*quemar un*	ke·*mar* oon
	disco	*dees·*ko
check my	*revisar mi*	re·vee·*sar* mee
email	*correo*	ko·*re·*o
download	*bajar mis*	ba·*khar* mees
my photos	*fotos*	*fo·*tos
get Internet	*tener acceso*	te·*ner* ak·*se·*so
access	*al internet*	al een·ter·*net*
use a printer	*usar una*	oo·*sar* oo·na
	impresora	eem·pre·*so·*ra
use a scanner	*usar un*	oo·*sar* oon
	escáner	es·*ka·*ner

Do you have …?	*¿Tiene …?*	*tye·*ne …
PCs	*PCs*	pe ses
Macs	*Macs*	maks
a Zip drive	*unidad de Zip*	oo·nee·*dad* de seep

Can I connect	*¿Puedo conectar*	*pwe·*do ko·nek·*tar*
my … to this	*mi … a esta*	mee … a *es·*ta
computer?	*computadora?*	kom·poo·ta·*do·*ra
camera	*cámara*	*ka·*ma·ra
media player	*reproductor*	re·pro·dook·*tor*
	media	*me·*dya
portable hard	*disco duro*	*dees·*ko *doo·*ro
drive	*portátil*	por·*ta·*teel

How much per ...?	¿Cuánto es por ...?	kwan·to es por ...
hour	hora	o·ra
(five) minutes	(cinco) minutos	(seen·ko) mee·noo·tos
page	página	pa·khee·na

How do I log on?	¿Cómo entro?	ko·mo en·tro
It's crashed.	Está caída.	es·ta ka·ee·da
I've finished.	Ya terminé.	ya ter·mee·ne

where the @!*# is it?

Spanish-language and English-language keyboard layouts differ because the two alphabets aren't quite the same. This shouldn't generally be a problem, but for one pesky – all too useful in the age of email – key.

The @ ('at') symbol – in Spanish this symbol is called *la arroa* la a·ro·a – isn't necessarily labeled on keyboards or may not be accessed by simply pressing the keys you're used to. Try the F2 key, use an ALT code – or ask for help:

Where's the @ key?
¿Dónde está la arroa? don·de es·ta la a·ro·a

mobile/cell phone

teléfono celular

I'd like a ...	Necesito ...	ne·se·see·to ...
charger for my phone	un cargador para mi celular	oon kar·ga·dor pa·ra mee se·loo·lar
mobile/cell phone for hire	alquilar un teléfono celular	al·kee·lar oon te·le·fo·no se·loo·lar
prepaid mobile/ cell phone	un celular prepagado	oon se·loo·lar pre·pa·ga·do
SIM card for your network	una tarjeta SIM para su red	oo·na tar·khe·ta seem pa·ra soo red

What are the call rates?
  ¿Cuánto es la tarifa?   *kwan·to es la ta·ree·fa*

(30) *colones* per (30) minutes.
  (Treinta) colones por   *(trayn·ta) ko·lo·nes por*
  (treinta) minutos.   *(trayn·ta) mee·noo·tos*

phone

el teléfono

What's your phone number?
  ¿Cuál es tu número   kwal es too *noo·me·ro*
  de teléfono?   de te·*le·*fo·no

Where's the nearest public phone?
  ¿Dónde está el teléfono   *don·*de es·*ta* el te·*le·*fo·no
  público más cercano?   poo·blee·ko mas ser·*ka·*no

Can I look at a phone book?
  ¿Puedo ver la   *pwe·*do ver la
  guía telefónica?   *gee·*a te·le·*fo·*nee·ka

What's the area/country code for (Panama)?
  ¿Cuál es el código de   kwal es el *ko·*dee·go de
  área/país para (Panamá)? *a·*re·a/pa·*ees* pa·ra (pa·na·*ma*)

The number is …
  El número es …   el *noo·*me·ro es …

I want to …	*Quiero …*	*kye·*ro …
buy a	*comprar una*	kom·*prar* oo·na
phonecard	*tarjeta*	tar·*khe·*ta
	telefónica	te·le·*fo·*nee·ka
call (Canada)	*llamar a*	ya·*mar* a
	(Canadá)	(ka·na·*da*)
make a (local)	*hacer una*	a·*ser* oo·na
call	*llamada (local)*	ya·*ma·*da (lo·*kal*)
reverse the	*llamar de cobro*	ya·*mar* de *ko·*bro
charges	*revertido*	re·ver·*tee·*do
speak for (three)	*hablar (tres)*	a·*blar* (tres)
minutes	*minutos*	mee·*noo·*tos

How much does … cost?	¿Cuánto cuesta …?	kwan·to kwes·ta …
a (three)-minute call	una llamada de (tres) minutos	oo·na ya·ma·da de (tres) mee·noo·tos
each extra minute	cada minuto extra	ka·da mee·noo·to eks·tra

It's engaged.	Está ocupado.	es·ta o·koo·pa·do
I've been cut off.	Se cortó.	se kor·to
The connection's bad.	La conexión está muy mala.	la ko·nek·syon es·ta mooy ma·la
Hello.	Aló.	a·lo
It's …	Es …	es …

listen for …

¿Con quién quiere hablar?	kon kyen kye·re a·blar	Who do you want to speak to?
No está.	no es·ta	He/She isn't here.
Número equivocado.	noo·me·ro e·kee·vo·ka·do	Wrong number.
¿Quién llama?	kyen ya·ma	Who's calling?
Un momento.	oon mo·men·to	One moment.

Please tell him/her I called.

¿Le podría decir que yo llamé, por favor? — le po·dree·a de·seer ke yo ya·me por fa·vor

Can I leave a message?

¿Le puedo dejar un mensaje? — le pwe·do de·khar oon men·sa·khe

I don't have a contact number.

No tengo un número dónde me pueda llamar. — no ten·go oon noo·me·ro don·de me pwe·da ya·mar

I'll call back later.

Yo llamo después. — yo ya·mo des·pwes

What time should I call?

¿A qué hora debo llamar? — a ke o·ra de·bo ya·mar

post office

I want to send a ...	Quiero mandar ...	kye·ro man·dar ...
fax	un fax	oon faks
letter	una carta	oo·na kar·ta
parcel	un paquete	oon pa·ke·te
postcard	una postal	oo·na pos·tal

I want to buy a/an ...	Quiero comprar...	kye·ro kom·prar...
(padded) envelope	un sobre (acolchonado)	oon so·bre (a·kol·cho·na·do)
stamp	una estampilla	oo·na es·tam·pee·ya

Please send it by air/surface mail to (Australia).
Por favor, envíelo por avión/tierra a (Australia).
por fa·vor en·vee·e·lo por a·vyon/tye·ra a (ow·stra·lya)

It contains (souvenirs).
Contiene (recuerdos).
kon·tye·ne (re·kwer·dos)

Is there any mail for me?
¿Me llegó algo?
me ye·go al·go

snail mail

... mail	correo ...	ko·re·o ...
air	aéreo	a·e·re·o
express	express	eks·pres
registered	certificado	ser·tee·fee·ka·do
sea	marítimo	ma·ree·tee·mo
surface	por tierra	por tye·ra

communications

81

customs declaration	*declaración de aduana* f	de·kla·ra·*syon* de a·*dwa*·na
domestic	*local* m&f	lo·*kal*
fragile	*frágil* m&f	*fra*·kheel
international	*internacional* m&f	een·ter·na·syo·*nal*
mail n	*correo* m	ko·*re*·o
mailbox	*buzón* m	boo·*son*
PO box	*apartado* m	a·par·*ta*·do
postcode	*código postal* m	*ko*·dee·go pos·*tal*

return to sender

Addresses in Costa Rica sometimes take a surprising form. For one thing, outside San José and other larger cities, numbered addresses and street names don't really exist. Instead, Costa Ricans use descriptive addresses.

People can get quite creative in their choice of landmarks, and rural addresses have even been known to make reference to natural features such as streams or trees! Most addresses include the name of the province and the name of the nearest large town or city. A house address may read something like:

Anna Fernández
2km después de la fábrica hacia el Aguila
(2km after the factory on the way to Aguila)
Pejibaye de Perez Zeledón
San Isidro el General (closest major town)
Costa Rica
Centroamérica

What times/days is the bank open?

¿A qué horas/días	a ke *o*·ras/*dee*·as	
está abierto el banco?	es·*ta* a·*byer*·to el *ban*·ko	

Where can I …?	*¿Dónde puedo …?*	*don*·de *pwe*·do …
I'd like to …	*Quisiera …*	kee·*sye*·ra …
cash a cheque	*cambiar un cheque*	kam·*byar* oon *che*·ke
change a travellers cheque	*cambiar un cheque de viajero*	kam·*byar* oon *che*·ke de vya·*khe*·ro
change money into *colones*	*cambiar dinero a colones*	kam·*byar* dee·*ne*·ro a ko·*lo*·nes
change money/ dollars	*cambiar plata/ dólares*	kam·*byar* pla·ta/ *do*·la·res
get a cash advance	*obtener un adelanto en efectivo*	ob·te·*ner* oon a·de·*lan*·to en e·fek·*tee*·vo
get change for this note	*cambiar este pagaré*	kam·*byar* es·te pa·ga·*re*
withdraw money	*sacar dinero*	sa·*kar* dee·*ne*·ro
Where's a/an …?	*¿Dónde hay …?*	*don*·de ai …
automated teller machine	*un cajero automático*	oon ka·*khe*·ro ow·to·*ma*·tee·ko
foreign exchange office	*una casa de cambio*	*oo*·na *ka*·sa de *kam*·byo

For more information on the Costa Rican currency, the *colón*, see the box **the colour of money**, page 40.

What's the exchange rate?
¿A cómo está el   a *ko*·mo es·*ta* el
tipo de cambio?   *tee*·po de *kam*·byo

What's the charge for that?
¿Cuánto cobran por eso?   *kwan*·to *ko*·bran por *e*·so

The automated teller machine took my card.
El cajero automático   el ka·*khe*·ro ow·to·*ma*·tee·ko
se dejó mi tarjeta.   se de·*kho* mee tar·*khe*·ta

I've forgotten my PIN.
Se me olvidó mi PIN.   se me ol·vee·*do* mee peen

Can I use my credit card to withdraw money?
¿Puedo usar mi tarjeta de   *pwe*·do oo·*sar* mee tar·*khe*·ta de
crédito para sacar plata?   *kre*·dee·to *pa*·ra sa·*kar pla*·ta

Has my money arrived yet?
¿Ya llegó mi plata?   ya ye·*go* mee *pla*·ta

How long will it take to arrive?
¿Cuánto va a durar   *kwan*·to va a doo·*rar*
en llegar?   en ye·*gar*

For other useful phrases, see **money**, page 39.

---

listen for ...

Firme aquí.		
feer·me a·*kee*		**Sign here.**
Hay un problema.		
ai oon pro·*ble*·ma		**There's a problem.**
No podemos hacer eso.		
no po·*de*·mos a·*ser e*·so		**We can't do that.**
Usted no tiene fondos.		
oos·*ted* no *tye*·ne *fon*·dos		**You have no funds left.**
identificación f	ee·den·tee·fee·ka·*syon*	**identification**
pasaporte m	pa·sa·*por*·te	**passport**

sightseeing
turismo

I'd like a …	Quisiera …	kee·sye·ra …
brochure	un panfleto	oon pan·fle·to
catalogue	un catálogo	oon ka·ta·lo·go
guide	un guía	oon gee·a
guidebook (in English)	una guía turística (en inglés)	oo·na gee·a too·rees·tee·ka (en een·gles)
(local) map	un mapa (local)	oon ma·pa (lo·kal)

Do you have information on … sights?	¿Tiene información sobre atracciones …?	tye·ne een·for·ma·syon so·bre a·trak·syo·nes …
cultural	culturales	kool·too·ra·les
historical	históricas	ees·to·ree·kas
religious	religiosas	re·lee·khyo·sas

I'd like to see …
Me gustaría ver …   me goos·ta·ree·a ver …

What's that?
¿Qué es eso?   ke es e·so

Who built/made it?
¿Quién lo construyó/hizo?   kyen lo kons·troo·yo/ee·so

How old is it?
¿Qué tan viejo es?   ke tan vye·kho es

Could you take a photo of me?
¿Podría/Podrías tomarme una foto? pol/inf   po·dree·a/po·dree·as to·mar·me oo·na fo·to

Can I take a photo (of you)?
¿(Le/Te) Puedo sacar una foto? pol/inf   (le/te) pwe·do sa·kar oo·na fo·to

I'll send you the photo.
Yo le/te mando la foto. pol/inf   yo le/te man·do la fo·to

getting in

What time does it open/close?
¿A qué hora abren/cierran?   a ke *o*·ra *a*·bren/*sye*·ran

What's the admission charge?
¿Cuánto cuesta la entrada?   *kwan*·to *kwes*·ta la en·*tra*·da

Is there a discount for …?	*¿Hay algún descuento para …?*	ai al·*goon* des·*kwen*·to *pa*·ra …
children	*niños*	*nee*·nyos
families	*familias*	fa·*mee*·lyas
groups	*grupos*	*groo*·pos
older people	*personas mayores*	per·*so*·nas ma·*yo*·res
pensioners	*pensionados*	pen·syo·*na*·dos
students	*estudiantes*	es·too·*dyan*·tes

tours

tours

Can you recommend a/an …?	¿Me podría recomendar un/una …? m/f	me po·*dree*·a re·ko·men·*dar* oon/*oo*·na …
When's the next …?	¿Cuándo es el/la próximo/a …? m/f	*kwan*·do es el/la *prok*·see·mo/a …
boat trip	excursión en lancha f	eks·koor·*syon* en *lan*·cha
day trip	tour de un día m	toor de oon *dee*·a
ecotour	ecotour m	e·ko·*toor*
natural history tour	tour de historia natural m	toor de ees·*to*·rya na·too·*ral*
tour	tour m	toor
I'd like to go …	Me gustaría …	me goos·ta·*ree*·a …
bird watching	ver pájaros	ver *pa*·kha·ros
canoeing	hacer canoa	a·*ser* ka·*no*·a
horse riding	hacer una cabalgata	a·*ser* *oo*·na ka·bal·*ga*·ta
on a guided trek	hacer trekking con guía	a·*ser* *tre*·keen kon *gee*·a
river rafting	ir rafting	eer *raf*·teen
walking on the beach	caminar en la playa	ka·mee·*nar* en la *pla*·ya
wildlife spotting	ver fauna	ver *fow*·na
Is … included?	¿Incluye …?	een·*kloo*·ye …
accommodation	la dormida	la dor·*mee*·da
food	la comida	la ko·*mee*·da
transport	el transporte	el trans·*por*·te

I want to hire a guide.
Quiero contratar un guía.   *kye*·ro kon·tra·*tar* oon *gee*·a

How much for one day?
¿Cuánto cuesta por un día?   *kwan*·to *kwes*·ta por oon *dee*·a

sightseeing

87

How long is the tour?
    ¿Cuánto dura el tour?   kwan·to doo·ra el toor

What time should we be back?
    ¿A qué hora volvemos?   a ke o·ra vol·ve·mos

Where will we meet?
    ¿Dónde nos encontramos?   don·de nos en·kon·tra·mos

I'm with them.
    Yo vengo con ellos.   yo ven·go kon e·yos

I've lost my group.
    Perdí mi grupo.   per·dee mee groo·po

biological reserve	*reserva biológica* f	re·ser·va byo·lo·khee·ka
botanical garden	*jardín botánico* m	khar·deen bo·ta·nee·ko
habitat	*hábitat* m	a·bee·tat
indigenous reserve	*reserva indígena* f	re·ser·va een·dee·khe·na
national park	*parque nacional* m	par·ke na·syo·nal
wildlife refuge	*refugio de fauna silvestre* m	re·foo·khyo de fow·na seel·ves·tre

For more on habitats and wildlife, see **ecotourism**, page 149.

---

costa rican national parks

Parque Nacional Chirripó	par·ke na·syo·nal chee·ree·po	Chirripó National Park
Parque Nacional Corcovado	par·ke na·syo·nal kor·ko·va·do	Corcovado National Park
Parque Nacional Santa Rosa	par·ke na·syo·nal san·ta ro·sa	Santa Rosa National Park
Parque Nacional Tortuguero	par·ke na·syo·nal tor·too·ge·ro	Tortuguero National Park
Reserva Monteverde	re·ser·va mon·te·ver·de	Monteverde Nature Reserve

I'm attending a …	Estoy aquí para …	es·toy a·kee pa·ra …
conference	una conferencia	oo·na kon·fe·ren·sya
course	un curso	oon koor·so
meeting	una reunión	oo·na re·oo·nyon
trade fair	una feria de comercio	oo·na fe·rya de ko·mer·syo

I'm here with …	Estoy aquí con …	es·toy a·kee kon …
my colleague(s)	mi(s) colega(s)	mee(s) ko·le·ga(s)
(two) others	(dos) personas más	(dos) per·so·nas mas

I'm alone.
Estoy aquí solo/a. m/f
es·toy a·kee so·lo/a

I have an appointment with …
Tengo una cita con …
ten·go oo·na see·ta kon …

I'm staying at (the Hotel Brisamar), room (200).
Me estoy quedando en (el Hotel Brisamar), habitación (doscientos).
me es·toy ke·dan·do en (el o·tel bree·sa·mar) a·bee·ta·syon (do·syen·tos)

I'm here for (two) days/weeks.
Voy a estar aquí (dos) días/semanas.
voy a es·tar a·kee (dos) dee·as/se·ma·nas

Can I have your business card?
¿Me podría dar su tarjeta de presentación?
me po·dree·a dar soo tar·khe·ta de pre·sen·ta·syon

Here's my ...	*Este es mi ...*	*es·*te es mee ...
What's your ...?	*¿Cuál es su ...?*	kwal es soo ...
address	*dirección*	dee·rek·*syon*
email address	*correo*	ko·*re·*o
	electrónico	e·lek·*tro·*nee·ko
fax number	*número*	*noo·*me·ro
	de fax	de faks
mobile/cell	*número de*	*noo·*me·ro de
phone number	*celular*	se·loo·*lar*
pager number	*número*	*noo·*me·ro
	de beeper	de *bee·*per
work number	*número de*	*noo·*me·ro de
	teléfono del	te·*le·*fo·no del
	trabajo	tra·*ba·*kho
Where's the ...?	*¿Dónde es la ...?*	*don·*de es la ...
business centre	*sala*	*sa·*la
	ejecutiva	e·khe·koo·*tee·*va
conference	*conferencia*	kon·fe·*ren·*sya
meeting	*reunión*	re·oo·*nyon*
I need (a/an) ...	*Necesito ...*	ne·se·*see·*to ...
computer	*una*	*oo·*na
	computadora	kom·poo·ta·*do·*ra
Internet	*una conexión*	*oo·*na ko·nek·*syon*
connection	*de internet*	de een·ter·*net*
interpreter	*un traductor*	oon tra·dook·*tor*
who speaks	*que hable*	ke *a·*ble
(English)	*(inglés)*	(een·*gles*)
to send a fax	*mandar un fax*	man·*dar* oon faks

Thank you for your attention.
Gracias por su atención.   *gra·*syas por soo a·ten·*syon*

That went very well.
Estuvo muy bien.   es·*too·*vo mooy byen

Shall we go for a drink/meal?
¿Vamos a comer/tomar algo?   *va·*mos a ko·*mer*/to·*mar al·*go

It's on me.
Yo invito.   yo een·*vee·*to

senior & disabled travellers
viajeros discapacitados o de edad avanzada

Costa Rica is making strides to implement facilities for the elderly and people with disabilities. There are already special seats, parking spots and, in government offices, express queues reserved for people with disabilities (*filas para discapacitados* fee·las pa·ra dees·ka·pa·see·ta·dos). Wheelchair ramps are increasingly common in San José, and the country has recently established its first disabled taxi service (*taxi para discapacitados* tak·see pa·ra dees·ka·pa·see·ta·dos).

I have a disability.
Tengo una discapacidad. ten·go oo·na dees·ka·pa·see·dad

I need assistance.
Necesito asistencia. ne·se·see·to a·sees·ten·sya

I'm deaf.
Soy sordo/a. m/f soy sor·do/a

I have a hearing aid.
Tengo un audífono. ten·go oon ow·dee·fo·no

My (companion) is blind.
Mi (compañero/a) mee (kom·pa·nyer·o/a)
es ciego/a. m/f es sye·go/a

What services do you have for people with a disability?
¿Qué servicios tiene ke ser·vee·syos tye·ne
para personas con pa·ra per·so·nas kon
discapacidad? dees·ka·pa·see·dad

Are guide dogs permitted?
¿Se permiten perros guías? se per·mee·ten pe·ros gee·as

Are there disabled parking spaces?
¿Hay parqueo para ai par·ke·o para
discapacitados? dees·ka·pa·see·ta·dos

Is there wheelchair access?
¿Hay acceso para ai ak·se·so pa·ra
silla de ruedas? see·ya de rwe·das

How wide is the entrance?
¿Qué tan ancha   ke tan *an*·cha
es la entrada?   es la en·*tra*·da

How many steps are there?
¿Cuántas gradas hay?   *kwan*·tas *gra*·das ai

Is there an elevator?
¿Hay ascensor?   ai a·sen·*sor*

Are there disabled toilets?
¿Hay baños para   ai *ba*·nyos *pa*·ra
discapacitados?   dees·ka·pa·see·*ta*·dos

Are there rails in the bathroom?
¿Hay barras para   ai *ba*·ras *pa*·ra
sostenerse en el baño?   sos·te·*ner*·se en el *ba*·nyo

Could you call me a disabled taxi?
¿Me podría llamar   me po·*dree*·a ya·*mar*
un taxi para   oon *tak*·see *pa*·ra
discapacitados?   dees·ka·pa·see·*ta*·dos

Could you help me cross the street safely?
¿Me podría ayudar   me po·*dree*·a a·yoo·*dar*
a cruzar la calle?   a kroo·*sar* la *ka*·ye

Is there somewhere I can sit down?
¿Hay algún lugar   ai al·*goon* loo·*gar*
donde me pueda sentar?   *don*·de me *pwe*·da sen·*tar*

guide dog	*perro guía* m	*pe*·ro *gee*·a
older person	*persona mayor* f	per·*so*·na ma·*yor*
person with a disability	*discapacitado/a* m/f	dees·ka·pa·see·*ta*·do/a
ramp	*rampa* f	*ram*·pa
walking frame	*baranda* f	ba·*ran*·da
walking stick	*bastón* m	bas·*ton*
wheelchair	*silla de ruedas* f	*see*·ya de *rwe*·das

---

golden age

Costa Rican senior citizens are designated *ciudadanos de oro* syoo·da·*da*·nos de *o*·ro (lit: golden citizens) and have ID cards which entitle them to special privileges.

travelling with children

Is there a ...?	¿Tienen ...?	tye·nen ...
baby change room	un lugar para cambiar bebés	oon loo·gar pa·ra kam·byar be·bes
child discount	un descuento para niños	oon des·kwen·to pa·ra nee·nyos
child-minding service	una guardería	oo·na gwar·de·ree·a
children's menu	un menú para niños	oon me·noo pa·ra nee·nyos
child's portion	una porción para niños	oo·na por·syon pa·ra nee·nyos
family ticket	un tiquete familiar	oon tee·ke·te fa·mee·lyar

I need a/an ...	Necesito ...	ne·se·see·to ...
baby seat	una silla para bebé	oo·na see·ya pa·ra be·be
(English-speaking) babysitter	una niñera (que hable inglés)	oo·na nee·nye·ra (ke a·ble een·gles)
booster seat	una silla de carro para niños	oo·na see·ya de ka·ro pa·ra nee·nyos
cot	un catre	oon ka·tre
highchair	una silla para comer	oo·na see·ya pa·ra ko·mer
plastic bag	una bolsa plástica	oo·na bol·sa plas·tee·ka
potty	una vacenilla	oo·na va·se·nee·ya
pram	un coche	oon ko·che
stroller	un coche sombrilla	oon ko·che som·bree·ya

Where's the nearest ...?	¿Dónde está el/la ... más cercano/a? m/f	don·de es·ta el/la ... mas ser·ka·no/a
drinking fountain	fuente de agua m	fwen·te de a·gwa
park	parque m	par·ke
playground	play m	plai
swimming pool	piscina f	pee·see·na
tap	tubo m	too·bo
toyshop	juguetería f	khoo·ge·te·ree·a

Do you sell ...?	¿Venden ...?	ven·den ...
baby wipes	pañitos desechables para bebé	pa·nyee·tos de·se·cha·bles pa·ra be·be
disposable nappies/diapers	pañales desechables	pa·nya·les de·se·cha·bles
painkillers for infants	pastillas pediátricas para el dolor	pas·tee·yas pe·dee·a·tree·kas pa·ra el do·lor
tissues	klíneks	klee·neks

Are there any good places to take children around here?

¿Hay algún lugar bonito para llevar niños por aquí?	ai al·goon loo·gar bo·nee·to pa·ra ye·var nee·nyos por a·kee

Are children allowed?

¿Se permiten niños?	se per·mee·ten nee·nyos

Where can I change a nappy/diaper?

¿Dónde puedo cambiar un pañal?	don·de pwe·do kam·byar oon pa·nyal

Do you mind if I breast-feed here?

¿Le molestaría si doy de mamar aquí?	le mo·les·ta·ree·a see doy de ma·mar a·kee

Could I have some paper and pencils, please?

¿Me podría dar un papel y lápices, por favor?	me po·dree·a dar oon pa·pel ee la·pee·ses por fa·vor

Is this suitable for (five)-year-old children?

¿Ésto está bien para niños de (cinco) años?	es·to es·ta byen pa·ra nee·nyos de (seen·ko) a·nyos

Do you know a dentist/doctor who is good with children?
  ¿Usted conoce algún   oos·*ted* ko·*no*·se al·*goon*
  dentista/doctor que sea   den·*tees*·ta/dok·*tor* ke *se*·a
  bueno con los niños?   *bwe*·no kon los *nee*·nyos

If your child is sick, see **health**, page 183.

talking with children

What's your name?
  ¿Cómo te llamás?   *ko*·mo te ya·*mas*

How old are you?
  ¿Cuántos años tenés?   *kwan*·tos *a*·nyos te·*nes*

When's your birthday?
  ¿Cuándo cumplís años?   *kwan*·do koom·*plees a*·nyos

Do you go to kindergarten?
  ¿Vas al kínder?   vas al *keen*·der

Do you go to school?
  ¿Vas a la escuela?   vas a la es·*kwe*·la

What grade are you in?
  ¿En qué grado estás?   en ke *gra*·do es·*tas*

Do you like (school)?
  ¿Te gusta (la escuela)?   te *goos*·ta (la es·*kwe*·la)

Do you learn (English)?
  ¿Aprendés (ingles)?   a·pren·*des* (een·*gles*)

What do you do after school?
  ¿Qué hacés después   ke a·*ses* des·*pwes*
  de la escuela?   de la es·*kwe*·la

talking about children

When's the baby due?
¿Para cuándo está el bebé?   pa·ra kwan·do es·ta el be·be

What are you going to call the baby?
¿Cómo le va/vas   ko·mo le va/vas
a poner? pol/inf   a po·ner

Is this your first child?
¿Es su primer hijo/a? pol m/f   es soo pree·mer ee·kho/a
¿Es tu primer hijo/a? inf m/f   es too pree·mer ee·kho/a

How many children do you have?
¿Cuántos hijos   kwan·tos ee·khos
tiene/tenés? pol/inf   tye·ne/te·nes

What a beautiful child!
¡Qué chiquito/a   ke chee·kee·to/a
más lindo/a! m/f   mas leen·do/a

Is it a boy or a girl?
¿Es chiquito o chiquita?   es chee·kee·to o chee·kee·ta

How many months is he/she?
¿Cuántos meses tiene?   kwan·tos me·ses tye·ne

How old is he/she?
¿Cuántos años tiene?   kwan·tos a·nyos tye·ne

What's his/her name?
¿Cómo se llama?   ko·mo se ya·ma

---

who's who in the zoo?

Ever wondered how a rooster says 'cock-a-doodle-do' in Costa Rica? To break the ice with the local domestic fauna, try addressing them in their native tongue:

cat	*miau*	myow
chicken	*pío pío*	pee·o pee·o
cow	*muu*	moo
dog	*guau guau*	wow wow
rooster	*ki ki ri ki*	kee kee ree kee

basics

lo básico

Yes.	*Sí.*	see
No.	*No.*	no
Please.	*Por favor.*	por fa·*vor*
Thank you (very much).	*(Muchas) Gracias.*	(*moo*·chas) *gra*·syas
You're welcome.	*Con mucho gusto.*	kon *moo*·cho *goos*·to
Excuse me. (to get attention/ to get past)	*Con permiso.*	kon per·*mee*·so
Excuse me. (apology)	*Discúlpeme.*	dees·*kool*·pe·me
Sorry. (apology)	*Perdón.*	per·*don*
Sorry. (condolence)	*Lo siento.*	lo *syen*·to

greetings & goodbyes

saludos y despedidas

Costa Ricans are very conscious of civilities in their public be-haviour. Never address a stranger without first extending a greeting such as *buenos días* (good morning), *buenas tardes* (good afternoon) or *buenas noches* (good evening). These may be abbreviated to simply *buenos* (for *buenos días*) and *buenas* (for *buenas tardes* and *buenas noches*).

Good ...		
day	*Buen día.*	bwen *dee*·a
morning	*Buenos (días).*	*bwe*·nos (*dee*·as)
afternoon	*Buenas (tardes).*	*bwe*·nas (*tar*·des)
evening	*Buenas (noches).*	*bwe*·nas (*no*·ches)

meeting people

97

In addition to the formal greetings on the preceding page, you can use the expressions below to greet a friend or someone you're familiar with. The expressions *pura vida* (lit: pure life) and *tuanis* (lit: too nice – from the English) are quintessential *tiquismos* tee·*kees*·mos (Costa Rican slang). If you bandy them about you might soon be taken for a *Tico* tee·ko or *Tica* tee·ka (Costa Rican man or woman) yourself. See the box **talking tiquismos**, page 134, for more on these expressions.

Hello/Hi.	*Hola.*	o·la
Hello. How's it going?	*Hola. ¿Pura vida?*	o·la poo·ra vee·da
Hello. How are things?	*Hola. ¿Todo bien?*	o·la to·do byen
Great, thanks.	*Tuanis.*	too·a·nees

How are you?

¿Cómo va/vas? sg pol/inf	ko·mo va/vas
¿Cómo van? pl	ko·mo van

Fine. And you?

Bien. ¿Y usted/vos? sg pol/inf	byen ee oos·ted/vos
Bien. ¿Y ustedes? pl	byen ee oos·te·des

What's your name?

¿Cómo se llama? pol	ko·mo se ya·ma
¿Cómo te llamás? inf	ko·mo te ya·mas

My name is …

Me llamo …	me ya·mo …

I'd like to introduce you to (Daniel).

Quiero presentarle/	kye·ro pre·sen·tar·le/
presentarte a (Daniel). pol/inf	pre·sen·tar·te a (da·nyel)

I'm pleased to meet you.

Mucho gusto.	moo·cho goos·to

knock knock …

If you're paying a visit to someone's house and can't find a doorbell, call out the following greeting to announce your presence:

¡Upe!	oo·pe	**Anyone home?**

This is my ...	*Él/Ella es mi ...* m/f	el/*e*·ya es mee ...
boyfriend	*novio*	*no*·vyo
child	*hijo/a* m/f	*ee*·kho/a
colleague	*colega* m&f	ko·*le*·ga
friend	*amigo/a* m/f	a·*mee*·go/a
girlfriend	*novia*	*no*·vya
husband	*esposo*	es·*po*·so
partner	*compañero/a* m/f	kom·pa·*nye*·ro/a
wife	*esposa*	es·*po*·sa

See you later.	*Nos vemos.*	nos *ve*·mos
Bye.	*Chao.*	chao
Goodbye.	*Adiós.*	a·*dyos*
Good night.	*Buenas (noches).*	*bwe*·nas (*no*·ches)
Bon voyage!	*¡Buen viaje!*	bwen *vya*·khe

addressing people

modos de saludar

The usual nonverbal greetings are either shaking hands or kissing once on the cheek. In a formal situation or when you're meeting someone for the first time, it's probably best to shake hands. For a more informal everyday encounter, one kiss on the cheek is the usual protocol – unless it's between men, who usually just shake hands. The following titles are used in formal situations, and they're frequently abbreviated in writing:

Mr/Sir	*Señor (Sr)*	se·*nyor*
Mrs/Madam	*Señora (Sra)*	se·*nyo*·ra
Miss	*Señorita (Srta)*	se·nyo·*ree*·ta

making conversation

empezando una conversación

Costa Ricans will do everything they can to *quedar bien* ke·*dar* byen (leave a good impression). To respond in kind, you should preface any conversation with enquiries about the other person's wellbeing and engage in a little small talk too.

Everything fine?
¿Pura vida?   poo·ra *vee*·da

What's going down?
¿Qué hay de nuevo?   ke ai de *nwe*·vo

Everything cool?
¿Qué, todo bien?   ke *to*·do byen

What's the news?
¿Qué me cuenta?   ke me *kwen*·ta

What a beautiful day!
¡Qué día más bonito!   ke *dee*·a mas bo·*nee*·to

Nice/Awful weather, isn't it?
Qué tiempo más   ke *tyem*·po mas
bonito/feo, ¿verdad?   bo·*nee*·to/*fe*·o ver·*dad*

Do you live here?
¿Vive/Vivís
por aquí? pol/inf
vee·ve/vee·vees
por a·kee

Where are you going?
¿Dónde va/vas? pol/inf
don·de va/vas

What are you doing?
¿Qué está/estás
haciendo? pol/inf
ke es·ta/es·tas
a·syen·do

Do you like it here?
¿Le/Te gusta aquí? pol/inf
le/te goos·ta a·kee

I love it here.
Me encanta aquí.
me en·kan·ta a·kee

Can I take a photo of you?
¿Puedo tomarle/
tomarte una foto? pol/inf
pwe·do to·mar·le/
to·mar·te oo·na fo·to

I'll send you the photo.
Yo le/te mando   yo le/te la *man*·do
la foto. pol/inf   la *fo*·to

That's (beautiful), isn't it?
Qué (bonito), ¿verdad?   ke (bo·*nee*·to) ver·*dad*

How long are you here for?
¿Cuánto tiempo va/vas   *kwan*·to *tyem*·po va/vas
a estar aquí? pol/inf   a es·*tar* a·*kee*

I'm here for (four) weeks/days.
Voy a estar aquí (cuatro)   voy a es·*tar* a·*kee* (*kwa*·tro)
semanas/días.   se·*ma*·nas/*dee*·as

Are you here on holiday?
¿Está/Estás aquí   es·*ta*/es·*tas* a·*kee*
de vacaciones? pol/inf   de va·ka·*syo*·nes

I'm here ...   *Estoy aquí ...*   es·*toy* a·*kee* ...
  for a holiday   *de vacaciones*   de va·ka·*syo*·nes
  on business   *de negocios*   de ne·*go*·syos
  to study   *estudiando*   es·too·*dyan*·do

local talk		
Hey!	*¡Hey!*	khe
Great!	*¡Tuanis!*	too·*a*·nees
Just a minute.	*Dame un toque.*	da·me oon *to*·ke
Just joking.	*Estoy*	es·*toy*
	vacilando.	va·see·*lan*·do
Maybe.	*Tal vez.*	tal ves
No problem.	*No te*	no te
	preocupés.	pre·o·koo·*pes*
No way!	*¡Qué va!*	ke va
Sure.	*Claro.*	*kla*·ro

nationalities

Where are you from?
¿De dónde es/sos? sg pol/inf   de *don*·de es/sos

I'm from ...	*Soy de ...*	soy de ...
Australia	*Australia*	ow·*stra*·lya
Canada	*Canadá*	ka·na·*da*
the USA	*los Estados*	los es·*ta*·dos
	Unidos	oo·*nee*·dos

ticomania

Costa Ricans are nicknamed *Ticos* tee·kos and *Ticas* tee·kas due to their affinity for adding endings such as *-tico/a* ·tee·ko/a, *-ito/a* ·ee·to/a or *-(c)illo/a* ·(s)ee·yo/a m/f, to the ends of words. These endings are known as diminutives. Diminutives can indicate the smallness of something – eg *gato* ga·to (cat) becomes *gatico* ga·tee·ko 'kitten' – but they also express how a speaker feels about something. Not surprisingly, many terms of endearment are in the form of diminutives – eg *palomita* pa·lo·*mee*·ta (darling) is a diminutive of *paloma* pa·*lo*·ma (dove). Diminutives can also give a friendly tone to a conversation. For instance, *un momentito* oon mo·men·*tee*·to (just a moment) sounds more light-hearted than *un momento* oon mo·*men*·to (one moment).

age

How old ...?	*¿Cuantos años ...?*	*kwan*·tos *a*·nyos ...
are you	*tiene/tenés* pol/inf	*tye*·ne/te·*nes*
is your	*tiene su hija* pol	*tye*·ne soo *ee*·kha
daughter	*tiene tu hija* inf	*tye*·ne too *ee*·kha
is your son	*tiene su hijo* pol	*tye*·ne soo *ee*·kho
	tiene tu hijo inf	*tye*·ne too *ee*·kho

I'm … years old.
  Tengo … años.   *ten*·go … *a*·nyos

He/She is … years old.
  Él/Ella tiene … años.   el/*e*·ya tye·ne … *a*·nyos

Too old!
  ¡Demasiado viejo/a! m/f de·ma·*sya*·do *vye*·kho/a

I'm younger than I look.
  Soy menor de lo que parezco. soy me·*nor* de lo ke pa·*res*·ko

For your age, see **numbers & amounts**, page 33.

occupations & studies

trabajo y estudio

What's your occupation?
  ¿Qué hace usted? pol   ke *a*·se oos·*ted*
  ¿Vos qué hacés? inf   vos ke a·*ses*

I'm self-employed.
  Tengo mi propio negocio. *ten*·go mee *pro*·pyo ne·*go*·syo

I'm a …	Soy …	soy …
chef	chef m&f	shef
engineer	ingeniero/a m/f	een·khe·*nye*·ro/a
journalist	periodista m&f	pe·ryo·*dees*·ta
student	estudiante m&f	es·too·*dyan*·te
teacher	profesor/	pro·fe·*sor*
	profesora m/f	pro·fe·*so*·ra

I work in …	Yo trabajo en …	yo tra·*ba*·kho en …
administration	administración	ad·mee·nees·tra·*syon*
health	salud	sa·*lood*
sales &	ventas y	*ven*·tas ee
marketing	mercadeo	mer·ka·*de*·o

I'm …	Soy …	soy …
retired	pensionado/a m/f	pen·syo·*na*·do/a
unemployed	desempleado/a m/f	de·sem·ple·*a*·do/a

What are you studying?
    ¿Qué estás estudiando?   ke es·*tas* es·too·*dyan*·do

I'm studying …	*Estudio …*	es·*too*·dyo …
humanities	*humanidades*	oo·ma·nee·*da*·des
science	*ciencias*	*syen*·syas
Spanish	*español*	es·pa·*nyol*

family

familia

Family is one of the sacred pillars of Costa Rican society, so this vocabulary could well come in handy.

Do you have	*¿Tiene …?* pol	*tye*·ne …
(a) …?	*¿Tenés …?* inf	te·*nes* …
I (don't) have	*(No) Tengo…*	(no) *ten*·go …
(a) …		
boyfriend	*novio*	*no*·vyo
brother	*un hermano*	oon er·*ma*·no
children	*hijos*	*ee*·khos
daughter	*una hija*	*oo*·na *ee*·kha
girlfriend	*novia*	*no*·vya
husband	*esposo*	es·*po*·so
partner	*una pareja* m&f	*oo*·na pa·*re*·kha
sister	*una hermana*	*oo*·na er·*ma*·na
son	*un hijo*	oon *ee*·kho
wife	*esposa*	es·*po*·sa

Are you married?
    ¿Está casado/a? pol m/f   es·*ta* ka·*sa*·do/a
    ¿Estás casado/a? inf m/f   es·*tas* ka·*sa*·do/a

I live with someone.
    Vivo con alguien.   *vee*·vo kon *al*·gyen

I'm …	*Soy …*	soy …
married	*casado/a* m/f	ka·*sa*·do/a
separated	*separado/a* m/f	se·pa·*ra*·do/a
single	*soltero/a* m/f	sol·*te*·ro/a

105

farewells

Tomorrow is my last day here.
Mañana es mi   ma·*nya*·na es mee
último día acá.   *ool*·tee·mo *dee*·a a·*ka*

If you come to (the States) you can stay with me.
Si usted venga a (los   see oos·*ted* ven·ga a (los
Estados Unidos) se puede   es·*ta*·dos oo·*nee*·dos) se *pwe*·de
quedar conmigo. **pol**   ke·*dar* kon·*mee*·go
Si venís a (los Estados   see ve·*nees* a (los es·*ta*·dos
Unidos) te podés   oo·*nee*·dos) te po·*des*
quedar conmigo. **inf**   ke·*dar* kon·*mee*·go

It's been great meeting you.
Fue un placer conocerle/   fwe oon pla·*ser* ko·no·*ser*·le/
conocerte. **pol/inf**   ko·no·*ser*·te

Here's my ...	*Este es mi ...*	es·*te* es mee ...
What's your ...?	*¿Cuál es*	kwal es
	su/tu ...? **pol/inf**	soo/too ...
address	*dirección*	dee·rek·*syon*
email address	*correo*	ko·*re*·o
	electrónico	e·lek·*tro*·nee·ko
phone number	*teléfono*	te·*le*·fo·no

well-wishing

All the best!	*¡Qué te vaya bien!*	ke te *va*·ya byen
Congratulations!	*¡Felicidades!*	fe·lee·see·*da*·des
Good luck!	*¡Buena suerte!*	*bwe*·na *swer*·te
Happy Birthday!	*¡Feliz*	fe·*lees*
	cumpleaños!	koom·ple·*a*·nyos
May God be	*¡Qué Dios te*	ke dee·*os* te
with you!	*acompañe!*	a·kom·*pa*·nye
God bless you!	*¡Qué Dios*	ke dee·*os*
	te bendiga!	te ben·*dee*·ga
Merry Christmas!	*¡Feliz Navidad!*	fe·*lees* na·vee·*dad*
Take care!	*¡Cuidate!*	*kwee*·da·te

In this chapter, phrases are given in the informal *tú* and *vos* forms. For more details on polite and informal forms, see the **phrasebuilder**, page 23.

common interests

intereses comunes

What do you do in your spare time?

¿Qué te gusta hacer en el tiempo libre?		ke te *goos*·ta a·*ser* en el *tyem*·po *lee*·bre

Do you like ...?	*¿Te gusta ...?*	te *goos*·ta ...
I (don't) like ...	*(No) Me gusta ...*	(no) me *goos*·ta ...
art	*el arte*	el *ar*·te
cooking	*cocinar*	ko·see·*nar*
dancing	*bailar*	bai·*lar*
drawing	*dibujar*	dee·boo·*khar*
gardening	*hacer el jardín*	a·*ser* el khar·*deen*
hiking	*ir a caminar*	eer a ka·mee·*nar*
listening to music	*escuchar música*	es·koo·*char moo*·see·ka
painting	*pintar*	peen·*tar*
reading	*leer*	le·*er*
shopping	*ir de compras*	eer de *kom*·pras
socialising	*socializar*	so·sya·lee·*sar*
sport	*hacer deporte*	a·*ser* de·*por*·te
surfing the Internet	*navegar el internet*	na·ve·*gar* el een·ter·*net*
travelling	*viajar*	vya·*khar*
watching films	*ver películas*	ver pe·*lee*·koo·las
watching TV	*ver tele*	ver *te*·le

For types of sports, see **sport**, page 135, and the **dictionary**.

music

Do you dance/sing?
  ¿Bailás/Cantás?   bai·*las*/kan·*tas*

Do you go to concerts?
  ¿Vas a conciertos?   vas a kon·*syer*·tos

Do you listen to music?
  ¿Escuchás música?   es·koo·*chas* moo·see·ka

Do you play an instrument?
  ¿Tocás algún   to·*kas* al·*goon*
  instrumento?   eens·troo·*men*·to

What music do you like?
  ¿Qué música te gusta?   ke *moo*·see·ka te *goos*·ta

Which bands/singers do you like?
  ¿Qué grupos/cantantes   ke *groo*·pos/kan·*tan*·tes
  te gustan?   te *goos*·tan

blues	*blues*	bloos
classical music	*música clásica*	*moo*·see·ka *kla*·see·ka
electronic	*música*	*moo*·see·ka
music	*electrónica*	e·lek·*tro*·nee·ka
folk music	*música*	*moo*·see·ka
	folklórica	fol·*klo*·ree·ka
jazz	*jazz*	shass
pop	*pop*	pop
rock	*rock*	rok
traditional	*música*	*moo*·see·ka
music	*tradicional*	tra·dee·syo·*nal*
world music	*música*	*moo*·see·ka
	internacional	een·ter·na·syo·*nal*

In Costa Rica you'll hear music from all over the world, but your ears will also become attuned to Latin American rhythms. Guanacaste province, in particular, is known for its traditional music, often based around the marimba. Here are some of the musical styles that may get you jumping:

cumbia *koom·bya*
Rhythmic dance music incorporating guitars, accordions, brass, drums and percussion. It encompasses indigenous, Spanish and African influences and was originally a courtship dance among slave populations.

merengue *me·ren·ge*
Lively dance music originating in the Dominican Republic, combining African and Spanish influences. Signature instruments include the tambora drum, saxophone and accordion.

reggaetón *re·ge·ton*
Reggae music reborn for a new generation. It's sung in Spanish and is a hip hop and dancehall hybrid originating in Puerto Rico and New York City. Eminently danceable and wildly popular with Costa Rican youth.

salsa *sal·sa*
Popular dance music originating in New York, which spread like wildfire throughout the Caribbean in the 1960s.

Planning to go to a concert? See **tickets**, page 42, and **going out**, page 119.

cinema & theatre

cine y teatro

I feel like going to a ...	*Tengo ganas de ir a ...*	*ten·go ga·nas de eer a ...*
concert	*un concierto*	oon kon·syer·to
film	*una película*	oo·na pe·lee·ko·la
play	*una obra de teatro*	oo·na o·bra de te·a·tro

interests

109

Did you like (the concert)?
¿Te gustó (el concierto)?   te goos·to (el kon·*syer*·to)

What's showing at the cinema/theatre tonight?
¿Qué están dando en el   ke es·*tan* dan·do en el
cine/teatro hoy en la noche?   *see*·ne/te·*a*·tro hoy en la *no*·che

Is it in (English)?
¿Es en (inglés)?   es en (een·*gles*)

Does it have (English) subtitles?
¿Tiene subtítulos en   *tye*·ne soob·*tee*·too·los en
(inglés)?   (een·*gles*)

Do you have tickets for ...?
¿Tenés entradas para ...?   te·*nes* en·*tra*·das *pa*·ra ...

Are there any extra tickets for ...?
¿Hay más entradas para ...?   ai mas en·*tra*·das *pa*·ra ...

Have you seen ...?
¿Has visto ...?   as *vees*·to ...

Who's in it?
¿Quién tiene?   kyen *tye*·ne

It stars ...
Protagoniza ...   pro·ta·go·*nee*·sa ...

Is this seat taken?
¿Está ocupado?   es·*ta* o·ko·*pa*·do

Is there a/an ...?	*¿Hay un ...?*	ai oon ...
intermission	*intermedio*	een·ter·*me*·dyo
programme	*programa*	pro·*gra*·ma
I thought it was ...	*Me pareció ...*	me pa·re·*syo* ...
excellent	*excelente*	ek·se·*len*·te
long	*larga*	*lar*·ga
OK	*bien*	byen

There are three ways of saying 'you' (singular) in Costa Rica. In formal situations or when you don't know someone well, it's best to use the polite (pol) form *usted* oos·*ted*. When the situation is informal or you're well acquainted with someone, the informal (inf) form *vos* vos is used. *Tú* too may also be used for informal situations, although it's less common than *vos*. In plural, however, there's only one 'you' form for both polite and informal situations – *ustedes* oos·*te*·des.

The words *usted*, *tú* and *vos* take different verb forms. Throughout this book the correct verb forms are given according to the real-life context of the phrases. Note that the pronouns are often left out in Spanish, as the verb endings tell you who's doing the action. For more information, see the **phrasebuilder**, page 23.

I (don't) like …	*(No) Me gusta/ gustan* … sg/pl	(no) me *goos*·ta/ *goos*·tan …
action movies	*las películas de acción* pl	las pe·*lee*·koo·las de ak·*syon*
animated films	*las películas animadas* pl	las pe·*lee*·koo·las a·nee·*ma*·das
(Costa Rican) cinema	*el cine (costarricense)* sg	el *see*·ne (kos·ta·ree·*sen*·se)
comedies	*las comedias* pl	las ko·*me*·dyas
documentaries	*los documentales* pl	los do·koo·men·*ta*·les
drama	*el drama* sg	el *dra*·ma
horror movies	*las películas de miedo* pl	las pe·*lee*·koo·las de *mye*·do
sci-fi	*la ciencia ficción* sg	la *syen*·sya feek·*syon*
short films	*los cortos* pl	los *kor*·tos
thrillers	*las películas de terror* pl	las pe·*lee*·koo·las de te·*ror*
war movies	*las películas de guerras* pl	las pe·*lee*·koo·las de *ge*·ras

interests

111

limón creole

If you're visiting popular destinations along the Caribbean coast, in the province of Limón, you'll notice striking differences in the language spoken by its Afro-Costa Rican community. This idiom, often referred to as *criollo limones* kree·o·yo lee·mo·nes (Limón Creole) is a mix of various languages and cultures in the region.

Limón Creole isn't a standardised language like English or Spanish – it changes from generation to generation and even from speaker to speaker. The idiom is a colourful hybrid of Jamaican Creole (a variation of English) and Spanish, which gradually developed among the descendents of the black 19th-century Jamaican immigrants.

An example that shows the great degree of Spanish influence in Limón Creole, particularly among younger people, is the y sound – just like the Costa Rican pronunciation of the Spanish letter *ll* – so that, for instance, the 'zh' sound in the word *gendarme* is actually pronounced as the 'y' in 'yes'.

Words in Limón Creole which are derived from English vocabulary don't necessarily have the same meaning. 'All right' often means 'hello' and 'OK' can mean 'thank you' or 'goodbye'. The Spanish phrase *es que* es ke (lit: it's that) is a common way to begin a sentence.

Looking at the same sentence in standard English, Spanish, Jamaican Creole and Limón Creole can give a good indication of the interaction between the languages and the way sentences are formed. Note that the sentences in both Jamaican and Limón Creole are spelled only phonetically to give a better idea of how they actually sound (and because the languages exist primarily in spoken form):

English	In three years, he will be ten.
Spanish	*Le faltan tres años para cumplir diez.*
	le *fal*·tan tres *a*·nyos *pa*·ra koom·*pleer* dyes
	(lit: him need three years to turn ten)
Jamaican Creole	heem *a*·ve tree *yee*·as lef fe toon ten
Limón Creole	*fal*·ta tree *yee*·as eem get ten

In this chapter, phrases are given in the informal *tú* and *vos* forms. For more details on polite and informal forms, see the **phrasebuilder**, page 23.

feelings

Feelings are described with either nouns or adjectives. The nouns use forms of the verb *tener* (have) in Spanish (eg 'I have hunger'), while the adjectives use forms of *estar* (be).

I'm (not) …	*(No) Tengo …*	(no) ten·go …
Are you …?	*¿Tenés …?*	te·nes …
cold	*frío*	free·o
hot	*calor*	ka·lor
hungry	*hambre*	am·bre
thirsty	*sed*	sed

I'm (not) …	*(No) Estoy …*	(no) es·toy …
Are you …?	*¿Estás …?*	es·tas …
happy	*contento/a* m/f	kon·ten·to/a
OK	*bien* m&f	byen
sad	*triste* m&f	trees·te
tired	*cansado/a* m/f	kan·sa·do/a

pregnant pause

If you want to say in Spanish that you're embarrassed, beware the following pitfall or you could end up with red faces all round. The word *embarazada* em·ba·ra·sa·da might look like the translation equivalent of 'embarrassed', but in actual fact means 'pregnant', as in the phrase *Estoy embarazada* es·toy em·ba·ra·sa·da (I'm pregnant). The correct word for embarrassed is *avergonzado/a* a·ver·gon·sa·do/a m/f.

mixed emotions		
not at all	*para nada*	pa·ra *na*·da
I don't care at all.	*No me importa*	no me eem·*por*·ta
	para nada.	pa·ra *na*·da
a little	*un poco*	oon *po*·ko
I'm a little sad.	*Estoy un poco*	es·*toy* oon *po*·ko
	triste.	*trees*·te
very	*muy*	mooy
I feel very tired.	*Estoy muy*	es·*toy* mooy
	cansado/a. m/f	kan·*sa*·do/a
extremely	*muchísimo*	moo·*chee*·see·mo
I'm extremely sorry.	*Lo siento*	lo *syen*·to
	muchísimo.	moo·*chee*·see·mo

If you're not feeling well, see **health**, page 183.

opinions

opiniones

Did you like it?
   ¿Te gustó?   te goos·*to*

What do you think of it?
   ¿Qué opinás?   ke o·pee·*nas*

I thought	*Pienso que*	pyen·so ke
it was …	*estuvo …*	es·*too*·vo …
It's …	*Es …*	es …
awful	*pésimo/a* m/f	*pe*·see·mo/a
bad	*malo/a* m/f	*ma*·lo/a
beautiful	*muy bonito/a* m/f	mooy bo·*nee*·to/a
boring	*aburrido/a* m/f	a·boo·*ree*·do/a
(too)	*(demasiado)*	(de·ma·*sya*·do)
expensive	*caro/a* m/f	*ka*·ro/a
great	*excelente* m&f	ek·se·*len*·te
interesting	*interesante* m&f	een·te·re·*san*·te
strange	*raro/a* m/f	*ra*·ro/a

politics & social issues

Costa Rica is a progressive country and has by far the most stable government and economy in Central America. The country hasn't had a military for over 50 years. Immigration, drugs, the ongoing battle against deforestation, political corruption and how to properly manage and develop the tourism boom are issues of social and political interest and debate. A growing problem in Costa Rica is also the high number of young thieves (*chapulines* cha·poo·*lee*·nes).

Who do you vote for?

¿Por quién votaste?		por kyen vo·*tas*·te

I support the ... party.	*Yo soy ...*	yo soy ...
I'm a member of the ... party.	*Yo soy ...*	yo soy ...
communist	*comunista* m&f	ko·moo·*nees*·ta
conservative	*conservador/*	kon·ser·va·*dor/*
	conservadora m/f	kon·ser·va·*do*·ra
democratic	*demócrata* m&f	de·*mo*·kra·ta
green	*verde* m&f	*ver*·de
liberal	*liberal* m&f	lee·be·*ral*
social	*social*	so·*syal*
democratic	*demócrata* m&f	de·*mo*·kra·ta
socialist	*socialista* m&f	so·sya·*lees*·ta

masculine or feminine?

In this phrasebook, masculine forms of nouns, pronouns and adjectives appear before the feminine forms. If you see a word ending in *-o/a*, it means the masculine form ends in *-o*, and the feminine form ends in *-a* (that is, you replace the *-o* ending with the *-a* ending to make it feminine). The same goes for the plural endings *-os/as*. In other cases we spell out the whole word.

feelings & opinions

The major political parties in Costa Rica are:

Partido Acción Ciudadana (PAC)
par·*tee*·do ak·*syon* · Citizens' Action Party
syoo·da·*da*·na

Partido Liberación Nacional (PLN)
par·*tee*·do lee·be·ra·*syon* · National Liberation
na·syo·*nal* · Party

Partido Unidad Social Cristiana (PUSC)
par·*tee*·do oo·nee·*dad* · United Christian
so·*syal* krees·*tya*·na · Social Party

Is there help	*¿Hay ayuda*	ai a·*yoo*·da
for (the) …?	*para los …?*	*pa*·ra los …
aged	*ancianos*	an·*sya*·nos
beggars	*mendigos*	men·*dee*·gos
disabled	*discapacitados*	dees·ka·pa·see·*ta*·dos
homeless	*indigentes*	een·dee·*khen*·tes
street kids	*niños de la calle*	*nee*·nyos de la *ka*·ye

Did you hear about …?
¿Escuchaste que …? es·koo·*chas*·te ke …

Do you agree with …?
¿Estás de acuerdo con …? es·*tas* de a·*kwer*·do kon …

I don't agree with …
No estoy de no es·*toy* de
acuerdo con … a·*kwer*·do kon …

How do people feel about …?
¿Qué piensa la ke *pyen*·sa la
gente sobre …? *khen*·te so·*bre* …

How can we protest against …?
¿Cómo podemos *ko*·mo po·*de*·mos
protestar contra …? pro·tes·*tar* kon·tra …

How can we support …?
¿Cómo podemos apoyar …? *ko*·mo po·*de*·mos a·po·*yar* …

abortion	*aborto* m	a·*bor*·to
animal rights	*derechos de*	de·*re*·chos de
	los animales m pl	los a·nee·*ma*·les
corruption	*corrupción* f	ko·roop·*syon*
crime	*crimen* m	*kree*·men
discrimination	*discriminación* f	dees·kree·mee·na·*syon*
drugs	*drogas* f pl	*dro*·gas
the economy	*economía* f	e·ko·no·*mee*·a
education	*educación* f	e·doo·ka·*syon*
the environment	*medio ambiente* m	*me*·dyo am·*byen*·te
equal	*igualdad de*	ee·gwal·*dad* de
opportunity	*oportunidades* f	o·por·too·nee·*da*·des
euthanasia	*eutanasia* f	e·oo·ta·*na*·sya
globalisation	*globalización* f	glo·ba·lee·sa·*syon*
human rights	*derechos*	de·*re*·chos
	humanos m pl	oo·*ma*·nos
immigration	*inmigración* f	een·me·gra·*syon*
indigenous	*Indígenas* m pl	een·*dee*·khe·nas
issues		
inequality	*desigualdad* f	des·ee·gwal·*dad*
party politics	*partidos*	par·*tee*·dos
	políticos m pl	po·*lee*·tee·kos
poverty	*pobreza* f	po·*bre*·sa
privatisation	*privatización* f	pree·va·tee·sa·*syon*
racism	*racismo* m	ra·*sees*·mo
sexism	*sexismo* m	sek·*sees*·mo
social welfare	*bienestar social* m	byen·es·*tar* so·*syal*
terrorism	*terrorismo* m	te·ro·*rees*·mo
the war in	*la guerra en*	la *ge*·ra en
(Iraq)	*(Irak)* f	(ee·*rak*)
unemployment	*desempleo* m	des·em·*ple*·o

feelings & opinions

tongue torture

Tongue twisters are known as *trabalenguas* tra·ba·*len*·gwas.
Try rolling this tricky number off the tip of your tongue:

Tres tristes tigres trigo comieron.

| tres *trees*·tes *tee*·gres | Three sad tigers |
| *tree*·go ko·*mye*·ron | ate wheat. |

117

the environment

Is there a … problem here?
¿Hay un problema   ai oon pro·*ble*·ma
de … aquí?   de … a·*kee*

What should be done about …?
¿Qué se debería   ke se de·be·*ree*·a
hacer con respecto a …?   a·*ser* kon re·*spek*·to a …

conservation	*protección del medio ambiente* f	pro·tek·*syon* del *me*·dyo am·*byen*·te
deforestation	*deforestación* f	de·fo·res·ta·*syon*
drought	*sequías* f pl	se·*kee*·as
ecosystem	*ecosistema* m	e·ko·sees·*te*·ma
endangered species	*especies en peligro de extinción* f pl	es·*pe*·syas en pe·*lee*·gro de eks·teen·*syon*
genetically modified food	*alimentos transgénicos* m pl	a·lee·*men*·tos trans·*khe*·nee·kos
hunting	*caza* f	*ka*·sa
hydroelectricity	*proyectos hidroeléctricos* m pl	pro·*yek*·tos ee·dro·e·*lek*·tree·kos
irrigation	*irrigación* f	ee·ree·ga·*syon*
nuclear energy	*energía nuclear* f	e·ner·*khee*·a noo·kle·*ar*
nuclear testing	*pruebas nucleares* f pl	*prwe*·bas noo·kle·*a*·res
ozone layer	*capa de ozono* f	*ka*·pa de o·*so*·no
pesticides	*pesticidas* m pl	pes·tee·*see*·das
pollution	*contaminación* f	kon·ta·mee·na·*syon*
recycling programme	*programas de reciclaje* m pl	pro·*gra*·mas de re·see·*kla*·khe
toxic waste	*desechos tóxicos* m pl	de·*se*·chos *tok*·see·kos
water supply	*suministro de agua* m	soo·mee·*nees*·tro de *a*·gwa
wildlife poaching	*caza ilegal* f	*ka*·sa ee·le·*gal*

In this chapter, phrases are given in the informal *tú* and *vos* forms. For more details on polite and informal forms, see the **phrasebuilder**, page 23.

where to go

a dónde ir

What's there to do in the evenings?

¿Qué se puede hacer		ke se *pwe*·de a·*ser*
en la noche?		en la *no*·che

What's on …? ¿Qué actividades ke ak·tee·vee·*da*·des
hay …? ai …

locally	por aquí	por a·*kee*
this weekend	este fin de	*es*·te feen de
	semana	se·*ma*·na
today	hoy	oy
tonight	hoy en la noche	oy en la *no*·che

out of the closet

Homosexuality is generally kept hidden in the closet in Costa Rica – as is the case throughout Central America. While most locals will be familiar with the terms *gay* gay and *lesbiana* les·*bya*·na, gay travellers should also be on the lookout for the term *playo pla*·yo. This is an offensive term for a gay man and might signal a potentially threatening situation.

On the bright side, Costa Rica does have some gay-friendly beaches and international resorts. Check ahead of your departure for information about these facilities.

Where are the ...?	¿Dónde hay ...?	don·de ai ...
bars	bares	ba·res
clubs	discotecas	dees·ko·te·kas
gay/lesbian venues	lugares gay/ lesbianas	loo·ga·res gay/ les·bya·nas
places to eat	lugares para comer	loo·ga·res pa·ra ko·mer
pubs	bares	ba·res

Is there a local ... guide?	¿Existe una guía local ...?	ek·sees·te oo·na gee·a lo·kal ...
entertainment	de entretenimiento	de en·tre·te·nee·myen·to
film	de películas	de pe·lee·koo·las
gay/lesbian	para personas gay/lesbianas	pa·ra per·so·nas gay/les·bya·nas
music	de música	de moo·see·ka

I feel like going to a ...	Tengo ganas de ir a ...	ten·go ga·nas de eer a ...
bar	un bar	oon bar
café	un café	oon ka·fe
concert	un concierto	oon kon·syer·to
film	ver una película	ver oo·na pe·lee·koo·la
(football) game	un partido de (fútbol)	oon par·tee·do de (foot·bol)
karaoke bar	un karaoke	oon ka·ra·o·ke
nightclub	un club	oon kloob
party	una fiesta	oo·na fyes·ta
performance	una presentación	oo·na pre·sen·ta·syon
play	una obra de teatro	oo·na o·bra de te·a·tro
pub	un bar	oon bar
restaurant	un restaurante	oon res·tow·ran·te

For more on bars, drinks and partying, see **romance**, page 125, and **eating out**, page 153.

invitations

What are you doing …?	¿Qué vas a hacer …?	ke vas a a·ser …
now	ahora	a·o·ra
this weekend	el fin de semana	el feen de se·ma·na
tonight	hoy en la noche	oy en la no·che
I feel like going (for a) …	Tengo ganas de ir a …	ten·go ga·nas de eer a …
Would you like to go (for a) …?	¿Querés ir a …?	ke·res eer a …
coffee	tomar un café	to·mar oon ka·fe
dancing	bailar	bai·lar
drink	tomar algo	to·mar al·go
meal	comer algo	ko·mer al·go
out somewhere	algún lado	al·goon la·do
walk	caminar	ka·mee·nar

My round.
Me toca. me to·ka

Do you know a good restaurant?
¿Conocés un buen restaurante? ko·no·ses oon bwen res·tow·ran·te

Do you want to come to the concert with me?
¿Querés acompañarme al concierto? ke·res a·kom·pa·nyar·me al kon·syer·to

We're having a party.
Tenemos una fiesta. te·ne·mos oo·na fyes·ta

You should come.
Vení. ve·nee

responding to invitations

Sure!
¡Claro!   kla·ro

Yes, I'd love to.
Si, me encantaría.   see me en·kan·ta·*ree*·a

That's very kind of you.
Qué amable.   ke a·*ma*·ble

Where shall we go?
¿Dónde vamos?   *don*·de *va*·mos

No, I'm afraid I can't.
No, no puedo.   no no *pwe*·do

What about tomorrow?
¿Y mañana?   ee ma·*nya*·na

Sorry, I can't sing/dance.
Perdoná, no sé   per·do·*na* no se
cantar/bailar.   kan·*tar*/bai·*lar*

arranging to meet

What time will we meet?
¿A qué hora nos vemos?   a ke o·ra nos *ve*·mos

Where will we meet?
¿Dónde nos vemos?   *don*·de nos *ve*·mos

Let's meet at …   *Veámonos …*   ve·*a*·mo·nos …
  (eight) o'clock   *a las (ocho)*   a las (*o*·cho)
  the entrance   *en la entrada*   en la en·*tra*·da

I'll pick you up.
Yo paso por vos.   yo *pa*·so por vos

Are you ready?
¿Estás listo/a? m/f   es·*tas* lees·to/a

I'm ready.
Yo estoy listo/a. m/f   yo es·*toy* lees·to/a

I'll be coming later.
Voy a llegar más tarde.   voy a ye·*gar* mas *tar*·de

Where will you be?
¿Dónde vas a estar?   *don*·de vas a es·*tar*

If I'm not there by (nine), don't wait for me.
Si no he llegado a (las   see no e ye·*ga*·do a (las
nueve) no me esperés.   *nwe*·ve) no me es·pe·*res*

I'll see you then.
Nos vemos.   nos *ve*·mos

See you later.
Nos vemos más tarde.   nos *ve*·mos mas *tar*·de

See you tomorrow.
Nos vemos mañana.   nos *ve*·mos ma·*nya*·na

Sorry I'm late.
Perdoná que llegara tarde.   per·*do*·na ke ye·*ga*·ra *tar*·de

Never mind.
No importa.   no eem·*por*·ta

don't worry, don't hurry

The ideas about punctuality are more relaxed in Costa Rica
than in English-speaking countries. You can expect *Ticos* to
be at least half an hour late for most social occasions. Costa
Ricans do differentiate, however, between formal and social
situations and are usually more punctual for the former.

Where punctuality is important, you could try adding the
expression *en punto* en *poon*·to – meaning 'exactly' – after
arranging to meet. If it's a rendez-vous for a football match
you're trying to arrange, you can count on your Costa Rican
friends being on time!

going out

123

drugs

drogas

I don't take drugs.
  Yo no uso drogas.   yo no *oo*·so *dro*·gas

Do you want to have a smoke?
  ¿Querés fumarte un puro?   ke·*res* foo·*mar*·te oon *poo*·ro

Do you have a light?
  ¿Tenés fuego?   te·*nes* fwe·go

If the police are talking to you about drugs, see **police**, page 180, for useful phrases.

fiesta fiends

Various local festivals, known as *fiestas fyes*·tas, add plenty of colour to life in Costa Rica. These are a few festivals of national significance:

Día de los Muertos   *dee*·a de los *mwer*·tos
  All Souls' Day (November 2nd) – families visit graveyards to make flower offerings to their loved ones. Religious parades are also held in honour of the deceased.

Semana Santa   se·*ma*·na *san*·ta
  Holy Week – the week leading up to Easter, celebrated with colourful religious processions and masses.

Virgen de los Ángeles   *veer*·khen de los *an*·khe·les
  Costa Rica's patron saint is celebrated on 2 August with a particularly important procession from San José to Cartago.

romance

In this chapter, phrases are given in the informal *tú* and *vos* forms. For more details on polite and informal forms, see the **phrasebuilder**, page 23.

asking someone out

invitando a alguien a salir

Where would you like to go (tonight)?
¿Dónde te gustaría   *don*·de te goos·ta·*ree*·a
ir (hoy en la noche)?   eer (oy en la *no*·che)

Would you like to do something (tomorrow)?
¿Querés hacer algo (mañana)? ke·*res* a·*ser* al·go (ma·*nya*·na)

Yes, I'd love to.
Sí, me encantaría.   see me en·kan·ta·*ree*·a

Sorry, I can't.
Perdoná, no puedo.   per·do·*na* no *pwe*·do

---

local talk

How ...!	¡Qué ...!	ke ...
cool	buena nota	*bwe*·na *no*·ta
sexy	sexy	*sek*·see
He/She ...	Él/Ella es ...	el/e·ya es ...
is hot	rico/a m/f	*ree*·ko/a
gets around	un perro/	oon *pe*·ro/
	una perra m/f	oo·na *pe*·ra

He/She is a babe.
Él/Ella está guapo/a. m/f   el/e·ya es·*ta gwa*·po/a

He's a bastard.
Él es un hijueputa.   el es oon ee·khwe·*poo*·ta

She's a bitch.
Ella es una zorra.   e·ya es oo·na *so*·ra

---

romance

125

pick-up lines

Would you like a drink?
¿Querés tomar algo?   ke·*res* to·*mar* al·go

You look like someone I know.
Me parecés conocido/a. m/f   me pa·re·*ses* ko·no·*see*·do/a

You're a fantastic dancer.
Sos un/una excelente   sos oon/*oo*·na ek·se·*len*·te
bailarín/bailarina. m/f   bai·la·*reen*/bai·la·*ree*·na

Can I ...?   *¿Puedo ...?*   *pwe*·do ...
   dance with you   *bailar contigo*   bai·*lar* kon·*tee*·go
   sit here   *sentarme acá*   sen·*tar*·me a·*ka*
   take you home   *llevarte a la casa*   ye·*var*·te a la *ka*·sa

macho a go go

When it comes to mating, *machismo* ma·*chees*·mo is Costa Rica's law of the jungle – men initiate most flirting. Typically a man will ask a woman to dance and will also buy drinks. Even merely striking up a conversation is usually left to the initiative of men. Feminists need not despair though, as in San José and other more cosmopolitan areas, women sometimes make the first move and have even been known to whistle at passing men.

rejections

You're cool, but no thanks.
Me caes muy bien,   me *ka*·es mooy byen
pero no gracias.   *pe*·ro no *gra*·syas

I love you like a friend.
Te quiero como amigo/a. m/f   te *kye*·ro *ko*·mo a·*mee*·go/a

I'm here with my girlfriend/boyfriend.
   Estoy aquí con mi
   novio/novia.

   es·*toy* a·*kee* kon mee
   no·vyo/*no*·vya

I'd rather not.
   Mejor no.

   me·*khor* no

No, thank you.
   No, gracias.

   no *gra*·syas

Excuse me, I have to go now.
   Con permiso, ya
   me tengo que ir.

   kon per·*mee*·so ya
   me *ten*·go ke eer

---

giving someone the flick

Get out of here!
   ¡Andáte ya!

   an·*da*·te ya

Leave me in peace!
   ¡Dejáme en paz!

   de·*kha*·me en pas

Piss off!
   ¡Largáte!

   lar·*ga*·te

---

getting closer

acercando

I really like you.
   Me gustás mucho.

   me goos·*tas moo*·cho

You're great.
   Sos muy tuanis.

   sos mooy too·*a*·nees

Can I kiss you?
   ¿Te puedo dar un beso?

   te *pwe*·do dar oon *be*·so

Do you want to come inside for a while?
   ¿Querés entrar un rato?

   ke·*res* en·*trar* oon *ra*·to

Do you want a massage?
   ¿Querés que te dé
   un masaje?

   ke·*res* ke te de
   oon ma·*sa*·khe

romance

127

Would you like to stay over?
¿Te querés quedar?   te ke·*res* ke·*dar*

Can I stay over?
¿Me puedo quedar?   me *pwe*·do ke·*dar*

sex

sexo

Kiss me.
Dáme un beso.   *da*·me oon *be*·so

I want you.
Te deseo.   te de·*se*·o

Let's go to bed.
Vamos a la cama.   *va*·mos a la *ka*·ma

Touch me here.
Tocáme aquí.   to·*ka*·me a·*kee*

Do you like this?
¿Ésto te gusta?   *es*·to te *goos*·ta

I (don't) like that.
Éso (no) me gusta.   *e*·so (no) me *goos*·ta

I think we should stop now.
Mejor paremos ya.   me·*khor* pa·*re*·mos ya

Do you have a (condom)?
¿Tenés (preservativo)?   te·*nes* (pre·ser·va·*tee*·vo)

Let's use a (condom).
Usémos (preservativo).   oo·*se*·mos (pre·ser·va·*tee*·vo)

I won't do it without protection.
No lo voy a hacer   no lo voy a a·*ser*
sin protección.   seen pro·tek·*syon*

It's my first time.
Es mi primera vez.   es mee pree·*me*·ra ves

Oh my God!
   ¡Dios mío!   dee·*os* mee·o

That's great.
   ¡Qué bueno!   ke *bwe*·no

Easy tiger!
   ¡Suave tigre!   swa·ve *tee*·gre

That was …	*Eso estuvo …*	e·so es·*too*·vo …
amazing	*increíble*	een·kre·*ee*·ble
romantic	*romántico*	ro·*man*·tee·ko
wild	*salvaje*	sal·*va*·khe

love

amor

I think we're good together.
   Hacemos buena pareja.   a·*se*·mos *bwe*·na pa·*re*·kha

I love you.
   Te amo.   te *a*·mo

Will you go out with me?
   ¿Saldrías conmigo?   sal·*dree*·as kon·*mee*·go

Will you marry me?
   ¿Te casarías conmigo?   te ka·sa·*ree*·as kon·*mee*·go

Will you meet my parents?
   ¿Conocerías a mis papás?   ko·no·se·*ree*·as a mees pa·*pas*

---

pillow talk

It's a peculiarity of Costa Rican Spanish that seemingly unflattering turns of phrase are, in fact, terms of endearment:

My …	*Mi …*	mee …
baby	*bebé* m&f	be·*be*
chicken	*pollo/a* m/f	*po*·yo/a
fatty	*gordo/a* m/f	*gor*·do/a
love	*amor* m&f	a·*mor*

romance

problems

Are you seeing someone else?
¿Me estás dando vuelta?   me es·*tas* dan·do *vwel*·ta

He's just a friend.
Él es sólo un amigo.   el/*e*·ya es *so*·lo oon a·*mee*·go

She's just a friend.
Ella es sólo una amiga.   el/*e*·ya es *so*·lo *oo*·na a·*mee*·ga

You're just using me for sex.
Sólo estás   *so*·lo es·*tas*
jugando conmigo.   khoo·*gan*·do kon·*mee*·go

I never want to see you again.
No te quiero ver   no te *kye*·ro ver
nunca más.   *noon*·ka mas

I don't think it's working out.
Creo que no está   *kre*·o ke no es·*ta*
funcionando.   foon·see·o·*nan*·do

We'll work it out.
Vamos a resolverlo.   *va*·mos a re·sol·*ver*·lo

leaving

I have to leave (tomorrow).
(Mañana) Me tengo que ir.   (ma·*nya*·na) me *ten*·go ke eer

I'll call you.
Yo te llamo.   yo te *ya*·mo

I'll write to you.
Yo te escribo.   yo te es·*kree*·bo

I'll miss you.
Me vas a hacer falta.   me vas a a·*ser fal*·ta

For more phrases, see **farewells**, page 106.

beliefs & cultural differences
creencias y diferencias culturales

religion

religión

What's your religion?
¿De qué religión es/sos? pol/inf   de ke re·lee·*khyon* es/sos

I'm not religious.
No soy religioso/a. m/f   no soy re·lee·*khyo*·so/a

I'm (a/an) ...	Soy ...	soy ...
agnostic	agnóstico/a m/f	ag·*nos*·tee·ko/a
Buddhist	budista m&f	boo·*dees*·ta
Catholic	católico/a m/f	ka·*to*·lee·ko/a
Christian	cristiano/a m/f	krees·*tya*·no/a
Hindu	hindú m&f	een·*doo*
Jewish	judío/a m/f	khoo·*dee*·o/a
Muslim	musulmán/	moo·sool·*man*/
	musulmána m/f	moo·sool·*ma*·na
Rastafarian	rastafarián/	ras·ta·fa·*ryan*/
	rastafariana m/f	ras·ta·fa·*rya*·na

I (don't)	Yo (no)	yo (no)
believe in ...	creo en ...	*kre*·o en ...
astrology	la astrología	la as·tro·lo·*khee*·a
fate	el destino	el des·*tee*·no
God	Dios	dee·*os*

Can I ... here?	¿Puedo ... aquí?	*pwe*·do ... a·*kee*
Where can I ...?	¿Dónde puedo ...?	*don*·de *pwe*·do ...
attend a	participar en	par·tee·see·*par* en
service	un servicio	oon ser·*vee*·syo
attend mass	ir a misa	eer a *mee*·sa
pray	rezar	re·*sar*

131

cultural differences

Is this a local or national custom?
¿Ésto es una costumbre local o del país?	es·to es oo·na kos·toom·bre lo·kal o del pa·ees

I don't want to offend you.
No quiero ofenderle/ ofenderte. pol/inf	no kye·ro o·fen·der·le/ o·fen·der·te

I'm not used to this.
No estoy acostumbrado/a a ésto. m/f	no es·toy a·kos·toom·bra·do/a a es·to

I'd rather not join in.
Prefiero no participar.	pre·fye·ro no par·tee·see·par

I'll try it.
Lo voy a probar.	lo voy a pro·bar

I didn't mean to do/say anything wrong.
No era mi intención hacer/decir algo malo.	no e·ra mee een·ten·syon a·ser/de·seer al·go ma·lo

I'm sorry, it's against my ...	*Lo siento, pero éso va en contra de ...*	lo syen·to pe·ro e·so va en kon·tra de ...
beliefs	*mis creencias*	mees kre·en·syas
religion	*mi religión*	mee re·lee·khyon

This is ...	*Ésto es ...*	es·to es ...
different	*diferente*	dee·fe·ren·te
fun	*divertido*	dee·ver·tee·do
interesting	*interesante*	een·te·re·san·te

---

mind your p's

As Roman Catholicism is the dominant religion in Costa Rica, be careful not to confuse *la papa* la pa·pa (with a lower case 'p'), which means 'potato', with *el Papa* el pa·pa (with an upper case 'P'), meaning 'Pope'. Best not to mix up your tubers and your pontiffs if you don't want to cause an unholy row.

In this chapter, phrases are given in the informal *tú* and *vos* forms. For more details on polite and informal forms, see the **phrasebuilder**, page 23.

When's the gallery open?
¿Cuándo está abierta la galería?
kwan·do es·ta a·byer·ta la ga·le·ree·a

When's the museum open?
¿Cuándo está abierto el museo?
kwan·do es·ta a·byer·to el moo·se·o

What's in the collection?
¿Qué hay en la colección?
ke ai en la ko·lek·syon

It's an exhibition of …
Es una exhibición de …
es oo·na ek·see·bee·syon de …

What do you think of …?
¿Qué opinas de …?
ke o·pee·nas de …

I like the works of …
Me gusta la obra de …
me goos·ta la o·bra de …

It reminds me of …
Me recuerda a …
me re·kwer·da a …

What kind of art are you interested in?
¿Qué tipo de arte te gusta?
ke tee·po de ar·te te goos·ta

I'm interested in … art.	Me interesa el arte …	me een·te·re·sa el ar·te …
graphic	gráfico	gra·fee·ko
impressionist	impresionista	eem·pre·syo·nees·ta
indigenous	autóctono	ow·tok·to·no
modern	moderno	mo·der·no
performance	de desempeño	de de·sem·pe·nyo
Renaissance	renacentista	re·na·sen·tees·ta
traditional	tradicional	tra·dee·syo·nal
tropical art	tropical	tro·pee·kal

architecture	arquitectura f	ar·kee·tek·*too*·ra
art	arte m	*ar*·te
artwork	obra de arte f	o·bra de *ar*·te
curator	curador m	koo·ra·*dor*
exhibit n	exhibición f	ek·see·bee·*syon*
installation	instalación f	eens·ta·la·*syon*
painter	pintor/pintora m/f	peen·*tor*/peen·*to*·ra
painting (artwork)	cuadro m	*kwa*·dro
painting (technique)	pintura f	peen·*too*·ra
period	periodo m	pe·*ryo*·do
collection	colección f	ko·lek·*syon*
pottery	alfarería f	al·fa·re·*ree*·a
print n	impresión f	eem·pre·*syon*
sculptor	escultor/ escultora m/f	es·kool·*tor*/ es·kool·*to*·ra
sculpture	escultura f	es·kool·*too*·ra
statue	estatua f	es·*ta*·too·a
studio	estudio m	es·*too*·dyo
style n	estilo m	es·*tee*·lo

talking *tiquismos*

Ticos (Costa Ricans) colour their speech with a healthy smattering of distinctively Costa Rican expressions and slang words called *tiquismos* tee·*kees*·mos. These two phrases are ubiquitous:

¡Pura vida!   poo·ra vee·da

This expression embodies Costa Rican life. Meaning literally 'pure life', it's really a more profound concept encompassing wellbeing, positivity and harmony. It can variously be translated as 'great, cool, right on' etc.

¡Tuanis!   too·*a*·nees

A very popular phrase with younger folk, similar in meaning to *pura vida*. It's thought to have come from the English expression 'too nice'.

For more *tiquismos*, see the box **talking like a *tico***, page 31.

In this chapter, phrases are given in the informal *tú* and *vos* forms. For more details on polite and informal forms, see the **phrasebuilder**, page 23.

sporting interests

intereses deportivos

What sport do you ...?	*¿Qué deporte ...?*	ke de·*por*·te ...
follow	*te gusta*	te *goos*·ta
play	*practicas*	prak·*tee*·kas
I follow ...	*Me gusta el ...*	me *goos*·ta el ...
I play/do ...	*Yo juego/ hago el ...*	yo *khwe*·go/ *a*·go el ...
athletics	*atletismo*	at·le·*tees*·mo
football/soccer	*fútbol*	*foot*·bol
scuba diving	*buceo*	boo·*se*·o
volleyball	*voleibol*	vo·lay·*bol*
I ...	*Yo ...*	yo ...
cycle (for fun)	*ando en bicicleta*	*an*·do en bee·see·*kle*·ta
cycle (in races)	*practico ciclismo*	prak·*tee*·ko see·*klees*·mo
run	*corro*	*ko*·ro

Do you like (surfing)?
¿Te gusta (surfear)? — te *goos*·ta (soor·fe·*ar*)

Yes, very much.
Sí, mucho. — see *moo*·cho

Not really.
No, en realidad no. — no en re·a·lee·*dad* no

I like watching it.
    Me gusta verlo.   me *goos*·ta *ver*·lo

Who's your favourite athlete/player?
    ¿Quién es tu atleta/   kyen es too at·*le*·ta/
    jugador preferido?   khoo·ga·*dor* pre·fe·*ree*·do

What's your favourite team?
    ¿Cuál es tu equipo   kwal es too e·*kee*·po
    preferido?   pre·fe·*ree*·do

For more sports, see the **dictionary**.

going to a game

Would you like to go to a game?
    ¿Querés ir a un partido?   ke·*res* eer a oon par·*tee*·do

Who are you supporting?
    ¿Con quién vas?   kon kyen vas

Who's ...?	*¿Quién ...?*	kyen ...
playing	*está jugando*	es·*ta* khoo·*gan*·do
winning	*va ganando*	va ga·*nan*·do

That was a ... game!	*¡Qué partido más ...!*	ke par·*tee*·do mas ...
bad	*malo*	*ma*·lo
boring	*aburrido*	a·boo·*ree*·do
great	*bueno*	*bwe*·no

scoring

What's the score?	*¿Cuánto van?*	*kwan*·to van
draw/even	*empate* m	em·*pa*·te
love/nil (zero)	*cero* m	*se*·ro
match-point	*punto de juego* m	*poon*·to de *khwe*·go

What a ...!	¡Qué ...!	ke ...
goal	golazo	go·la·so
hit	tiro	tee·ro
kick	patada	pa·ta·da
pass	pase	pa·se
performance	buena	bwe·na
	presentación	pre·sen·ta·syon

playing sport

practicando deporte

Do you want to play?
¿Querés jugar?　　　　ke·res khoo·gar

Can I join in?
¿Puedo jugar?　　　　pwe·do khoo·gar

Sure.
Claro.　　　　kla·ro

Yes, I'd love to.
Sí, me encantaría.　　　　see me en·kan·ta·ree·a

I can't.
No puedo.　　　　no pwe·do

I have an injury.
Estoy lesionado/a. m/f　　　　es·toy le·syo·na·do/a

Your/My point.
Punto mío/tuyo.　　　　poon·to mee·o/too·yo

Kick/Pass it to me!
¡Pasámela!　　　　pa·sa·me·la

You're a good player.
Jugás bien.　　　　khoo·gas byen

Thanks for the game.
Gracias por el partido.　　　　gra·syas por el par·tee·do

sport

137

Where's a good place to ...?	¿Dónde hay un buen lugar para ...?	don·de ai oon bwen loo·gar pa·ra ...
fish	pescar	pes·kar
go horse riding	montar a caballo	mon·tar a ka·ba·yo
run	correr	ko·rer
snorkel	esnorclear	e·snor·kle·ar
surf	surfear	soor·fe·ar

Where's the nearest ...?	¿Dónde está ... más cercano/a? m/f	don·de es·ta ... mas ser·ka·no/a
golf course	el campo de golf m	el kam·po de golf
gym	el gimnasio m	el kheem·na·syo
swimming pool	la piscina f	la pee·see·na
tennis court	la cancha de tenis m	la kan·cha de te·nees

What's the charge per ...?	¿Cuánto cobra por ...?	kwan·to ko·bra por ...
day	día	dee·a
game	juego	khwe·go
hour	hora	o·ra
visit	visita	vee·see·ta

Can I hire a ...?	¿Puedo alquilar una ...?	pwe·do al·kee·lar oo·na ...
ball	bola	bo·la
bicycle	bicicleta	be·see·kle·ta
court	cancha	kan·cha
racquet	raqueta	ra·ke·ta

Do I have to be a member to attend?
  ¿Tengo que ser   ten·go ke ser
  miembro para ir?   myem·bro pa·ra eer

Is there a women-only session?
  ¿Hay alguna sesión   ai al·goo·na se·syon
  sólo para mujeres?   so·lo pa·ra moo·khe·res

Where are the changing rooms?
  ¿Dónde están   don·de es·tan
  los vestidores?   los ves·tee·do·res

diving

Where's a good diving site?
  ¿Dónde hay un buen   don·de ai oon bwen
  sitio para bucear?   see·tyo pa·ra boo·se·ar

Is the visibility good?
  ¿La visibilidad es buena?   la vee·see·bee·lee·dad es bwe·na

How deep is the dive?
  ¿Qué tan hondo es el buzo?   ke tan on·do es el boo·so

Is it a boat dive?
  ¿Es un buzo desde un bote?   es oon boo·so des·de oon bo·te

Is it a shore dive?
  ¿Es un buzo desde la orilla?   es oon boo·so des·de la o·ree·ya

I'd like to …	Me gustaría …	me goos·ta·ree·a …
explore caves/	explorar	eks·plo·rar
wrecks	cuevas/ruinas	kwe·vas/rwee·nas
go night diving	bucear de	boo·se·ar de
	noche	no·che
go scuba diving	ir a bucear	eer a boo·se·ar
go snorkelling	ir a esnorclear	eer a es·nor·kle·ar
join a diving	ir a bucear con	eer a boo·se·ar kon
tour	un tour	oon toor
learn to dive	aprender a	a·pren·der a
	bucear	boo·se·ar

sport

Are there ...?	¿Hay ...?	ai ...
currents	corrientes	ko·ryen·tes
sharks	tiburones	tee·boo·ro·nes
whales	ballenas	ba·ye·nas

I want to hire (a) ...	Quiero alquilar ...	kye·ro al·kee·lar ...
buoyancy vest	un chaleco salvavidas	oon cha·le·ko sal·va·vee·das
diving equipment	equipo de buceo	e·kee·po de boo·se·o
fins	unas patas de rana	oo·nas pa·tas de ra·na
mask	una mascarilla	oo·na mas·ka·ree·ya
regulator	un regulador	oon re·goo·la·dor
snorkel	un esnórquel	oon e·snor·kel
tank	un tanque	oon tan·ke
weight belt	un cinturón de pesas	oon seen·too·ron de pe·sas
wetsuit	un traje de buzo	oon tra·khe de boo·so

buddy	compañero/a m/f	kom·pa·nye·ro/a
cave n	cueva f	kwe·va
dive n	buceo m	boo·se·o
dive v	bucear	boo·se·ar
diving boat	bote de buceo m	bo·te de boo·se·o
diving course	curso de buceo m	koor·so de boo·se·o
night dive	buceo nocturno m	boo·se·o nok·toor·no
wreck n	ruinas f pl	rwee·nas

extreme sports

I'd like to go ...	Quiero ...	kye·ro ...
bungee jumping	tirarme de bungee	tee·rar·me de boon·gee
caving	ir a explorar cavernas	eer a eks·plo·rar ka·ver·nas
canopying	ir al canopy	eer al ka·no·pee
game fishing	ir de pesca	eer de pes·ka
mountain biking	practicar ciclismo de montaña	prak·tee·kar see·klees·mo de mon·ta·nya
sea-kayaking	andar en kayak en el mar	an·dar en ka·yak en el mar
sky-diving	tirarme en paracaídas	tee·rar·me en pa·ra·ka·ee·das
white-water rafting	ir a los rápidos	eer a los ra·pee·dos

Is the equipment secure?
¿Está bien puesto el equipo?   es·ta byen pwes·to el e·kee·po

Is this safe?
¿Ésto es seguro?   es·to es se·goo·ro

This is insane.
Ésto es de locos.   es·to es de lo·kos

football/soccer

Who plays for (Saprissa)?
¿Quién juega con (Saprissa)?   kyen khwe·ga kon (sa·pree·sa)

He's a great (player).
Él es un (jugador) buenísimo.   el es oon (khoo·ga·dor) bwe·nee·see·mo

He played brilliantly in the match against (Brazil).

Jugó muy bien en
el partido contra (Brasil).

khoo-*go* mooy byen en
el par-*tee*-do *kon*-tra (bra-*seel*)

Which team is at the top of the league?

¿Cuál equipo está de
primero en la tabla?

kwal e-*kee*-po es-*ta* de
pree-*me*-ro en la *ta*-bla

What a great/terrible team!

¿Qué equipo más
bueno/malo!

ke e-*kee*-po mas
bwe-no/*ma*-lo

ball	bola f	*bo*-la
coach n	entrenador m	en-tre-na-*dor*
corner (kick) n	tiro de esquina m	*tee*-ro de es-*kee*-na
fan	aficionado/a m/f	a-fee-syo-*na*-do/a
foul n	falta f	*fal*-ta
free kick	tiro libre m	*tee*-ro *lee*-bre
goal	gol m	gol
goalkeeper	portero/a m/f	por-*te*-ro/a
manager	director m	dee-rek-*tor*
offside	posición	po-see-*syon*
	prohibida f	pro-ee-*bee*-da
penalty	penal m	pe-*nal*
red card	tarjeta roja f	tar-*khe*-ta *ro*-kha
referee	árbitro m	*ar*-bee-tro
throw in v	meter	me-*ter*

Off to see a match? Check out **going to a game**, page 136.

surfing

surfeo

How do I get to the surf beaches?

¿Cómo llego a las
playas de surfear?

ko-mo *ye*-go a las
pla-yas de soor-fe-*ar*

Which beach has the best conditions today?

¿Cuál playa tiene las
mejores condiciones hoy?

kwal *pla*-ya *tye*-ne las
me-*kho*-res kon-dee-*syo*-nes oy

Where's the nearest beach/point break?

¿Dónde está el beach/   *don·de es·ta el beech/*
point break más cerca?   *poynt brek mas ser·ka*

Where's the best beach/point break?

¿Dónde está el mejor   *don·de es·ta el me·khor*
beach/point break?   *beech/poynt brek*

What are the best times to surf there?

¿Cuál es la mejor   *kwal es la me·khor*
hora para surfear ahí?   *o·ra pa·ra soor·fe·ar a·ee*

Is the swell big?

¿Son grandes las olas?   *son gran·des las o·las*

Does it barrel?

¿Hay tubos?   *ai too·bos*

Does it work at high/low tide?

¿Sirve en marea   *seer·ve en ma·re·a*
alta/baja?   *al·ta/ba·kha*

Do you know any secret spots?

¿Conocés algún   *ko·no·ses al·goon*
lugar secreto?   *loo·gar se·kre·to*

Where can I find a surf shop?

¿Dónde hay una   *don·de ai oo·na*
tienda de surf?   *tyen·da de soorf*

Where can I ...	¿Dónde puedo ...	*don·de pwe·do ...*
(equipment)?	(equipo)?	*(e·kee·po)*
buy	comprar	*kom·prar*
rent	alquilar	*al·kee·lar*
repair	arreglar	*a·re·glar*

board bag	*bolsa para la tabla* f	bol·sa pa·ra la ta·bla
body board	*bodyboard* m	bo·dee·bord
fin(s)	*pata(s) de rana* f	pa·ta(s) de ra·na
sailboarding	*tabla de vela* f	ta·bla de ve·la
sailing boat	*bote de vela* m	bo·te de ve·la
set n	*set* m	set
surfing n	*surf* m	soorf
surf v	*surfear*	soor·fe·ar
surfboard	*tabla de surf* f	ta·bla de soorf
wave n	*ola* f	o·la
wax n	*cera* f	se·ra

water sports

Can I book a lesson?
¿Puedo apuntarme   pwe·do a·poon·tar·me
en una clase?   en oo·na kla·se

Can I hire (a) …?	*¿Puedo alquilar …?*	pwe·do al·kee·lar …
boat	*un bote*	oon bo·te
canoe	*una canoa*	oo·na ka·no·a
kayak	*un kayak*	oon ka·yak
life jacket	*un chaleco*	oon cha·le·ko
	salvavidas	sal·va·vee·das
snorkelling	*equipo para*	e·kee·po pa·ra
gear	*esnorclear*	e·snor·kle·ar
water-skis	*esquís de agua*	es·kees de a·gwa
wetsuit	*un traje de*	oon tra·khe de
	neoprene	ne·o·pre·ne

Are there	*¿Hay algunos/*	ai al·goo·nos/
any …?	*algunas …?* m/f	algunas …
reefs	*arrecifes* m	a·re·see·fes
rips	*corrientes* f	ko·ryen·tes

guide n	*guía* m	gee·a
motorboat	*bote de motor* m	bo·te de mo·tor
oars	*paletas* f pl	pa·le·tas

hiking

caminatas

Where can I ...?	¿Dónde puedo ...?	don·de pwe·do ...
buy supplies	comprar provisiones	kom·prar pro·vee·syo·nes
find someone who knows this area	encontrar a alguien que conozca la zona	en·kon·trar a al·gyen ke ko·nos·ka la so·na
get a map	conseguir un mapa	kon·se·geer oon ma·pa
hire hiking gear	alquilar equipo para la caminata	al·kee·lar e·kee·po pa·ra la ka·mee·na·ta

How ...?	¿Qué tan ...?	ke tan ...
high is the climb	alta es la subida	al·ta es la soo·bee·da
long is the trail	largo es el sendero	lar·go es el sen·de·ro

Is the route scenic?
¿Es panorámica la ruta?
es pa·no·ra·mee·ka la roo·ta

Do we need a guide?
¿Ocupamos un guía?
o·koo·pa·mos oon gee·a

Are there guided treks?
¿Hay caminatas con guía?
ai ka·mee·na·tas kon gee·a

Is it safe?
¿Es seguro?
es se·goo·ro

Is there a hut?
¿Hay un rancho?
ai oon ran·cho

When does it get dark?
¿A qué hora oscurece?
a ke o·ra os·koo·re·se

Do we need to take ...?	¿Tenemos que llevar ...?	te·*ne*·mos ke ye·*var* ...
bedding	ropa de cama	*ro*·pa de *ka*·ma
food	comida	ko·*mee*·da
water	agua	*a*·gwa
Is the track ...?	¿El sendero está ...?	el sen·*de*·ro es·*ta* ...
(well) marked	(bien) marcado	(byen) mar·*ka*·do
open	abierto	a·*byer*·to
Which is the ... route?	¿Cuál es el camino más ...?	kwal es el ka·*mee*·no mas ...
easiest	fácil	*fa*·seel
shortest	corto	*kor*·to
Where can I find the ...?	¿Dónde queda/quedan ...? sg/pl	*don*·de ke·da/ke·dan ...
camping ground	la zona para acampar sg	la *so*·na *pa*·ra a·kam·*par*
showers	las duchas pl	las *doo*·chas
toilets	los baños pl	los *ba*·nyos

Where have you come from?
¿De dónde viene/vienen? sg/pl   de *don*·de *vye*·ne/*vye*·nen

How long did it take you?
¿Cuánto duró/duraron   kwan·to doo·ro/doo·ra·ron
en llegar? sg/pl   en ye·gar

Does this path go to (Arenal)?
¿Este camino   es·te ka·mee·no
llega a (Arenal)?   ye·ga a (a·re·nal)

Can I go through here?
¿Puedo pasar por aquí?   pwe·do pa·sar por a·kee

Is the water OK to drink?
¿Se puede beber el agua?   se pwe·de be·ber el a·gwa

I'm lost.
Estoy perdido/a. m/f   es·toy per·dee·do/a

beach

playa

Where's the … beach?	¿Dónde está la …?	don·de es·ta la …
best	mejor playa	me·khor pla·ya
nearest	playa más cercana	pla·ya mas ser·ka·na
How much to rent a/an …?	¿Cuánto cuesta alquilar …?	kwan·to kwes·ta al·kee·lar …
chair	una silla	oo·na see·ya
hut	un rancho	oon ran·cho
umbrella	una sombrilla	oo·na som·bree·ya

signs

Prohibido Hacer Clavados	pro·ee·bee·do a·ser kla·va·dos	**No Diving**
Prohibido Nadar	pro·ee·bee·do na·dar	**No Swimming**

outdoors

Is it dangerous to dive/swim here?
¿Será peligroso bucear/   se·*ra* pe·lee·*gro*·so boo·se·*ar*/
nadar aquí?   na·*dar* a·*kee*

What time is high/low tide?
¿A qué hora es la   a ke *o*·ra es la
marea alta/baja?   ma·*re*·a *al*·ta/*ba*·kha

listen for ...

¡Cuidado con las corrientes de resaca!
    kwee·*da*·do kon las   **Be careful of the undertow!**
    ko·*ryen*·tes de re·*sa*·ka

¡Es peligroso!
    es pe·lee·*gro*·so   **It's dangerous!**

weather

tiempo

What's the weather like?
¿Cómo está el tiempo?   *ko*·mo es·*ta* el *tyem*·po

It's ...	*Está ...*	es·*ta* ...
cloudy	*nublado*	noo·*bla*·do
cold	*frío*	*free*·o
hot	*haciendo*	a·*syen*·do
	mucho calor	*moo*·cho ka·*lor*
raining	*lloviendo*	yo·*vyen*·do
sunny	*haciendo sol*	a·*syen*·do sol
warm	*caliente*	ka·*lyen*·te
windy	*ventoso*	ven·*to*·so

Where can I	*¿Dónde puedo*	*don*·de *pwe*·do
buy a/an ...?	*comprar una ...?*	kom·*prar* oo·na ...
rain jacket	*capa*	*ka*·pa
umbrella	*sombrilla*	som·*bree*·ya

dry season	*estación seca* f	es·ta·*syon* *se*·ka
wet season	*estación lluviosa* f	es·ta·*syon* yoo·*vyo*·sa

SOCIAL

148

ecotourism

Costa Rica boasts some of the most diverse flora and fauna in the world, and opportunities for wildlife enthusiasts are endless. The country is known for its serious approach to conservation and protection of the environment, which includes one of the best park systems in the Western Hemisphere. Costa Rica also has numerous privately owned parks and ecotourism projects.

What … is that?	¿Qué es …?	ke es …
animal	ese animal	e·se a·nee·mal
flower	esa flor	e·sa flor
plant	esa mata	e·sa ma·ta
tree	ese árbol	e·se ar·bol

What's it used for?
¿Para qué se usa?   pa·ra ke se oo·sa

Can you eat the fruit?
¿Esa fruta se come?   e·sa froo·ta se ko·me

Is it …?	¿Es …?	es …
dangerous	peligroso/a m/f	pe·lee·gro·so/a
poisonous	venenoso/a m/f	ve·ne·no·so/a

Is it …?	¿Está …?	es·ta …
endangered	en peligro	en pe·lee·gro
	de extinción	de eks·teen·syon
protected	protegido/a m/f	pro·te·khee·do/a

Is this a	¿Este/Esta es …	es·te/es·ta es …
protected …?	protegido/a? m/f	pro·te·khee·do/a
park	un parque m	oon par·ke
species	una especie f	oo·na es·pe·sye

outdoors

149

What time is best for seeing …?
¿Cuál es la mejor   kwal es la me·*khor*
hora para ver …?   *o*·ra *pa*·ra ver …

Can I see … here?
¿Puedo ver … aquí?   *pwe*·do ver … a·*kee*

Are there active volcanoes in this area?
¿Hay volcanes activos   ai vol·*ka*·nes ak·*tee*·vos
en esta zona?   en *es*·ta *so*·na

Is that an active volcano?
¿Es un volcán activo?   es oon vol·*kan* ak·*tee*·vo

wildlife & habitat

geography

cave	*cueva* f	*kwe*·va
cliff	*acantilado* m	a·kan·tee·*la*·do
estuary	*estuario* m	es·too·*a*·ryo
forest	*bosque* m	*bos*·ke
hill	*colina* f	ko·*lee*·na
island	*isla* f	*ees*·la
lake	*lago* m	*la*·go
lava	*lava* f	*la*·va
mountain	*montaña* f	mon·*ta*·nya
mountain range	*sierra* f	*sye*·ra
ocean	*océano* m	o·*se*·a·no
river	*río* m	*ree*·o
sea	*mar* m	mar
swamp	*pantano* m	pan·*ta*·no
valley	*valle* m	*va*·ye
volcano	*volcán* m	vol·*kan*
waterfall	*salto* m	*sal*·to
wildlife	*flora y fauna*	*flo*·ra ee *fow*·na
	silvestre f	seel·*ves*·tre

flora

ceiba (silk cotton tree)	*ceiba* f	*say·*ba
cloud forest	*bosque nuboso* m	*bos·*ke noo·*bo·*so
guanacaste tree (national tree)	*árbol de guanacaste* m	*ar·*bol de gwa·na·*kas·*te
jungle	*selva* f	*sel·*va
mangrove	*manglar* m	man·*glar*
orchid	*orquídea* f	or·*kee·*de·a
palm tree	*palma* f	*pal·*ma
purple orchid (national flower)	*guaria morada* f	*gwa·*ree·a mo·*ra·*da
rain forest	*bosque lluvioso* m	*bos·*ke yoo·*vyo·*so
tropical dry forest	*bosque seco tropical* m	*bos·*ke *se·*ko tro·pee·*kal*
tropical plains	*llanura tropical* f	ya·*noo·*ra tro·pee·*kal*

mammals

agouti	*guatusa* f	gwa·*too·*sa
anteater	*oso hormiguero* m	*o·*so or·mee·*ge·*ro
armadillo	*armadillo* m	ar·ma·*dee·*yo
capuchin monkey	*mono capuchín* m	*mo·*no ka·poo·*cheen*
coati	*pizote* m	pee·*so·*te
howler monkey	*mono congo* m	*mo·*no *kon·*go
jaguar	*jaguar* m	kha·*gwar*
kinkajou	*martilla* f	mar·*tee·*ya
monkey	*mono* m	*mo·*no
opossum	*zorro* m	*so·*ro
paca	*tepezcuintle* m	te·pes·*kweent·*le
peccary	*chancho del monte* m	*chan·*cho del *mon·*te
sloth	*oso perezoso* m	*o·*so pe·re·*so·*so
spider monkey	*mono araña* m	*mo·*no a·*ra·*nya
squirrel	*ardilla* f	ar·*dee·*ya
squirrel monkey	*mono tití* m	*mo·*no tee·*tee*
tapir	*danta* f	*dan·*ta

insects & birds

ant	*hormiga* f	or·*mee*·ga
butterfly	*mariposa* f	ma·ree·*po*·sa
eagle	*águila* m	*a*·gee·la
heron	*garza* f	*gar*·sa
hummingbird	*colibrí* m	ko·lee·*bree*
jacana	*jacana* f	kha·*ka*·na
macaw	*lapa* f	*la*·pa
morpho butterfly	*morfo* m	*mor*·fo
mosquito	*zancudo* m	san·*koo*·do
parakeet	*perico* m	pe·*ree*·ko
pelican	*pelícano* m	pe·*lee*·ka·no
pigeon	*paloma* f	pa·*lo*·ma
quetzal	*quetzal* m	ket·*sal*
toucan	*tucán* m	too·*kan*
vulture	*buitre* m	*bwee*·tre
yigüirro (national bird)	*yigüirro* m	yee·*gwee*·ro

reptiles

bushmaster (snake)	*cascabel muda* f	kas·ka·*bel moo*·da
crocodile	*cocodrilo* m	ko·ko·*dree*·lo
fer-de-lance (snake)	*terciopelo* m	ter·syo·*pe*·lo
iguana	*iguana* f/*garrobo* m	ee·*gwa*·na/ga·*ro*·bo
lizard	*lagarto* m	la·*gar*·to
snake	*culebra* f	koo·*le*·bra

marine life

dolphin	*delfín* m	del·*feen*
fish	*pes* m	pes
frog	*rana* f	*ra*·na
manatee	*manatí* m	ma·na·*tee*
otter	*nutria* f	noo·*tree*·a
turtle	*tortuga* f	tor·*too*·ga
whale	*ballena* f	ba·*ye*·na

basics

lo básico

breakfast	*desayuno* m	de·sa·*yoo*·no
lunch	*almuerzo* m	al·*mwer*·so
dinner	*cena* f	*se*·na
snack n	*merienda* f	me·*ryen*·da
eat v	*comer*	ko·*mer*
drink v	*beber*	be·*ber*
I'd like …	*Me gustaría* … pol	me goos·ta·*ree*·a …
	Quiero … inf	*kye*·ro …
Please.	*Por favor.*	por fa·*vor*
Thank you.	*Gracias.*	*gra*·syas
Enjoy your meal.	*(Buen) Provecho.*	(bwen) pro·*ve*·cho
Cheers!	*¡Salud!*	sa·*lood*

a match made in heaven

The traditional lunch and dinner are variations on the famous *casado* ka·*sa*·do (lit: married couple). This match-made-in-heaven is a hearty combination plate of rice, beans, shredded cabbage salad, vegetable or fruit *picadillo* pee·ka·*dee*·yo (mince) and a meat of choice (beef, fish, pork or chicken). The whole is garnished with fried plantains, tortillas and a slice or two of tomato. It's cheap and more than enough to keep body and soul together! Specify what meat you want by asking for *bife* *bee*·fe (beef), *pescado* pes·*ka*·do (fish), *puerco* *pwer*·ko (pork) or *pollo* *po*·yo (chicken).

finding a place to eat

Can you recommend a …?	¿Podría recomendar …?	po·dree·a re·ko·men·dar …
bar	un bar	oon bar
café	un café	oon ka·fe
lunch counter	una soda	oo·na so·da
(Chinese) restaurant	un restaurante (chino)	oon res·tow·ran·te (chee·no)

Where would you go for (a) …?	¿Dónde podría ir para …?	don·de po·dree·a eer pa·ra …
celebration	una celebración	oo·na se·le·bra·syon
cheap meal	comer barato	ko·mer ba·ra·to
local specialities	comer comida local	ko·mer ko·mee·da lo·kal

I'd like to reserve a table for …	Quiero reservar una mesa para …	kye·ro re·ser·var oo·na me·sa pa·ra …
(two) people	(dos) personas	(dos) per·so·nas
(eight) o'clock	las (ocho)	las (o·cho)

at the counter

If it's snacks you're after, you should be on the lookout for a *soda* so·da. You shouldn't have to look too far because they abound and come in various guises ranging from a lean-to or shack with a couple of makeshift tables to a small café-style restaurant.

Sodas dispense drinks and *casados* ka·sa·dos (combination plates of rice and meat or vegetables) in addition to snacks. They usually also sell *empanadas* em·pa·na·das (turnovers), *gallos* ga·yos (tortilla sandwiches) or *enchiladas* en·chee·la·das (pastries with spicy meat). Grilled beef or pork kebabs known as *pinchos* peen·chos are also a popular snack on the go. For more on these items and Costa Rican cuisine generally, see the **menu decoder**.

Are you still serving food?

¿Todavía están sirviendo comida?	to·da·*vee*·a es·*tan* seer·*vyen*·do ko·*mee*·da

How long is the wait?

¿Cuánto tengo que esperar?	*kwan*·to *ten*·go ke es·pe·*rar*

listen for ...

Está cerrado.	es·*ta* se·*ra*·do	**We're closed.**
Está lleno.	es·*ta* ye·no	**We're full.**
Un momento.	oon mo·*men*·to	**One moment.**

at the restaurant

en el restaurante

I'd like (a/the) ...	*Quisiera ..., por favor.*	kee·*sye*·ra ... por fa·*vor*
(non)smoking section	*el área de (no) fumado*	el *a*·re·a de (no) foo·*ma*·do
table for (five)	*una mesa para (cinco)*	*oo*·na *me*·sa pa·ra (*seen*·ko)
that dish	*ese plato*	*e*·se *pla*·to

What would you recommend?

¿Qué me recomienda?	ke me re·ko·*myen*·da

What's in that dish?

¿Ese plato qué trae?	*e*·se *pla*·to ke *tra*·e

What's that called?

¿Éso cómo se llama?	*e*·so *ko*·mo se *ya*·ma

I'll have that.

Yo quiero éso.	yo *kye*·ro *e*·so

Does it take long to prepare?

¿Se dura mucho preparándolo?	se *doo*·ra *moo*·cho pre·pa·*ran*·do·lo

Is it self-serve?

¿Es de auto-servicio?	es de ow·to·ser·*vee*·syo

eating out

155

Is there a cover/service charge?

¿Hay que pagar	ai ke pa·*gar*
entrada/servicio?	en·*tra*·da/ser·*vee*·syo

Is service included in the bill?

¿El servicio está incluído?	el ser·*vee*·syo es·*ta* een·kloo·*ee*·do

Are these complimentary?

¿Son gratis?	son *gra*·tees

Could I see the wine list?

¿Podría ver la lista	po·*dree*·a ver la *lees*·ta
de vinos, por favor?	de *vee*·nos por fa·*vor*

Bring me a/the ..., please.	*Tráigame ..., por favor.*	*trai*·ga·me ... por fa·*vor*
children's menu	*el menú para niños*	el me·*noo* pa·ra *nee*·nyos
drink list	*la lista de tragos*	la *lees*·ta de *tra*·gos
half portion	*media porción*	*me*·dya por·*syon*
local speciality	*una especialidad local*	*oo*·na es·pe·sya·lee·*dad* lo·*kal*
menu (in English)	*el menú (en inglés)*	el me·*noo* (en een·*gles*)

---

listen for ...

¿Cómo lo/la quiere? m/f		
ko·mo lo/la *kye*·re		How would you like that?
¿Dónde se quiere sentar?		
don·de se *kye*·re sen·*tar*		Where would you like to sit?
¿Qué le puedo traer?		
ke le *pwe*·do tra·*er*		What can I get for you?
¡Aquí está!	a·*kee* es·*ta*	Here you go!
Buen provecho.	bwen pro·*ve*·cho	Enjoy your meal.
¿Le gusta ...?	le *goos*·ta ...	Do you like ...?
Le recomiendo ...	le re·ko·*myen*·do ...	I suggest the ...

I'd like it with/	*Lo quiero*	lo *kye*·ro
without …	*con/sin …*	kon/seen …
cheese	*queso*	*ke*·so
chilli sauce	*salsa picante*	*sal*·sa pee·*kan*·te
garlic	*ajo*	*a*·kho
ketchup	*ketchup*	ke·*tchoop*
nuts	*nueces*	*nwe*·ses
oil	*aceite*	a·*say*·te
pepper	*pimienta*	pee·*myen*·ta
Salsa Lizano	*Salsa Lizano*	*sal*·sa lee·*sa*·no
salt	*sal*	sal
vinegar	*vinagre*	vee·*na*·gre

For other specific meal requests, see **vegetarian & special meals**, page 169.

at the table

en la mesa

Please bring	*Por favor*	por fa·*vor*
(a/the) …	*tráigame …*	*trai*·ga·me …
bill	*la cuenta*	la *kwen*·ta
cutlery	*los cubiertos*	los koo·*byer*·tos
glass	*un vaso*	oon *va*·so
serviette	*una servilleta*	oo·na ser·vee·*ye*·ta

There's a mistake in the bill.
Hay un error en la cuenta.   ai oon e·*ror* en la *kwen*·ta

I didn't order this.
No pedí esto.   no pe·*dee* es·to

talking food

I'm starving!
*¡Me estoy muriendo
de hambre!*
me es·*toy* moo·*ryen*·do
de *am*·bre

The food is very good.
La comida está muy rica.
la ko·*mee*·da es·*ta* mooy *ree*·ka

I love the local cuisine.
*Me encanta la
comida de aquí.*
me en·*kan*·ta la
ko·*mee*·da de a·*kee*

I love this dish.
Me encanta este plato.
me en·*kan*·ta *es*·te *pla*·to

That was delicious!
¡Estuvo delicioso!
es·*too*·vo de·lee·*syo*·so

I'm full.
Estoy lleno/a. m/f
es·*toy* ye·no/a

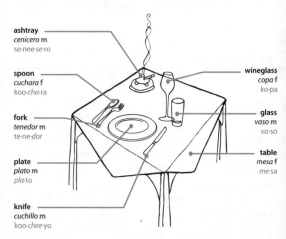

ashtray
cenicero m
se·nee·*se*·ro

spoon
cuchara f
koo·*cha*·ra

fork
tenedor m
te·ne·*dor*

plate
plato m
pla·to

knife
cuchillo m
koo·*chee*·yo

wineglass
copa f
ko·pa

glass
vaso m
va·so

table
mesa f
me·sa

FOOD

158

This is …	Está …	es·ta …
burnt	quemado	ke·ma·do
cold	frío	free·o
hot	caliente	ka·lyen·te
(too) spicy	(demasiado)	(de·ma·sya·do)
	condimentado	kon·dee·men·ta·do

look for …

Aperitivos	a·pe·ree·tee·vos	Appetisers
Sopas	so·pas	Soups
Entradas	en·tra·das	Entrées
Ensaladas	en·sa·la·das	Salads
Platos Fuertes	pla·tos fwer·tes	Main Courses
Guarniciónes	gwar·nee·syo·nes	Side Dishes (at restaurants)
Acompañamientos	a·kom·pa·nya·myen·tos	Side Dishes (at bars & lunch counters)
Postres	pos·tres	Desserts
Bebidas	be·bee·das	Drinks
Refrescos	re·fres·kos	Soft Drinks
Cocteles	kok·te·les	Spirits
Cervezas	ser·ve·sas	Beers
Vinos …	vee·nos …	… Wines
Blancos	blan·kos	White
Digestivos	dee·khes·tee·vos	Dessert
Espumantes	es·poo·man·tes	Sparkling
Tintos	teen·tos	Red

For more words you might see on a menu, see the **menu decoder**, page 171.

eating out

159

methods of preparation

I'd like it …	Lo quiero …	lo kye·ro …
I don't want it …	No lo quiero …	no lo kye·ro …
boiled	hervido	er·vee·do
broiled	asado	a·sa·do
fried	frito	free·to
grilled	a la parrilla	a la pa·ree·ya
mashed	en puré	en poo·re
medium	término medio	ter·mee·no me·dyo
rare	crudo	kroo·do
reheated	recalentado	re·ka·len·ta·do
steamed	al vapor	al va·por
well-done	bien cocinado	byen ko·see·na·do
with the dressing	con el aderezo	kon el a·de·re·so
on the side	al lado	al la·do
without …	sin …	seen …

nonalcoholic drinks

bebidas sin alcohol

boiled water	agua hervida f	a·gwa er·vee·da
bottled water	agua embotellada f	a·gwa em·bo·te·ya·da
freshly-squeezed fruit drink	fresco m	fres·ko
fruit shake	batido m	ba·tee·do
hot water	agua caliente f	a·gwa ka·lyen·te
iced tea	té con hielo m	te kon ye·lo
(orange) juice	jugo (de naranja) m	khoo·go (de na·ran·kha)
mineral water	agua mineral f	a·gwa mee·ne·ral
soft drink	gaseosa f	ga·se·o·sa
sparkling mineral water	soda f	so·da
with/without ice	con/sin hielo	kon/seen ye·lo

(cup of) coffee ...	(taza de) café ...	(ta·sa de) ka·fe ...
(cup of) tea ...	(taza de) té ...	(ta·sa de) te ...
with (milk)	con (leche)	kon (le·che)
without (sugar)	sin (azúcar)	seen (a·soo·kar)
... coffee	café ...	ka·fe ...
black	negro	ne·gro
decaffeinated	descafeinado	des·ka·fay·na·do
strong	fuerte	fwer·te
weak	ralo	ra·lo
white	con leche	kon le·che

juicy treats

There are many delicious ways to quench your thirst in Costa Rica. Top of the list are the seemingly infinite varieties of *refrescos naturales* re·fres·kos na·too·ra·les, usually known simply as *frescos* fres·kos. These consist of almost any kind of fruit squeezed or blended with water and sugar or milk. You can specify whether you want water or milk by saying *con agua* kon a·gwa (with water) or *con leche* kon le·che (with milk). When ordering, simply refer to the flavour you want, eg *mora con leche* mo·ra kon le·che (blackberry with milk). Also popular are *batidos* ba·tee·dos (fruit shakes) which are essentially the same as *frescos* but thicker. Below are some of the most popular fruit flavours for both *frescos* and *batidos*:

barley	cebada f	se·ba·da
blackberry	mora f	mo·ra
cantaloupe	melón m	me·lon
carrot	zanahoria f	sa·na·o·rya
cas	cas m	kas
mango	mango m	man·go
naranjilla	naranjilla f	na·ran·khee·ya
papaya	papaya f	pa·pa·ya
pineapple	piña f	pee·nya
soursop	guanábana f	gwa·na·ba·na
star fruit	carambola f	ka·ram·bo·la
strawberry	fresa f	fre·sa
tamarind	tamarindo m	ta·ma·reen·do
watermelon	sandía f	san·dee·a

Coffee is the most popular beverage in the country and wherever you go, someone is likely to offer you a *cafecito* ka·fe·*see*·to (an affectionate term for a cup of coffee). Traditionally it's served strong and mixed with hot milk to taste. This is known as a *café con leche* ka·fe kon *le*·che. Some prefer a *café negro* ka·fe *ne*·gro (black coffee), but those who want a little milk can ask for *leche al lado* le·che al *la*·do (milk on the side). Many trendier places also serve capuccinos and espressos which you can ask for by these names.

alcoholic drinks

		bebidas alcohólicas
a bottle/glass	*una botella/copa*	oo·na bo·*te*·ya/*ko*·pa
of ... wine	*de vino ...*	de *vee*·no ...
dessert	*digestivo*	dee·khes·*tee*·vo
red	*tinto*	*teen*·to
rosé	*rosado*	ro·*sa*·do
sparkling	*espumante*	es·poo·*man*·te
white	*blanco*	*blan*·ko
a ... of beer	*... de cerveza*	... de ser·*ve*·sa
glass	*un vaso*	oon *va*·so
jug	*una jarra*	oo·na *kha*·ra
large bottle	*una botella grande*	oo·na bo·*te*·ya *gran*·de
pitcher	*un pichel*	oon pee·*chel*
small bottle	*una botella pequeña*	oo·na bo·*te*·ya pe·*ke*·nya
champagne	*champán* m	cham·*pan*
cocktail	*coctél* m	kok·*tel*
gin	*ginebra* f	khee·*ne*·bra
rum	*ron* m	ron
tequila	*tequila* f	te·*kee*·la
vodka	*vodka* m	*vod*·ka
whisky	*whisky* m	*wee*·skee

in the bar

Most bars offer bar snacks called *bocas* bo·kas (lit: mouths). Typical offerings include black beans, *ceviche* se·vee·che (marinated shrimp or raw fish), chicken stew, potato chips, varieties of tacos or pieces of beef.

Excuse me!	¡Con permiso!	kon per·mee·so
I'm next.	Sigo yo.	see·go yo
I'll have (Cacique).	Quiero (Cacique).	kye·ro (ka·see·ke)
No ice, thanks.	Sin hielo, gracias.	seen ye·lo gra·syas

Same again, please.
   Lo mismo, por favor.   lo mees·mo por fa·vor

I'll buy you a drink.
   Te invito a un trago.   te en·vee·to a oon tra·go

It's my round.
   Me toca.   me to·ka

What would you like?
   ¿Que querés?   ke ke·res

I don't drink alcohol.
   Yo no tomo.   yo no to·mo

Do you serve meals here?
   ¿Sirven comida aquí?   seer·ven ko·mee·da a·kee

---

down the hatch

The most popular alcoholic drinks are *cerveza* ser·ve·sa (beer) and the cane alcohol *guaro* gwa·ro which has the kick of a mule and a hangover to match. Beer is served *cruda* kroo·da (as a draft), in a *jarra* kha·ra (jug) or in a *pichel* pee·chel (pitcher). *Guaro* comes in a shot or is mixed with a soft drink or juice. The most popular brand of *guaro* is *Cacique* ka·see·ke (meaning 'chief').

eating out

163

listen for...

Creo que ya tomaste suficiente.
   kre·o ke ya to·*mas*·te
   soo·fee·*syen*·te   **I think you've had enough.**

¿Que vas a pedir?
   ke vas a pe·*deer*   **What are you having?**

Última orden.
   ool·tee·ma *or*·den   **Last orders.**

drinking up

tomando

Cheers!
   ¡Salud!   sa·*lood*

I feel fantastic!
   ¡Me siento fenomenal!   me *syen*·to fe·no·me·*nal*

I think I've had one too many.
   Ya me llegaron.   ya me ye·*ga*·ron

I'm feeling drunk.
   Estoy tapis.   es·*toy* ta·pees

I'm pissed.
   Estoy hasta el culo.   es·*toy as*·ta el *koo*·lo

I feel ill.
   Me siento mal.   me *syen*·to mal

Where's the toilet?
   ¿Dónde está el baño?   *don*·de es·*ta* el *ba*·nyo

I'm tired, I'd better go home.
   Estoy cansado/a,   es·*toy* kan·*sa*·do/a
   mejor me voy. m/f   me·*khor* me voy

I don't think you should drive.
   No deberías manejar.   no de·be·*ree*·as ma·ne·*khar*

Can you call a taxi for me?
   ¿Me podrías llamar   me po·*dree*·as ya·*mar*
   un taxi?   oon *tak*·see

buying food

comprando comida

What's the local speciality?
¿Cuál es la
especialidad local?
kwal es la
es·pe·sya·lee·*dad* lo·*kal*

What's that?
¿Qué es éso?
ke es *e*·so

Can I taste it?
¿Puedo probarlo?
pwe·do pro·*bar*·lo

How much is (a kilo of cheese)?
¿Cuánto cuesta
(un kilo de queso)?
kwan·to *kwes*·ta
(oon *kee*·lo de *ke*·so)

Can I have a bag, please?
¿Me da una bolsa, por favor?
me da *oo*·na *bol*·sa por fa·*vor*

I don't need a bag, thanks.
No necesito bolsa, gracias.
no ne·se·*see*·to *bol*·sa *gra*·syas

I'd like ...	*Quiero ...*	*kye*·ro ...
(200) grams	*(doscientos)* *gramos*	(do·*syen*·tos) *gra*·mos
a kilo	*un kilo*	oon *kee*·lo
half a kilo	*medio kilo*	*me*·dyo *kee*·lo
(two) kilos	*(dos) kilos*	(dos) *kee*·los
a dozen	*una docena*	*oo*·na do·*se*·na
half a dozen	*media docena*	*me*·dya do·*se*·na
a bottle	*una botella*	*oo*·na bo·*te*·ya
a jar	*una jarra*	*oo*·na *kha*·ra
a packet	*un paquete*	oon pa·*ke*·te
a piece	*un pedazo*	oon pe·*da*·so
(three) pieces	*(tres) pedazos*	(tres) pe·*da*·sos
a slice	*una tajada*	*oo*·na ta·*kha*·da
(six) slices	*(seis) tajadas*	(says) ta·*kha*·das

I'd like …	Quiero …	kye·ro …
a little	un poquitito	oon po·kee·*tee*·to
some (of …)	un poco (de …)	oon *po*·ko (de …)
more	más	mas
that one	ése/a m/f	e·se/a
this one	éste/a m/f	es·te/a

Less.	Menos.	me·nos
A bit more.	Un poquito más.	oon po·*kee*·to mas
Enough.	Suficiente.	soo·fee·*syen*·te

Do you have …?	¿Tiene …?	tye·ne …
anything	algo más	al·go mas
cheaper	barato	ba·ra·to
other kinds	otros tipos	o·tros tee·pos

Where can I find the … section?	¿Dónde está/ están … sg/pl	don·de es·ta/ es·tan …
dairy	los lácteos pl	los lak·te·yos
fish	el pescado sg	el pes·ka·do
frozen goods	las comidas congeladas pl	las ko·mee·das kon·khe·la·das
fruit and vegetable	las frutas y verduras pl	las froo·tas ee ver·doo·ras
meat	las carnes pl	las kar·nes
poultry	las aves pl	las a·ves

For food items, see the **menu decoder**, page 171.

food stuff		
cooked	cocinado/a m/f	ko·see·na·do/a
cured	adobado/a m/f	a·do·ba·do/a
dried	seco/a m/f	se·ko/a
fresh	fresco/a m/f	fres·ko/a
frozen	congelado/a m/f	kon·khe·la·do/a
raw	crudo/a m/f	kroo·do/a
smoked	ahumado/a m/f	a·oo·ma·do/a

FOOD

¿Algo más?
al·go mas   **Anything else?**

¿Le puedo ayudar en algo?
le pwe·do a·yoo·dar
en al·go   **Can I help you**
                                   with something?

No hay.
no ai   **There isn't any.**

¿Qué quiere?
ke kye·re   **What would you like?**

cooking utensils

utensilios de cocina

Can I borrow a ...?	¿Podría prestarme ...?	po·dree·a pres·tar·me ...
I need a ...	Necesito ...	ne·se·see·to ...
can opener	un abrelatas	oon a·bre·la·tas
chopping board	una tabla para picar	oo·na ta·bla pa·ra pee·kar
corkscrew	un sacacorchos	oon sa·ka·kor·chos
cup	una taza	oo·na ta·sa
frying pan	un sartén	oon sar·ten
knife	un cuchillo	oon koo·chee·yo
saucepan	un sartén hondo	oon sar·ten on·do
spoon	una cuchara	oo·na koo·cha·ra

For more cooking implements, see the **dictionary**.

self-catering

167

One of the joys of a trip to Costa Rica is to sample some of the delicious varieties of healthy tropical fruits on offer. Some of these you'll discover in the guise of refreshing drinks called *frescos* fres·kos (see the box **juicy treats**, page 161). Note that not all local fruits have names in English.

caimito m   kai·*mee*·to
   star apple – similar to a star fruit but has a purplish skin and soft sweet flesh

cas m   kas
   small sour guava-like fruit which is whitish on the inside and frequently used in *frescos*

guanábana f   gwa·*na*·ba·na
   soursop – large dark green fruit with spines on the outside and tart white flesh on the inside

jocote m   kho·*ko*·te
   plum-sized fruit with a large pit, sometimes eaten green with salt (an acquired taste) or eaten when red and ripe – popular street snack

manzana de agua f   man·*sa*·na de *a*·gwa
   'water apple' (relative of the rose apple) – has a crisp white juicy apple-like flesh

manzana rosa f   man·*sa*·na *ro*·sa
   'rose apple' – round whitish-green to apricot-yellow fruit with a rose perfume and a sweet crispy and juicy flesh

naranjilla f   na·ran·*khee*·ya
   orange tomato-like fruit with a juicy acidic pulp used in drinks and sherbets

zapote m   sa·*po*·te
   sapote – fruit with a pinky-red flesh that has a sweet pumpkin-like flavour

zapote negro m   sa·*po*·te *ne*·gro
   'black sapote' – fruit with a delicious jelly-like flesh, similar in flavour to a chocolate pudding (unrelated to sapote)

ordering food

If you don't mind rice and beans, Costa Rica is a relatively comfortable place for vegetarians to travel. Most restaurants will do *casados vegetarianos* ka·*sa*·dos ve·khe·ta·*rya*·nos (ie vegetarian *casados*) on request – see the box **a match made in heaven**, page 153, for more information on this dish.

Is there a ...	¿Hay un	ai oon
restaurant	restaurante ...	res·tow·*ran*·te ...
near here?	cerca de aquí?	ser·ka de a·*kee*
Do you have	¿Tienen	*tye*·nen
... food?	comida ...?	ko·*mee*·da ...
halal	halal	a·*lal*
kosher	kosher	*ko*·sher
vegetarian	vegetariana	ve·khe·ta·*rya*·na

I don't eat ...	No como ...	no *ko*·mo ...
Is it cooked	¿Está cocinado	es·*ta* ko·see·*na*·do
with ...?	con ...?	kon ...
butter	mantequilla	man·te·*kee*·ya
eggs	huevos	*we*·vos
fish (stock)	(caldo de)	(*kal*·do de)
	pescado	pes·*ka*·do
meat (stock)	(caldo de) carne	(*kal*·do de) *kar*·ne
oil	aceite	a·*say*·te
pork	cerdo	*ser*·do
poultry	ave	*a*·ve
red meat	carne roja	*kar*·ne *ro*·kha

Could you prepare a meal without …?

| ¿Podría preparar | po·*dree*·a pre·pa·*rar* |
| un plato sin …? | oon *pla*·to seen … |

Does it contain animal produce?

| ¿Tiene productos | *tye*·ne pro·*dook*·tos |
| animales? | a·nee·*ma*·les |

Is this …?   ¿Es …?   es …

decaffeinated	descafeinado	des·ka·fay·*na*·do
genetically	genéticamente	khe·*ne*·tee·ka·men·te
modified	modificado	mo·dee·fee·*ka*·do
gluten-free	sin gluten	seen *gloo*·ten
low-fat	de poca grasa	de *po*·ka *gra*·sa
low in sugar	de poca azúcar	de *po*·ka a·*soo*·kar
organic	orgánico	or·*ga*·nee·ko
salt-free	sin sal	seen sal

special diets & allergies

dietas especiales y alergias

I'm on a special diet.

Estoy en una dieta especial.   es·*toy* en *oo*·na *dye*·ta es·pe·*syal*

I'm a vegan.

Soy vegano/a. m/f   soy ve·*ga*·no/a

I'm allergic to …   *Soy alérgico/a …* m/f   soy a·*ler*·khee·ko/a …

dairy produce	a los lácteos	a los *lak*·te·os
eggs	a los huevos	a los *we*·vos
gelatine	a la gelatina	a la khe·la·*tee*·na
gluten	al gluten	al *gloo*·ten
honey	a la miel	a la myel
MSG	al GMS	al khe *e*·me *e*·se
nuts	a las nueces	a las *nwe*·ses
peanuts	al maní	al ma·*nee*
seafood	a los mariscos	a los ma·*rees*·kos
shellfish	a las conchas	a las *kon*·chas

To explain your dietary restrictions with reference to religious beliefs, see **beliefs & cultural differences**, page 131.

menu decoder
léxico culinario

This miniguide to Costa Rican cuisine lists ingredients in Spanish alphabetical order (see the box **spanish alphabet**, page 13). It's designed to help you navigate menus and get the most out of your gastronomic experience in Costa Rica. ¡Buen provecho!

A

aceitunas ① pl a-say-*too*-nas *olives*
 — **negras** ne-gras *black olives*
 — **rellenas** re-*ye*-nas *stuffed olives*
 — **verdes** *ver*-des *green olives*
adobo ⓜ a-*do*-bo *garlic, oregano, paprika, peppercorn, salt, olive, lime juice & vinegar paste for seasoning meat*
agua ⓜ *a*-gwa *water*
 — **del tubo** del *too*-bo *tap water*
 — **de manantial** de ma-nan-*tyal* *spring water*
 — **mineral** mee-ne-*ral* *mineral water*
 — **sin gas** seen gas *still water*
aguacate ⓜ a-gwa-*ka*-te *avocado*
ahumado/a ⓜ/① a-oo-*ma*-do/a *smoked*
ají ⓜ a-*khee* *red chilli pepper*
ajillo, al a-*khee*-yo, al *cooked in garlic*
ajo ⓜ *a*-kho *garlic*
albahaca ① al-ba-*a*-ka *basil*
albaricoque ⓜ al-ba-ree-*ko*-ke *apricot*
albóndigas ① pl al-*bon*-dee-gas *meatballs*
alcachofa ① al-ka-*cho*-fa *artichoke*
alcaparra ① al-ka-*pa*-ra *caper*
alita ① a-*lee*-ta *wing (poultry)*
almejas ① pl al-*me*-khas *clams*
almendra ① al-*men*-dra *almond*
alubias ① pl a-*loo*-byas *red kidney beans*
anchoas ① pl an-*cho*-as *anchovies*
anguila ① an-*gee*-la *eel*
anís ⓜ a-*nees* *anise • aniseed*
apio ⓜ *a*-pyo *celery*
arreglado ⓜ a-re-*gla*-do *sandwich or tiny puff pastry stuffed with beef cheese or chicken*
arrollado/a ⓜ/① a-ro-*ya*-do/a *rolled*
arroz ⓜ a-*ros* *rice*
 — **con atún** kon a-*toon* *rice & tuna*
 — **con camarones** kon ka-ma-*ro*-nes *rice with shrimps*
 — **con leche** kon *le*-che *milky sweet rice pudding with a hint of cinnamon*
 — **con pollo** kon *po*-yo *rice & chicken*
 — **guacho** *gwa*-cho *rice with onion, garlic, pork & cilantro (coriander)*
 — **y frijoles** ee free-*kho*-les *rice with black beans*
arvejas ① pl ar-*ve*-khas *peas (also known as **petipoas**)*
 — **secas** *se*-kas *split peas*
asado ⓜ a-*sa*-do *mixed grill*
atún ⓜ a-*toon* *tuna*
ave ① *a*-ve *poultry*
avellana ① a-ve-*ya*-na *hazelnut*
avena ① a-*ve*-na *oats*
ayote ⓜ a-*yo*-te *gourd • squash*
azafrán ⓜ a-sa-*fran* *saffron*
azúcar ⓜ a-*soo*-kar *sugar*

B

bacalao ⓜ ba-ka-*low* *cod*
 — **seco** *se*-ko *dried salted cod*
bagre ⓜ *ba*-gre *catfish*
banano ⓜ ba-*na*-no *banana*
batido ⓜ ba-*tee*-do *fresh fruit shake made with water (**con agua**) or milk (**con leche**) – see the box **juicy treats**, page 161, for popular flavours*
berberechos ⓜ pl be-be-re-*chos* *cockles*
berenjena ① be-ren-*khe*-na *aubergine • eggplant*
berro ⓜ *be*-ro *watercress*
bien asado/a ⓜ/① byen a-*sa*-do/a *well done*
bien cocido/a ⓜ/① byen ko-*see*-do/a *well done*

bien hecho/a ⓜ/ⓕ byen e-cho/a *well done*
bistec ⓜ bees-*tek* *steak*
— **con papas** kon *pa*-pas *steak & chips*
bocadillo ⓜ bo-ka-*dee*-yo *snack*
bocas ⓕ pl *bo*-kas
bar snacks such as black beans, **ceviche**, *chicken stew, potato chips, varieties of* **tacos**, *or pieces of beef – served with drinks*
bollos ⓜ pl *bo*-yos *bread rolls*
brócoli ⓜ bro-ko-lee *broccoli*
budín ⓜ boo-*deen* *pudding*
buey ⓜ bwey *ox*

C

cabra ⓕ *ka*-bra *goat*
cacho ⓜ *ka*-cho *sweet horn-shaped pastry filled with* **dulce de leche**
caimito ⓜ kai-*mee*-to
star apple – similar to a star fruit but has a purplish skin & a soft sweet flesh
cajeta ⓕ ka-*khe*-ta *thick caramel fudge*
calabaza ⓕ ka-la-*ba*-sa *pumpkin*
calamares ⓜ pl ka-la-*ma*-res *squid*
— **a la romana** a la ro-*ma*-na
squid rings fried in butter
caldo ⓜ *kal*-do *broth • consommé • stock*
camarón ⓜ ka-ma-*ron* *shrimp*
— **grande** *gran*-de *large prawn*
camote ⓜ ka-*mo*-te *sweet potato*
canela ⓕ ka-*ne*-la *cinnamon*
canelones ⓜ pl ka-ne-*lo*-nes *cannelloni*
cangrejo ⓜ kan-*gre*-kho *crab*
caracol ⓜ ka-ra-*kol* *snail*
carambola ⓕ ka-ram-*bo*-la
star fruit – mild sweet tropical fruit eaten fresh or juiced in **frescos**
carbón, al kar-*bon*, al *chargrilled*
carne ⓕ *kar*-ne
meat – usually synonymous with beef
— **de caballo** de ka-*ba*-yo *horsemeat*
— **de res** de res *beef*
— **de vaca** de *va*-ka *beef*
— **dorada al horno** do-*ra*-da al or-no *roast meat*
— **fría** *free*-ya *cold meat*
— **molida** mo-*lee*-da *ground meat*
— **picada** pee-*ka*-da *minced meat*
— **rotisada** ro-tee-*sa*-da *roast meat*
carpa ⓕ *kar*-pa *carp*

cas ⓜ kas *tropical fruit – relative of the guava but very sour & whitish on the inside*
casado ⓜ ka-*sa*-do *set platter with rice, black beans, fried plantains, chopped cabbage, tomato & usually a choice of beef, chicken or fish (often an egg, a lime or an avocado are included)*
— **vegetariano** ve-khe-ta-*rya*-no *casado without the meat*
castaña ⓕ kas-*ta*-nya *chestnut*
caza ⓕ *ka*-sa *game (meat)*
— **de temporada** de tem-po-*ra*-da *game in season*
cazuela ⓕ ka-*swe*-la *casserole*
cebada ⓕ se-*ba*-da *barley*
cebolla ⓕ se-*bo*-ya *onion*
cebollín ⓜ se-bo-*yeen* *shallot • spring onion*
cele ⓜ *se*-le
green mango – usually eaten with salt
cerdo ⓜ *ser*-do *pork*
cereza ⓕ se-*re*-sa *cherry*
cerveza ⓕ ser-*ve*-sa *beer*
— **en botella** en bo-*te*-ya *bottled beer*
ceviche ⓜ se-*vee*-che *raw fish, shrimp or conch marinated in lemon juice, chilli, cilantro (coriander) & onions*
chancho ⓜ *chan*-cho *pork*
chayote ⓜ cha-*yo*-te *pear-shaped vegetable similar in flavour to a squash*
chicharrón ⓜ chee-cha-*ron*
fried pork crackling – popular as ingredient
chifrijo ⓜ chee-*free*-kho
beans & **chicharrón** *with minced tomato, onion, cilantro (coriander) & lime juice*
chile ⓜ *chee*-le *chilli pepper*
chirimoya ⓕ chee-ree-*mo*-ya *custard apple*
chivo ⓜ *chee*-vo *kid*
choclo ⓜ *cho*-klo *corn • maize (off the cob)*
chorizo ⓜ cho-*ree*-so
spicy red or white pork sausage
— **al horno** al or-no
spicy sausage baked in the oven
chorreadas ⓕ pl cho-re-*a*-das
fried pancakes of fresh corn mash served with sour cream
chuleta ⓕ choo-*le*-ta *chop • cutlet*
— **de cerdo** de *ser*-do *pork cutlet*
churrasco ⓜ choo-*ras*-ko *rib steak*
chuzo ⓜ *choo*-so
kebab – also know as **pincho**

FOOD

172

ciruela ① *see·rwe·*la *plum*
cocinado/a ⓜ/① ko·see·*na·*do/a *cooked*
coco ⓜ *ko·*ko *coconut*
coctel ⓜ kok·*tel appetiser in sauce · cocktail*
codorniz ① ko·dor·*nees quail*
coles de bruselas ⓜ pl *ko·*les de broo·se·las *Brussels sprouts*
coliflor ① ko·lee·*flor cauliflower*
con agua kon *a·*gwa
  'with water' – refers to the preparation of a **batido** *or* **refresco natural** *with water*
conejo ⓜ ko·*ne·*kho *rabbit*
con leche kon *le·*che
  'with milk' – refers to the preparation of a **batido** *or* **refresco natural** *with milk*
corazón ⓜ ko·ra·*son heart*
cordero ⓜ kor·*de·*ro *lamb*
corvina ① kor·*vee·*na *bass*
costilla ① kos·*tee·*ya *loin · spare rib*
costillas de cordero ⓜ
  kos·*tee·*yas de kor·*de·*ro *rack of lamb*
crema ① *kre·*ma *cream*
  — **chantillí** chan·tee·*lee whipped cream*
crudo/a ⓜ/① *kroo·*do/a *raw*
crustáceos ⓜ pl kroos·*ta·*se·os *shellfish*
cuajada ① kwa·*kha·*da
  milk junket with honey
culantro ⓜ koo·*lan·*tro *cilantro · coriander*

D

dátil ⓜ *da·*teel *date*
dorado ① do·*ra·*do *sea bass*
dorado/a ⓜ/① do·ra·do/a *seared*
dulce ⓜ&① *dool·*se *sweet* a
dulce de leche ⓜ *dool·*se de *le·*che
  caramelised condensed milk used as a filling for pastries or eaten on bread

E

ejote ⓜ e·*kho·*te *string bean*
elote ⓜ e·*lo·*te *corn · maize (on the cob)*
  — **asado** a·*sa·*do *corn roasted on the cob*
  — **hervido** er·*vee·*do *boiled corn*
empanada ① em·pa·*na·*da *baked or fried turnover usually containing fried meat & vegetables though it can have fruit fillings*
enchilada ① en·chee·*la·*da *pastry stuffed with potatoes & cheese & sometimes meat*

eneldo ⓜ e·*nel·*do *dill*
ensalada ① en·sa·*la·*da *salad*
  — **de remolacha** de re·mo·*la·*cha *beetroot salad*
  — **mixta** *mees·*ta *mixed salad*
  — **rusa** roo·sa *'Russian salad' – vegetable salad with mayonnaise*
  — **verde** *ver·*de *green salad*
espagueti ⓜ es·pa·*ge·*tee *spaghetti*
espárragos ⓜ pl es·*pa·*ra·gos *asparagus*
espinaca ① es·pee·*na·*ka *spinach*
estofado ⓜ es·to·*fa·*do *stew*
estofado/a ⓜ/① es·to·*fa·*do/a *braised*

F

faisán ⓜ fai·*san pheasant*
fideos ⓜ pl fee·*de·*os *noodles*
filete ⓜ fee·*le·*te *fillet*
  — **de carne** de *kar·*ne *beef fillet*
  — **de pescado** de pes·*ka·*do *fish fillet*
flan ⓜ flan *crème caramel · egg custard*
frambuesa ① fram·*bwe·*sa *raspberry*
fresa ① *fre·*sa *strawberry*
fresco ⓜ *fres·*ko
  fresh fruit drink – short for **refresco natural**
frijol ⓜ free·*khol bean*
  — **blanco** *blan·*ko *large butter bean*
frijoles ⓜ pl free·*kho·*les *beans*
  — **con arroz** kon a·*ros beans & rice*
frito ⓜ *free·*to *scraps of fried or roast pork*
frito/a ⓜ/① *free·*to/a *fried*
  — **al sartén** al sar·*ten pan-fried*
fruta ① *froo·*ta *fruit*
frutilla ① froo·*tee·*ya *berry*

G

galleta ① ga·*ye·*ta *biscuit · cookie*
  — **salada** sa·*la·*da *cracker*
gallo ⓜ *ga·*yo *tortilla sandwich containing a meat, bean, cheese or* **picadillo** *filling*
  — **de queso con cebolla** de *ke·*so kon se·*bo·*ya *soft cheese & onions folded in a* **tortilla**
  — **pinto** *peen·*to *'spotted rooster' – lighty spiced mixture of rice & black beans traditionally served for breakfast, sometimes with sour cream or fried eggs (Costa Rica's signature dish)*

ganso ⓜ *gan*·so *goose*

garbanzo ⓜ gar·*ban*·so
chickpea • garbanzo bean

gazpacho ⓜ gas·*pa*·cho
cold tomato & vegetable soup

granadilla ⓕ gra·na·*dee*·ya *pomegranate*

grasa ⓕ *gra*·sa
*fat • grease (also called **manteca**)*

gratinado ⓜ gra·tee·*na*·do
dish cooked au gratin

guacamole ⓜ gwa·ka·*mo*·le
*mashed avocado combined with onion,
chilli, lemon & tomato*

guanábana ⓕ gwa·*na*·ba·na *prickly custard
apple • soursop (fruit with a tart pulp)*

guaro ⓜ *gwa*·ro
local firewater made from sugar cane

guayaba ⓕ gwa·*ya*·ba *guava*

guineo ⓜ gee·*ne*·o
small banana similar to a plantain

guisantes ⓜ pl gee·*san*·tes *peas*

guiso ⓜ *gee*·so *stew*

H

haba ⓕ *a*·ba *broad bean*

hamburguesa ⓕ am·boor·*ge*·sa
hamburger

harina ⓕ a·*ree*·na *flour*

helado ⓜ e·*la*·do *ice cream*

helado/a ⓜ/ⓕ e·*la*·do/a *chilled • iced*

hervido/a ⓜ/ⓕ er·*vee*·do/a *boiled*
— a fuego lento a *fwe*·go *len*·to
simmered

hielo ⓜ *ye*·lo *ice*

hierba ⓕ *yer*·ba *herb*

hígado ⓜ *ee*·ga·do *liver*

higo ⓜ *ee*·go *fig*

hocico ⓜ o·*see*·ko *snout*

hongo ⓜ *on*·go *button mushroom*

hongos al ajillo ⓜ pl *on*·gos al a·*khee*·yo
garlic mushrooms

horchata ⓕ or·*cha*·ta
rice-based drink flavoured with cinnamon

horneado/a ⓜ/ⓕ or·ne·*a*·do/a *baked*

horno, al *or*·no, al *baked*

hueso ⓜ *we*·so *bone*

huevos ⓜ pl *we*·vos *eggs*
— de tortuga de tor·*too*·ga
*turtle eggs – be aware that turtles are an
endangered species*

— duros *doo*·ros *hard-boiled eggs*

— fritos *free*·tos *fried eggs*

— hervidos er·*vee*·dos *boiled eggs*

— pateados pa·te·*a*·dos *scrambled eggs*

— revueltos re·*vwel*·tos *scrambled eggs*

J

jabalí ⓜ kha·ba·*lee* *wild boar*

jalea ⓕ kha·*le*·a *jam*

jamón ⓜ kha·*mon* *ham*
— dulce *dool*·se *boiled ham*
— serrano se·*ra*·no *cured ham*

jarrete ⓜ kha·*re*·te
bone marrow • knuckle • shank

jengibre ⓜ khen·*khee*·bre *ginger*

jocote ⓜ kho·*ko*·te
*plum-sized fruit with a large pit,
sometimes eaten green with salt (an
acquired taste) or eaten when red & ripe*

jugo ⓜ *khoo*·go *juice*
— de naranja de na·*ran*·kha *orange juice*
— natural na·too·*ral*
freshly-squeezed juice
— puro *poo*·ro *pure juice*

L

langosta ⓕ lan·*gos*·ta *spiny lobster*

langostino ⓜ lan·gos·*tee*·no
crawfish • crayfish

leche ⓕ *le*·che *milk*
— descremada des·kre·*ma*·da
skimmed milk
— de soya de *so*·ya *soya milk*

lechón ⓜ le·*chon* *suckling pig*

lechuga ⓕ le·*choo*·ga *lettuce*

legumbre ⓕ le·*goom*·bre *pulse*

lengua ⓕ *len*·gwa *tongue*

lenguado ⓜ len·*gwa*·do *dab • lemon sole*

lentejas ⓕ len·*te*·khas *lentils*

limón ⓜ lee·*mon* *lemon • lime*

lomo ⓜ *lo*·mo *sirloin*

M

macarela ⓕ ma·ka·*re*·la *mackerel*

macarrones ⓜ pl ma·ka·*ro*·nes *macaroni*

maduro/a ⓜ/ⓕ ma·*doo*·ro/a *ripe*

maíz ⓜ ma·*ees* *corn • maize*

mandarina ① man-da-*ree*-na
  mandarin • tangerine
mango ⓜ *man*-go mango
maní ⓜ ma-*nee* peanut
manteca ① man-*te*-ka
  grease • fat (also known as **grasa**)
mantequilla ① man-te-*kee*-ya butter
manzana ① man-*sa*-na apple
  — **de agua** de *a*-gwa
  'water apple' (relative of the rose apple) –
  has a crisp, white, juicy, apple-like flesh
  — **rosa** *ro*-sa 'rose apple' – fruit with an
  apple-like taste but with a rose perfume
maracuyá ① ma-ra-koo-*ya* passionfruit
margarina ① mar-ga-*ree*-na margarine
marinado/a ⓜ/① ma-*ree*-na-do/a
  marinated
mariscos ⓜ pl ma-*rees*-kos
  seafood • shellfish
mayonesa ① ma-yo-*ne*-sa mayonnaise
mazapán ⓜ ma-sa-*pan*
  almond paste • marzipan
medio crudo/a ⓜ/① *me*-dyo kroo-do/a
  rare
mejilla ① me-*khee*-ya cheek
mejillones ⓜ pl me-khee-*yo*-nes mussels
  — **al vapor** al va-*por* steamed mussels
melocotón ⓜ me-lo-ko-*ton* peach
melón ⓜ me-*lon* melon
menta ⓜ *men*-ta mint
menudo de pollo ⓜ me-*noo*-do de *po*-yo
  gizzard • poultry entrails
menudos ⓜ pl me-*noo*-dos giblets
merluza ① mer-*loo*-sa hake
  — **a la plancha** a la *plan*-cha fried hake
mermelada ① mer-me-*la*-da marmalade
miel ⓜ myel honey
milanesa ① mee-la-*ne*-sa
  schnitzel – pounded, breaded & fried meat
mil hojas ⓜ pl meel *o*-khas
  'thousand leaves' – layers of thin pastry
  filled with an almond & honey paste
mojarra ① mo-*kha*-ra perch
mondongo ⓜ mon-*don*-go tripe
mora ① *mo*-ra blackberry
morcilla ① mor-*see*-ya black pudding •
  blood sausage – common **asado** dish
mostaza ① mos-*ta*-sa mustard
muslo ⓜ *moo*-slo thigh
muy cocinado/a ⓜ/①
  mooy ko-see-*na*-do/a well done

N
nabo ⓜ *na*-bo turnip
naranja ① na-*ran*-kha orange
naranjilla ① na-ran-*khee*-ya
  orange-coloured, tomato-like fruit with a
  juicy acidic pulp used in drinks & sherbets
nata ① *na*-ta cream
natilla ① na-*tee*-ya sour cream
natural ⓜ na-too-*ral*
  fresh fruit drink – short for **refresco natural**
nuez ⓜ nwes nut • walnut

O
olla de carne ① *o*-ya de *kar*-ne
  hearty soup containing beef, potatoes,
  corn, **chayote**, plantains & cassava
omelet ⓜ o-me-*let*
  omelette (also known as **torta de huevo**)
oreja ① o-*re*-kha
  'ear' – sweet biscuit of flaky pastry
ostión ⓜ os-tee-*on* scallop
ostra ① *os*-tra oyster
oveja ① o-*ve*-kha ewe

P
paleta ① pa-*le*-ta shoulder
palmitos ⓜ pl pal-*mee*-tos palm hearts –
  usually served in a vinegar dressing
paloma ① pa-*lo*-ma pigeon
pan ⓜ pan bread
  — **dulce** *dool*-se sweet bread
panqueque ⓜ pan-*ke*-ke pancake
papas ① pl *pa*-pas potatoes
  — **fritas** *free*-tas chips • French fries
papaya ① pa-*pa*-ya papaya
papitas ① pl pa-*pee*-tas crisps • potato chips
pargo ⓜ *par*-go red snapper
parrilla ① pa-*ree*-ya grill
parrilla, a la a la pa-*ree*-ya, a la
  grilled over charcoal
parrillada ① pa-ree-*ya*-da
  mixed grill – huge slabs of grilled meat
  prepared over hot coals & served with spicy
  sauces & vegetables
pasa ① *pa*-sa raisin
pasado/a al agua ⓜ/① pa-*sa*-do/a al *a*-gwa
  boiled

menu decoder

175

pasta ① *pas*-ta pasta
pastel ⓜ *pas*-tel cake • pastry
pata ① *pa*-ta leg
patacones ⓜ pl pa-ta-ko-nes
  fried green plantains cut into thin pieces,
  salted & then pressed & fried – popular on
  the Caribbean coast
patita de cerdo/chancho ①
  pa-*tee*-ta de *ser*-do/*chan*-cho pig's trotter
pato ⓜ *pa*-to duck
pavo ⓜ *pa*-vo turkey
pechuga ① pe-*choo*-ga breast meat
pejibaye ⓜ pe-khee-*ba*-ye
  starchy palm fruit boiled & frequently
  eaten with mayonnaise
pepinillo ⓜ pe-pee-*nee*-yo pickle
pepino ⓜ pe-*pee*-no cucumber
pera ① *pe*-ra pear
perejil ⓜ pe-re-*kheel* parsley
pescado ⓜ pes-*ka*-do fish
  — ahumado a-oo-*ma*-do smoked fish
  — al ajillo al a-*khee*-yo fish in garlic sauce
  — de agua dulce de *a*-gwa *dool*-se
    freshwater fish
  — de mar de mar saltwater fish
pescaito ⓜ pes-ka-*ee*-to tiny fried fish
petipoas ⓜ pl pe-tee-*po*-as
  peas – another word for **arvejas**
pez espada ⓜ pes es-*pa*-da swordfish
pez hoja ⓜ pes *o*-kha bottom fish • flounder
picadillo ⓜ pee-ka-*dee*-yo
  'minced' – side dish of minced vegetables
  and/or fruit & ground meat (usually beef)
picante ⓜ&① pee-*kan*-te spicy
pimentón ⓜ pee-men-*ton*
  bell pepper • capsicum
pimienta ① pee-*myen*-ta pepper
pincho ⓜ *peen*-cho
  kebab – also know as **chuzo**
piña ① *pee*-nya pineapple
pipa ① *pee*-pa
  green coconut – picked for its milk which is
  often drunk straight from the shell
pistacho ⓜ pees-*ta*-cho pistachio nut
plancha ① *plan*-cha grill • hot plate
plancha, a la *plan*-cha, a la grilled
plátano ⓜ *pla*-ta-no
  plantain – savoury banana-like fruit that's
  cooked & often served with main dishes
poco cocido/a ⓜ/① po-ko ko-*see*-do/a rare
poco hecho/a ⓜ/① po-ko e-*cho*/a rare

pollo ⓜ *po*-yo chicken
polvo ⓜ *pol*-vo powder
postre ⓜ *pos*-tre dessert
prestiño ⓜ pres-*tee*-nyo
  very thin fried pastry eaten with syrup
puerco ⓜ *pwer*-ko pork
pulpo ⓜ *pool*-po octopus
  — a la gallega a la ga-*ye*-ga
    octopus in a garlicky wine & tomato sauce
    with bell pepper & potatoes thrown in
punto, a *poon*-to, a medium (steak)

Q

queque ⓜ *ke*-ke cake • pastry
  — seco *se*-ko pound cake
queso ⓜ *ke*-so cheese

R

rábano ⓜ *ra*-ba-no radish
rabo ⓜ *ra*-bo tail
rape ⓜ *ra*-pe monkfish
refresco ⓜ re-*fres*-ko soft drink
  — natural na-too-*ral*
    frequently referred to simply as **frescos** or
    naturales, these are fruit juices made to
    order **con agua** (with water) or **con leche**
    (with milk) – see the box **juicy treats**, page
    161, for common flavours
relleno/a ⓜ/① re-*ye*-no/a stuffed
remolacha ① re-mo-*la*-cha beetroot
repollo ⓜ re-*po*-yo cabbage
res, carne de ① res, *kar*-ne de beef
riñón ⓜ ree-*nyon* kidney
romero ⓜ ro-*me*-ro rosemary
rosado/a ⓜ/① ro-*sa*-do rosé
rostisado/a ⓜ/① ros-tee-*sa*-do/a roasted
  — al espiedo al es-*pye*-do spit-roasted
  — a la parilla a la pa-*ree*-ya grilled
  — al horno al *or*-no oven roasted

S

sal ① sal salt
salado/a ⓜ/① sa-*la*-do/a salted • salty
salchichas ① pl sal-*chee*-chas
  sausages similar to hot dogs
salmón ⓜ sal-*mon* salmon

salsa ⓕ *sal*-sa *sauce*
— **de carne** de *kar*-ne *gravy*
— **picante** pee-*kan*-te *chilli sauce*
Salsa Lizano ⓕ *sal*-sa lee-*sa*-no
the secret sauce of Costa Rica (added to everything, especially **gallo pinto***) – a tangy, yet somewhat sweet concoction, with tamarind as the main ingredient*
salteado/a ⓜ/ⓕ sal-te-*a*-do/a *sautéed*
salvaje ⓜ&ⓕ sal-*va*-khe *wild*
sandía ⓕ san-*dee*-a *watermelon*
sandwich ⓜ *sand*-weech *sandwich*
sandwiche ⓜ *sand*-wee-che
alternate spelling of **sandwich**
sangre ⓕ *san*-gre *blood*
sangría ⓕ san-*gree*-a
sangria (red-wine punch)
sardina ⓕ sar-*dee*-na *sardine*
secado/a ⓜ/ⓕ se-*ka*-do/a *dried*
seco/a ⓜ/ⓕ se-*ko*/a *dry • dried*
semilla de marañón ⓕ
se-*mee*-ya de ma-ra-*nyon cashew*
semolina ⓕ se-mo-*lee*-na *semolina*
sepia ⓕ *se*-pya *cuttlefish*
sésamo ⓜ *se*-sa-mo *sesame*
sesos ⓜ pl *se*-sos *brains*
sidra ⓕ *see*-dra *cider*
sin grasa seen *gra*-sa *lean*
sopa ⓕ *so*-pa *soup*
— **de albóndigas** de al-*bon*-dee-gas
meatball soup
— **de espinacas** de es-pee-*na*-kas
spinach soup
— **de frijoles negros**
de free-*kho*-les ne-gros *black bean soup*
— **de mariscos** de ma-*rees*-kos
shellfish soup
— **de mondongo** de mon-*don*-go
tripe soup
— **de pescado** de pes-*ka*-do *fish soup*
— **de pollo** de *po*-yo *chicken soup*
— **negra** ne-gra *creamy black bean soup, often with a hard-boiled egg & vegetables soaking in the bean broth*
soya ⓕ *so*-ya *soy*
suflé ⓜ soo-*fle soufflé*

T

tacos ⓜ pl *ta*-kos *Costa Rican-style tacos (tortillas filled with meat, beans & other ingredients) – deep-fried & served with shredded cabbage, mayonnaise & ketchup*

tajadas ⓕ pl ta-*kha*-das *slices*
tallarines ⓜ pl ta-ya-*ree*-nes *noodles mixed with pork, chicken, beef or vegetables*
tamales ⓜ pl ta-*ma*-les
cornmeal dough filled with spiced beef or pork, vegetables & potatoes, then wrapped in a maize husk or banana leaf & fried, grilled or baked
— **asado** a-*sa*-do *sweet cornmeal cake*
tamarindo ⓜ ta-ma-*reen*-do *tamarind*
té ⓜ te *tea*
término medio *ter*-mee-no *me*-dyo
medium
ternera ⓕ ter-*ne*-ra *veal*
tiburón ⓜ tee-boo-*ron shark*
tinto ⓜ *teen*-to *red (wine)*
tocineta ⓕ to-see-*ne*-ta *bacon*
— **ahumada** a-oo-*ma*-da *smoked bacon*
tocino ⓜ to-*see*-no *cold bacon*
— **con queso** ⓜ kon *ke*-so
cold bacon & cheese
tomate ⓜ to-*ma*-te *tomato*
toronja ⓕ to-*ron*-kha *grapefruit*
— **rellena** ⓕ re-*ye*-na *caramelised grapefruit peel filled with milk* **cajeta**
torta ⓕ *tor*-ta *cake • tart*
— **de huevo** de *we*-vo
plain omelette also known as **omelet**
— **española** es-pa-*nyo*-la
egg & potato omelette
tortilla ⓕ tor-*tee*-ya *thin round of pressed corn (or sometimes wheat) dough cooked on a griddle • another name for an* **omelet**
— **con queso** kon *ke*-so
tortilla with cheese
tortuga ⓕ tor-*too*-ga *turtle – be aware that turtles are an endangered species*
tostada ⓕ tos-*ta*-da *toast*
tres leches ⓜ tres *le*-ches
moist cake prepared with cream, condensed & evaporated milk
tripas ⓕ pl *tree*-pas *offal*
trucha ⓕ *troo*-cha *trout*
trufa ⓕ *troo*-fa *truffle*
turrón ⓜ too-*ron* *almond nougat*

U

ubre ⓕ *oo*-bre *udder*
uva ⓕ *oo*-va *grape*

menu decoder

V

vaca, carne de ① *va*-ka, *kar*-ne de *beef*
vainilla ① vai-*nee*-ya *vanilla*
vapor ⓜ va-*por* *steam*
vapor, al va-*por*, al *steamed*
vegetal ⓜ ve-khe-*tal* *vegetable* n
vegetales ⓜ pl ve-khe-*ta*-les *vegetables*
venado ⓜ ve-*na*-do *venison*
verdes ⓜ pl *ver*-des *greens*
verduras ① pl ver-*doo*-ras *green vegetables*
vieira ① *vyay*-ra *scallop*
vigorón ⓜ vee-go-*ron* *boiled cassava top served with cabbage salad,* **chicharrón***, tomatoes, onions & lime juice*
vinagre ⓜ vee-*na*-gre *vinegar*
vino ⓜ *vee*-no *wine*
— **blanco** *blan*-ko *white wine*
— **espumoso** es-poo-*mo*-so *sparkling wine*
— **rosado** ro-*sa*-do *rosé*
— **tinto** *teen*-to *red wine*
vualve a la vida caribeño ⓜ *vwal*-ve a la *vee*-da ka-ree-be-nyo *thick seafood-based soup blended with coconut milk*

Y

yogur ⓜ yo-*gur* *yogurt*
yuca ① *yoo*-ka *cassava – common staple in Latin American cuisine*

Z

zanahoria ① sa-na-o-*rya* *carrot*
zapote ⓜ sa-*po*-te *sapote – fruit with a pinky red flesh & a pumpkin-like flavour*

emergencies

emergencias

Help!	¡Socorro!	so·ko·ro
Stop!	¡Pare!	pa·re
Go away!	¡Váyase!	va·ya·se
Thief!	¡Ladrón!	la·dron
Fire!	¡Incendio!	een·sen·dyo
Watch out!	¡Cuidado!	kwee·da·do

Call ...	*Llame a ...*	ya·me a ...
an ambulance	*una ambulancia*	oo·na am·boo·lan·sya
a doctor	*un doctor*	oon dok·tor
the police	*la policía*	la po·lee·see·a

It's an emergency.
Es una emergencia.   es oo·na e·mer·khen·sya

There's been an accident.
Hubo un accidente.   oo·bo oon ak·see·den·te

Could you please help me/us?
¿Me/Nos podría ayudar,   me/nos po·dree·a a·yoo·dar
por favor?   por fa·vor

signs

Emergencias	e·mer·khen·syas	**Emergency Department**
Estación Policial	es·ta·syon po·lee·syal	**Police Station (city)**
Guardia Rural	gwar·dya roo·ral	**Police Station (rural)**
Hospital	os·pee·tal	**Hospital**
Policía	po·lee·see·a	**Police**

essentials

179

Can I use your phone?
¿Usted me prestaría el teléfono?
oos·*ted* me pres·ta·*ree*·a el te·*le*·fo·no

I'm lost.
Estoy perdido/a. m/f
es·*toy* per·*dee*·do/a

Where are the toilets?
¿Dónde está el baño?
don·de es·*ta* el *ba*·nyo

Is it dangerous …?	*¿Es peligroso …?*	es pe·lee·*gro*·so …
at night	*en la noche*	en la *no*·che
for gay people	*para*	*pa*·ra
	homosexuales	o·mo·sek·*swa*·les
for travellers	*para turistas*	*pa*·ra too·*rees*·tas
for women	*para mujeres*	*pa*·ra moo·*khe*·res
on your own	*si uno va*	see *oo*·no va
	solo/a m/f	*so*·lo/a

police

policía

Where's the police station?
¿Dónde está la estación de policía?
don·de es·*ta* la es·ta·*syon* de po·lee·*see*·a

Please telephone the police.
Por favor, llame a la policía.
por fa·*vor ya*·me a la po·lee·*see*·a

I want to report an offence.
Quiero reportar un delito.
kye·ro re·por·*tar* oon de·*lee*·to

It was him/her.
Fue él/ella.
fwe el/*e*·ya

I've been …	*Me …*	me …
He/She has been …	*Lo/La …*	lo/la …
assaulted	*asaltaron*	a·sal·*ta*·ron
raped	*violaron*	vyo·*la*·ron
robbed	*robaron*	ro·*ba*·ron

SAFE TRAVEL

180

My ... was/were stolen.	Me robaron ...	me ro·ba·ron ...
I've lost my ...	Perdí ...	per·dee ...
backpack	mi mochila	mee mo·chee·la
credit card	mi tarjeta de crédito	mee tar·khe·ta de kre·dee·to
handbag	mi bolso	mee bol·so
jewellery	mis joyas	mees kho·yas
money	mi plata	mee pla·ta
papers	mis documentos	mees do·koo·men·tos
passport	mi pasaporte	mee pa·sa·por·te
travellers cheques	mis cheques de viajero	mee che·kes de vya·khe·ro
wallet	mi billetera	mee bee·ye·te·ra

the police may say ...

Es una multa por ...	es oo·na mool·ta por ...	It's a ... fine.
exceso de velocidad	ek·se·so de ve·lo·see·dad	speeding
parquear donde no se permite	par·ke·ar don·de no se per·mee·te	parking
A usted se le acusa de ...	a oos·ted se le a·koo·sa de ...	You're charged with ...
asaltar a alguien	a·sal·tar a al·gyen	assault
no tener visa	no te·ner vee·sa	not having a visa
permanecer ilegalmente en el país con documentos vencidos	per·ma·ne·ser ee·le·gal·men·te en el pa·ees kon do·koo·men·tos ven·see·dos	overstaying a visa
robo	ro·bo	theft
tenencia (de sustancias ilegales)	te·nen·sya (de soos·tan·syas ee·lee·ga·les)	possession (of illegal substances)

What am I accused of?
¿De que me están acusando?   de ke me es·*tan* a·koo·*san*·do

I apologise.
Lo siento.   lo *syen*·to

I didn't realise I was doing anything wrong.
No sabía que estaba   no sa·*bee*·a ke es·*ta*·ba
haciendo algo malo.   a·*syen*·do *al*·go *ma*·lo

I didn't do it.
Yo no fui.   yo no fwee

Can I pay an on-the-spot fine?
¿Puedo pagar la   *pwe*·do pa·*gar* la
multa aquí mismo?   *mool*·ta a·*kee* mees·mo

I have insurance.
Tengo seguro.   *ten*·go se·*goo*·ro

Do you have this form in (English)?
¿Tiene este formulario   *tye*·ne *es*·te for·moo·*la*·ryo
en (inglés)?   en (een·*gles*)

I want to contact my embassy/consulate.
Quiero contactar a mi   *kye*·ro kon·tak·*tar* a mee
embajada/consulado.   em·ba·*kha*·da/kon·soo·*la*·do

Can I make a phone call?
¿Puedo hacer una   *pwe*·do a·*ser* oo·na
llamada telefónica?   ya·*ma*·da te·le·*fo*·nee·ka

Can I have a lawyer (who speaks English)?
¿Me pueden traer un   me *pwe*·den tra·*er* oon
abogado (que hable inglés)?   a·bo·*ga*·do (ke *a*·ble een·*gles*)

I want to speak to a female police officer.
Quiero hablar con   *kye*·ro ab·*lar* kon
una mujer policía.   oo·na moo·*kher* po·lee·*see*·a

I have a prescription for this drug.
Tengo receta para   *ten*·go re·*se*·ta *pa*·ra
este medicamento.   *es*·te me·dee·ka·*men*·to

This drug is for personal use.
Esta droga es de   *es*·ta *dro*·ga es de
uso personal.   *oo*·so per·so·*nal*

health
salud

doctor

doctor

Where's the nearest ...?	¿Dónde está ... más cercano/a? m/f	don·de es·ta ... mas ser·ka·no/a
dentist	el dentista m	el den·tees·ta
doctor	el doctor m	el dok·tor
emergency department	la sección de emergencias f	la sek·syon de e·mer·khen·syas
hospital	el hospital m	el os·pee·tal
medical centre	la clínica f	la klee·nee·ka
optometrist	el optometrista m	el op·to·me·trees·ta
(24-hour) pharmacist	la farmacia (abierta 24 horas) f	la far·ma·sya (a·byer·ta vayn·tee·kwa·tro o·ras)

I need a doctor (who speaks English).
Necesito un doctor (que hable inglés).
ne·se·see·to oon dok·tor (ke a·ble een·gles)

Could I see a female doctor?
¿Podría atenderme una doctora?
po·dree·a a·ten·der·me oo·na dok·to·ra

Could the doctor come here?
¿El doctor podría venir acá? el dok·tor po·dree·a ve·neer a·ka

Is there an after-hours emergency number?
¿Hay un número de emergencias fuera de horas hábiles?
ai oon noo·me·ro de e·mer·khen·syas fwe·ra de o·ras a·bee·les

I've run out of my medication.
Se me acabó mi medicamento.
se me a·ka·bo mee me·dee·ka·men·to

health

183

This is my usual medicine.
Esta es mi medicina normal.
es·ta es mee me·dee·*see*·na nor·*mal*

My son/daughter weighs (20 kilos).
Mi hijo/hija pesa (20 kilos).
me ee·*kho*/ee·*kha* pe·sa (*vayn*·te *kee*·los)

What's the correct dosage?
¿Cuál es la dosis correcta?
kwal es la *do*·sees ko·*rek*·ta

I don't want a blood transfusion.
No quiero que me hagan una transfusión.
no *kye*·ro ke me *a*·gan oo·na trans·foo·*syon*

Please use a new syringe.
Por favor, use una jeringa nueva.
por fa·*vor* oo·se oo·na khe·*reen*·ga *nwe*·va

I have my own syringe.
Yo tengo mi propia jeringa.
yo *ten*·go mee *pro*·pya khe·*reen*·ga

---

the doctor may say ...

¿Cuál es el problema? kwal es el pro·*ble*·ma	**What's the problem?**
¿Dónde le duele? *don*·de le *dwe*·le	**Where does it hurt?**
¿Qué tiene? ke *tye*·ne	**What do you have?**
¿Tiene fiebre? *tye*·ne *fye*·bre	**Do you have a temperature?**
¿Cuánto tiene de estar así? *kwan*·to *tye*·ne de es·*tar* a·*see*	**How long have you been like this?**
¿Ha tenido esto mismo antes? ha te·*nee*·do *es*·to *mees*·mo *an*·tes	**Have you had this before?**
¿Es usted alérgico/a a algo? m/f es oos·*ted* a·*ler*·khee·ko/a a *al*·go	**Are you allergic to anything?**

the doctor may say ...

¿Está usted tomando algún medicamento?
es·ta oos·ted to·man·do
al·goon me·dee·ka·men·to
Are you on medication?

¿Usted es sexualmente activo/a? m/f
oos·ted es sek·swal·men·te
ak·tee·vo/a
Are you sexually active?

¿Ha tenido relaciones sexuales sin protección?
ha te·nee·do re·la·syo·nes
sek·swa·les seen pro·tek·syon
Have you had unprotected sex?

¿Usted fuma?
oos·ted foo·ma
Do you smoke?

¿Usted toma licor?
oos·ted to·ma lee·kor
Do you drink?

¿Usted usa drogas?
oos·ted oo·sa dro·gas
Do you take drugs?

¿Por cuánto tiempo es su viaje?
por kwan·to tyem·po
es soo vya·khe
How long are you travelling for?

Debería ir a revisarse eso cuando llegue a su casa.
de·be·ree·a eer a
re·vee·sar·se e·so kwan·do
ye·ge a soo ka·sa
You should have it checked when you go home.

Debería devolverse a su casa para que le den tratamiento.
de·be·ree·a de·vol·ver·se a
soo ka·sa pa·ra ke le
den tra·ta·myen·to
You should return home for treatment.

Vamos a tener que internarlo en el hospital.
va·mos a te·ner ke
een·ter·nar·lo en el
os·pee·tal
You need to be admitted to hospital.

Usted es hipocondríaco.
oos·ted es
ee·po·kon·dree·a·ko
You're a hypochondriac.

I've been	Yo estoy	yo es·*toy*
vaccinated	vacunado/a	va·koo·*na*·do/a
against …	contra … m/f	kon·tra …
He/She has been	El/Ella está	el/*e*·ya es·*ta*
vaccinated	vacunado/a	va·koo·*na*·do/a
against …	contra …	kon·tra …
hepatitis	hepatitis	e·pa·*tee*·tees
A/B/C	A/B/C	a/be/se
tetanus	tétano	*te*·ta·no
typhoid	fiebre tifoidea	*fye*·bre tee·foy·*de*·a

I need new …	Necesito …	ne·se·*see*·to …
	nuevos/as. m/f	*nwe*·vos/as
contact	lentes de	*len*·tes de
lenses	contacto f	kon·*tak*·to
glasses	anteojos m	an·te·o·khos

My prescription is …
   Mi receta está …   mee re·*se*·ta es·*ta* …

How much will it cost?
   ¿Cuánto me va a costar?   kwan·to me va a kos·*tar*

Can I have a receipt for my insurance?
   ¿Me podría dar una   me po·*dree*·a dar oo·na
   factura para mi   fak·*too*·ra *pa*·ra mee
   seguro médico?   se·*goo*·ro *me*·dee·ko

symptoms & conditions

condiciones y síntomas

I'm sick.
   Estoy enfermo/a. m/f   es·*toy* en·*fer*·mo/a

My friend is (very) sick.
   Mi amigo/a está   mee a·*mee*·go/a es·*ta*
   (muy) enfermo/a. m/f   (mooy) en·*fer*·mo/a

My son/daughter is (very) sick.
   Mi hijo/hija está   mee ee·kho/*ee*·kha es·*ta*
   (muy) enfermo/a.   (mooy) en·*fer*·mo/a

I've been injured.
Estoy herido/a. m/f   es·*toy* e·*ree*·do/a

He/She has been injured.
El/Ella está herido/a.   el/*e*·ya es·*ta* e·*ree*·do/a

I've been vomiting.
He estado vomitando.   e es·*ta*·do vo·mee·*tan*·do

He/She has been vomiting.
El/Ella ha estado   el/*e*·ya a es·*ta*·do
vomitando.   vo·mee·*tan*·do

She's having a baby.
Está teniendo el bebé.   es·*ta* te·*nyen*·do el be·*be*

He/She is having a/an …	*Le está dando …*	le es·*ta dan*·do …
allergic reaction	*una reacción alérgica*	*oo*·na re·ak·*syon* a·*ler*·khee·ka
asthma attack	*un ataque de asma*	oon a·*ta*·ke de *as*·ma
epileptic fit	*un ataque epiléptico*	oon a·*ta*·ke e·pee·*lep*·tee·ko
heart attack	*un ataque cardíaco*	oon a·*ta*·ke kar·*dee*·a·ko

I feel …	*Me siento …*	me *syen*·to …
anxious	*ansioso/a* m/f	an·*syo*·so/a
better	*mejor* m&f	me·*khor*
depressed	*deprimido/a* m/f	de·pree·*mee*·do/a
dizzy	*mareado/a* m/f	ma·re·a·do/a
hot and cold	*con calor y con frío*	kon ka·*lor* ee kon *free*·o
strange	*raro/a* m/f	*ra*·ro/a
weak	*débil* m&f	*de*·beel
worse	*peor* m&f	pe·*or*

I feel nauseous.
Tengo náuseas. — *ten·go now·se·as*

I feel shivery.
Tengo escalofríos. — *ten·go es·ka·lo·free·os*

It hurts here.
Me duele aquí. — *me dwe·le a·kee*

I'm dehydrated.
Estoy deshidratado/a. m/f — *es·toy de·see·dra·ta·do/a*

I can't sleep.
No puedo dormir. — *no pwe·do dor·meer*

I think it's the medication I'm on.
Creo que son las medicinas que estoy tomando. — *kre·o ke son las me·dee·see·nas ke es·toy to·man·do*

I'm on medication for …
Estoy tomando medicinas para … — *es·toy to·man·do me·dee·see·nas pa·ra …*

He/She is on medication for …
Él/Ella está tomando medicinas para … — *el/e·ya es·ta to·man·do me·dee·see·nas pa·ra …*

I have (a/an) …
Tengo (un/una) … m/f — *ten·go (oon/oo·na) …*

He/She has (a/an) …
Él/Ella tiene (un/una) … m/f — *el/e·ya tye·ne (oon/oo·na) …*

asthma	*asma* f	*as·ma*
cold n	*resfrío* m	*res·free·o*
constipation	*estreñimiento* m	*es·tre·nyee·myen·to*
cough n	*tos* m	*tos*
diabetes	*diabetes* m	*dee·a·be·tees*
diarrhoea	*diarrea* f	*dee·a·re·a*
fever	*fiebre* f	*fye·bre*
flu	*gripe* f	*gree·pe*
headache	*dolor de cabeza* m	*do·lor de ka·be·sa*
migraine	*migraña* f	*mee·gra·nya*
nausea	*náuseas* f pl	*now·se·as*
pain n	*dolor* m	*do·lor*
sore throat	*dolor de garganta* m	*do·lor de gar·gan·ta*

women's health

(I think) I'm pregnant.
(Creo que) Estoy embarazada. (kre·o ke) es·*toy* em·ba·ra·*sa*·da

I'm on the pill.
Estoy tomando pastillas es·*toy* to·*man*·do pas·*tee*·yas
anticonceptivas. an·tee·kon·sep·*tee*·vas

I haven't had my period for (six) weeks.
No me ha bajado la no me a ba·*kha*·do la
regla en (seis) semanas. *re*·gla en (says) se·*ma*·nas

I've noticed a lump here.
Noté una pelota aquí. no·*te oo*·na pe·*lo*·ta a·*kee*

Do you have something for (period pain)?
¿Tiene algo para *tye*·ne *al*·go *pa*·ra
(dolores menstruales)? (do·*lo*·res mens·*trwa*·les)

I have a …	*Tengo una …*	*ten*·go *oo*·na …
urinary tract infection	*infección urinaria*	een·fek·*syon* oo·ree·*na*·rya
yeast infection	*infección vaginal*	een·fek·*syon* va·khee·*nal*

I need (a/the) …	*Necesito …*	ne·se·*see*·to …
contraception	*un anti- conceptivo*	oon an·tee· kon·sep·*tee*·vo
morning-after pill	*una pastilla del día siguiente*	*oo*·na pas·*tee*·ya del *dee*·a see·*gyen*·te
pregnancy test	*una prueba de embarazo*	*oo*·na *prwe*·ba de em·ba·*ra*·so

¿Cuándo fue la última vez que tuvo la regla?		
kwan·do fwe la *ool*·tee·ma		**When did you last have**
ves ke *too*·vo la *re*·gla		**your period?**
¿ Está con la regla?		
es·*ta* kon la *reg*·la		**Are you menstruating?**
¿Está embarazada?		
es·*ta* em·ba·ra·*sa*·da		**Are you pregnant?**
Está embarazada.		
es·*ta* em·ba·ra·*sa*·da		**You're pregnant.**
¿Está usando algún anticonceptivo?		
es·*ta* oo·*san*·do al·*goon*		**Are you using contraception?**
an·tee·kon·sep·*tee*·vo		

allergies

alergias

I'm allergic	*Soy alérgico/*	soy a·*ler*·khee·ko/
to ...	*alérgica* ... m/f	a·*ler*·khee·ka ...
He/She is	*Él/Ella es*	el/e·ya es
allergic to ...	*alérgico/a* ...	a·*ler*·khee·ko/a ...
antibiotics	*a los*	a los
	antibióticos	an·tee·*byo*·tee·kos
anti-	*a los anti-*	a los an·tee·
inflammatories	*inflamatorios*	een·fla·ma·*to*·ryos
aspirin	*a la aspirina*	a la as·pee·*ree*·na
bees	*a las abejas*	a las a·*be*·khas
codeine	*a la codeína*	a la ko·de·*ee*·na
penicillin	*a la*	a la
	penicilina	pe·nee·see·*lee*·na
pollen	*al polen*	al *po*·len
sulphur-based	*a los*	a los
drugs	*medicamentos*	me·dee·ka·*men*·tos
	a base de azufre	a *ba*·se de a·*soo*·fre

I have a skin allergy.

Tengo una alergia
en la piel.

ten·go oo·na a·ler·khee·a
en la pyel

antihistamines	*antihista-* *mínicos* m pl	an·tee·ees·ta· mee·nee·kos
inhaler	*inhalador* m	een·a·la·dor
injection	*inyección* f	een·yek·syon

For phrases on food-related allergies, see **special diets &**
allergies, page 170.

alternative treatments

I don't use (Western medicine).

Yo no uso (la medicina
occidental).

yo no oo·so (la me·dee·see·na
ok·see·den·tal)

I prefer ...	*Prefiero ...*	pre·fye·ro ...
Can I see someone	*¿Podría ver a*	po·dree·a ver a
who practises ...?	*alguien que*	al·gyen ke
	practique la ...?	prak·tee·ke la ...
acupuncture	*acupuntura*	a·koo·poon·too·ra
aromatherapy	*aromaterapia*	a·ro·ma·te·ra·pee·a
homeopathy	*homeopatía*	o·me·o·pa·tee·a
meditation	*meditación*	me·dee·ta·syon
naturopathy	*neuropatía*	ne·oo·ro·pa·tee·a
reflexology	*reflexología*	re·flek·so·lo·khee·a

health

191

parts of the body

partes del cuerpo

My ... hurts.
   Me duele el/la ... m/f   me *dwe·*le el/la ...
I can't move my ...
   No puedo mover el/la ... m/f   no *pwe·*do mo·*ver* el/la ...
   No puedo mover   no *pwe·*do mo·*ver*
   los/las ... m/f pl   los/las ...
My ... is swollen.
   Tengo el/la ...   *ten·*go el/la ...
   hinchado/a. m/f   een·*cha·*do/a

For other parts of the body, see the **dictionary**.

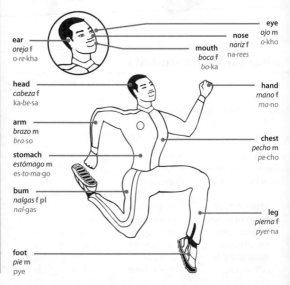

ear
oreja f
o·*re·*kha

head
cabeza f
ka·*be·*sa

arm
brazo m
*bra·*so

stomach
estómago m
es·*to·*ma·go

bum
nalgas f pl
*nal·*gas

foot
pie m
pye

eye
ojo m
o·kho

nose
nariz f
na·*rees*

mouth
boca f
*bo·*ka

hand
mano f
*ma·*no

chest
pecho m
*pe·*cho

leg
pierna f
*pyer·*na

pharmacist

I need something for (a headache).
Necesito algo para   ne·se·*see*·to *al*·go *pa*·ra
(el dolor de cabeza).   (el do·*lor* de ka·*be*·sa)

Do I need a prescription for (antihistamines)?
¿Necesito una receta   ne·se·*see*·to *oo*·na re·*se*·ta
para (antihistamínicos)?   *pa*·ra (an·tee·ees·ta·*mee*·nee·kos)

I have a prescription.
Tengo una receta.   *ten*·go *oo*·na re·*se*·ta

How many times a day?
¿Cuántas veces al día?   *kwan*·tas *ve*·ses al *dee*·a

Will it make me drowsy?
¿Me va a dar sueño?   me va a dar *swe*·nyo

antiseptic n	*antiséptico* m	an·tee·*sep*·tee·ko
contraceptives	*anticonceptivo* m	an·tee·kon·sep·*tee*·vo
insect repellent	*repelente* m	re·pe·*len*·te
painkillers	*medicinas para*	me·dee·*see*·nas *pa*·ra
	el dolor f pl	el do·*lor*
rehydration	*sales*	*sa*·les
salts	*hidratantes* f pl	ee·dra·*tan*·tes
sunblock	*bloqueador* m	blo·ke·a·*dor*
thermometer	*termómetro* m	ter·*mo*·me·tro

---

the pharmacist may say ...

Antes de comer.	*an*·tes de ko·*mer*	**Before food.**
Con la comida.	kon la ko·*mee*·da	**With food.**
Después de comer.	des·*pwes* de ko·*mer*	**After food.**

Dos/Tres veces al día.
  dos/tres *ve*·ses al *dee*·a   **Twice/Three times a day.**

¿Ha tomado esto antes?
  ha to·*ma*·do *es*·to *an*·tes   **Have you taken this before?**

Tiene que terminar el tratamiento completo.
  tye·ne ke ter·mee·*nar* el   **You must complete the**
  tra·ta·*myen*·to kom·*ple*·to   **course.**

dentist

dentista

I have a …	Tengo …	ten·go …
broken tooth	un diente quebrado	oon dyen·te ke·bra·do
cavity	una caries	oo·na ka·ryes
toothache	un dolor de muela	oon do·lor de mwe·la

I need a/an …	Necesito …	ne·se·see·to …
anaesthetic	un anestésico	oon a·nes·te·see·ko
filling	una calza	oo·na kal·sa

I've lost a filling.
Se me cayó una calza. se me ka·yo oo·na kal·sa

My dentures are broken.
Mi dentadura mee den·ta·doo·ra
está quebrada. es·ta ke·bra·da

My gums hurt.
Me duelen las encías. me dwe·len las en·see·as

I don't want it extracted.
No quiero que me la saque. no kye·ro ke me la sa·ke

Ouch!
Ay! ai

the dentist may say …

Abra grande.	a·bra gran·de	Open wide.
Enjuague.	en·khwa·ge	Rinse.
Esto no le va a doler.	es·to no le va a do·ler	This won't hurt a bit.
Muerda esto.	mwer·da es·to	Bite down on this.
No se mueva.	no se mwe·va	Don't move.
Vuelva, no he terminado.	vwel·va no e ter·mee·na·do	Come back, I haven't finished.

Spanish nouns in this dictionary have their gender indicated with ⓜ (masculine) and ⓕ (feminine). If adjectives and nouns have just one form for both genders, it's marked as ⓜ&ⓕ. Where adjectives and nouns have separate masculine and feminine forms, the endings are divided by a slash (eg *bello/a* ⓜ/ⓕ). In other cases we spell out the masculine and feminine forms in full for clarity of pronunciation (eg *embajador/ embajadora* ⓜ/ⓕ). See the **phrasebuilder** for more on gender. Words are also marked as n (noun), a (adjective), adv (adverb), v (verb), pl (plural), sg (singular), inf (informal) and pol (polite) where necessary. Verbs are given in the infinitive – for details on how to change verbs for use in a sentence, see the **phrasebuilder**, page 28.

A

aboard *a bordo* a bor-do
abortion *aborto* ⓜ a-bor-to
about *sobre* so-bre
above *sobre* so-bre
abroad *en el extranjero*
en el eks-tran-*khe*-ro
accident *accidente* ⓜ ak-see-*den*-te
accommodation *alojamiento* ⓜ
a-lo-kha-*myen*-to
account (bill) *cuenta* ⓕ *kwen*-ta
acid *ácido* ⓐ *a*-see-do
across *a través* a tra-*ves*
activist *activista* ⓜ&ⓕ ak-tee-*vees*-ta
actor *actor/actriz* ⓜ/ⓕ ak-*tor*/ak-*trees*
acupuncture *acupuntura* ⓕ
a-koo-poon-*too*-ra
adaptor *adaptador* ⓜ a-dap-ta-*dor*
addiction *adicción* ⓕ a-deek-*syon*
address *dirección* ⓕ dee-rek-*syon*
administration *administración* ⓕ
ad-mee-nees-tra-*syon*
admission (price) *admisión* ⓕ ad-mee-*syon*
admit *admitir* ad-mee-*teer*
adult n&a *adulto/a* ⓜ/ⓕ a-*dool*-to/a
advertisement *anuncio* ⓜ a-*noon*-syo
advice *consejo* ⓜ kon-*se*-kho
aerobics *aeróbicos* ⓜ a-e-ro-*bee*-kos
aeroplane *avión* ⓜ a-*vyon*
Africa *África* ⓕ *a*-free-ka
after *después* des-*pwes*

afternoon *tarde* ⓕ *tar*-de
aftershave *loción para despues del afeitado*
ⓕ lo-*syon* pa-ra des-*pwes* del a-fay-*ta*-do
again *otra vez* o-tra ves
age *edad* ⓕ e-*dad*
(three days) ago *hace (tres días)*
a-se (tres *dee*-as)
agree *estar de acuerdo* es-*tar* de a-*kwer*-do
agriculture *agricultura* ⓕ a-gree-kool-*too*-ra
ahead *adelante* a-de-*lan*-te
AIDS *SIDA* ⓜ *see*-da
air *aire* ⓜ *ai*-re
air-conditioned *con aire acondicionado*
kon *ai*-re a-kon-dee-syo-*na*-do
air conditioning *aire acondicionado* ⓜ
ai-re a-kon-dee-syo-*na*-do
airline *aerolínea* ⓕ a-e-ro-*lee*-ne-a
airmail *correo aéreo* ⓜ ko-*re*-o a-e-re-o
airplane *avión* ⓜ a-*vyon*
airport *aeropuerto* ⓜ a-e-ro-*pwer*-to
airport tax *impuesto de salida* ⓜ
eem-*pwes*-to de sa-*lee*-da
aisle (on plane) *pasillo* ⓜ pa-*see*-yo
alarm clock *reloj despertador* ⓜ
re-*lokh* des-per-ta-*dor*
alcohol *alcohol* ⓜ al-*kol*
all *todo/a* ⓜ/ⓕ *to*-do/a
allergy *alergia* ⓕ a-*ler*-khe-a
all-terrain vehicle *camión de todo-terreno*
ⓜ ka-*myon* de *to*-do te-*re*-no
almond *almendra* ⓕ al-*men*-dra
almost *casi ka*-see
alone *solo/a* ⓜ/ⓕ *so*-lo/a

already *ya* ya
also *también* tam-*byen*
altar *altar* ⓜ al-*tar*
altitude *altura* ① al-*too*-ra
always *siempre* syem-pre
ambassador *embajador/embajadora* ⓜ/①
em-ba-kha-dor/em-ba-kha-do-ra
ambulance *ambulancia* ① am-boo-lan-sya
anaemia *anemia* ① a-ne-mya
anarchist n&a *anarquista* ⓜ&①
a-nar-kees-ta
ancient *antiguo/a* ⓜ/① an-tee-gwo/a
and *y* ee
angry *enfadado/a* ⓜ/① en-fa-da-do/a
animal *animal* ⓜ a-nee-mal
ankle *tobillo* ⓜ to-bee-yo
another *otro/a* ⓜ/① o-tro/a
answer *respuesta* ① res-pwes-ta
answer v *responder* res-pon-der
ant *hormiga* ① or-mee-ga
antibiotics *antibióticos* ⓜ pl
an-tee-byo-tee-kos
antinuclear *antinuclear* an-tee-noo-kle-ar
antique *antigüedad* ① an-tee-gwe-dad
antiseptic *antiséptico* ⓜ an-tee-sep-tee-ko
any *cualquier/cualquiera* ⓜ/①
kwal-kyer/kwal-kye-ra
apartment *apartamento* ⓜ a-par-ta-men-to
appendix (body) *apéndice* ⓜ a-pen-dee-se
apple *manzana* ① man-sa-na
appointment *cita* ① see-ta
apricot *albaricoque* ⓜ al-ba-ree-ko-ke
April *abril* ⓜ a-breel
archaeological *arqueológico/a* ⓜ/①
ar-ke-o-lo-khee-ko/a
architect *arquitecto/a* ⓜ/① ar-kee-tek-to/a
architecture *arquitectura* ① ar-kee-tek-too-ra
argue *argumentar* ar-goo-men-tar
arm (body) *brazo* ⓜ bra-so
aromatherapy *aromaterapia* ①
a-ro-ma-te-ra-pya
arrest *arrestar* a-res-tar
arrivals *llegadas* ① pl ye-ga-das
arrive *llegar* ye-gar
art *arte* ⓜ ar-te
art gallery *galería de arte* ①
ga-le-ree-a de ar-te
artist *artista* ⓜ&① ar-tees-ta
ashtray *cenicero* ⓜ se-nee-se-ro
Asia *Asia* ① a-sya

ask (a question) *preguntar* pre-goon-tar
ask (for something) *pedir* pe-deer
asparagus *espárragos* ⓜ es-pa-ra-gos
aspirin *aspirina* ① as-pee-ree-na
asthma *asma* ① as-ma
at *en* en
athletics *atletismo* ⓜ at-le-tees-mo
Atlantic Ocean *Océano Atlántico* ⓜ
o-se-a-no at-lan-tee-ko
ATM *cajero automático* ⓜ
ka-khe-ro ow-to-ma-tee-ko
atmosphere *atmósfera* ① at-mos-fe-ra
aubergine *berenjena* ① be-ren-khe-na
August *agosto* ⓜ a-gos-to
aunt *tía* ① tee-a
Australia *Australia* ① ows-tra-lya
autumn *otoño* ⓜ o-to-nyo
avenue *avenida* ① a-ve-nee-da
avocado *aguacate* ⓜ a-gwa-ka-te
awful *horrible* ⓜ&① o-ree-ble

B

B&W (film) a *blanco y negro*
blan-ko ee ne-gro
baby *bebé* ⓜ&① be-be
baby food *comida de bebé* ①
ko-mee-da de be-be
baby powder *talcos* ⓜ pl tal-kos
babysitter *niñera* ① nee-nye-ra
back (body) *espalda* ① es-pal-da
back (position) *atrás* a-tras
backpack *mochila* ① mo-chee-la
bacon *tocineta* ① to-see-ne-ta
bad *malo/a* ⓜ/① ma-lo/a
bag *bolsa* ① bol-sa
baggage *equipaje* ⓜ e-kee-pa-khe
baggage allowance *límite de equipaje* ⓜ
lee-mee-te de e-kee-pa-khe
baggage claim *reclamo de equipaje* ⓜ
re-kla-mo de e-kee-pa-khe
bakery *panadería* ① pa-na-de-ree-a
balance (account) *saldo* ⓜ sal-do
balcony *balcón* ⓜ bal-kon
ball (sport) *bola* ① bo-la
ballet *ballet* ⓜ ba-let
banana *banano* ⓜ ba-na-no
band (music) *grupo musical* ⓜ
groo-po moo-see-kal

bandage *vendaje* m ven-*da*-khe
Band-Aid *curita* ① koo-*ree*-ta
bank *banco* m *ban*-ko
bank account *cuenta bancaria* ①
  kwen-ta ban-*ka*-rya
banknote *billete de banco* m
  bee-*ye*-te de *ban*-ko
baptism *bautismo* m bow-*tees*-mo
bar *bar* m bar
barber *barbero* m bar-*be*-ro
bar work *trabajo en el bar* m
  tra-*ba*-kho en el bar
baseball *béisbol* m *bays*-bol
basket *canasta* ① ka-*nas*-ta
basketball *básquetbol* m *bas*-ket-bol
bath *baño* m *ba*-nyo
bathing suit *vestido de baño* m
  ves-*tee*-do de *ba*-nyo
bathroom *baño* m *ba*-nyo
battery *batería* ① ba-te-*ree*-a
be (permanent) *ser* ser
be (temporary) *estar* es-*tar*
beach *playa* ① *pla*-ya
beach volleyball *volibol de playa* m
  vo-lee-*bol* de *pla*-ya
bean *frijol* m free-*khol*
beansprout *frijol nacido* m
  free-*khol* na-*see*-do
beautician *estilista* m&① es-tee-*lees*-ta
beautiful *bello/a* m/① *be*-yo/a
beauty salon *salón de belleza* m
  sa-*lon* de be-*ye*-sa
because *porque* por-*ke*
bed *cama* ① *ka*-ma
bedding *ropa de cama* ① *ro*-pa de *ka*-ma
bed linen *sábana* ① *sa*-ba-na
bedroom *cuarto* m *kwar*-to
bee *abeja* ① a-*be*-kha
beef *carne de res/vaca* ① *kar*-ne de res/*va*-ka
beer *cerveza* ① ser-*ve*-sa
before *antes* an-*tes*
beggar *mendigo/a* m/① men-*dee*-go/a
behind *detrás* de-*tras*
Belgium *Bélgica* ① *bel*-khee-ka
below *debajo de-ba-kho*
berth *litera* ① lee-*te*-ra
beside *junto a* khoon-to a
(the) best *el/la mejor* m/① el/la me-*khor*
bet *apuesta* ① a-*pwes*-ta
bet v *apostar* a-pos-*tar*

better *mejor* me-*khor*
between *entre* en-*tre*
Bible *Biblia* ① *bee*-blya
bicycle *bicicleta* ① bee-see-*kle*-ta
big *grande* m&① *gran*-de
bigger *más grande* m&① mas *gran*-de
(the) biggest *el/la más grande* m/①
  el/la mas *gran*-de
bike *bicicleta* ① bee-see-*kle*-ta
bike chain *cadena de bicicleta* ①
  ka-*de*-na de bee-see-*kle*-ta
bike lock *candado de bicicleta* m
  kan-*da*-do de bee-see-*kle*-ta
bike trail *sendero de bicicleta* m
  sen-*de*-ro de bee-see-*kle*-ta
bike shop *ciclo* m *see*-klo
bill (account/restaurant) *cuenta* ① *kwen*-ta
binoculars *binoculares* m pl
  bee-no-koo-*la*-res
bird *pájaro* m *pa*-kha-ro
birth certificate *certificado de nacimiento* m
  ser-tee-fee-*ka*-do de na-see-*myen*-to
birthday *cumpleaños* m koom-ple-*a*-nyos
biscuit (savoury) *pancito* m pan-*see*-to
biscuit (sweet) *galleta* ① ga-*ye*-ta
bite (dog) *mordida* ① mor-*dee*-da
bite (insect) *picada* ① pee-*ka*-da
bitter *amargo/a* m/① a-*mar*-go/a
black *negro/a* m/① *ne*-gro/a
black market *mercado negro* m
  mer-*ka*-do *ne*-gro
bladder *vejiga* ① ve-*khee*-ga
blanket *cobija* ① ko-*bee*-kha
blind *ciego/a* m/① *sye*-go/a
blister *ampolla* ① am-*po*-ya
blocked *bloqueado/a* m/① blo-ke-*a*-do/a
blood *sangre* ① *san*-gre
blood group *grupo sanguíneo* m
  groo-po san-*gee*-ne-o
blood pressure *presión sanguínea* ①
  pre-*syon* san-*gee*-ne-a
blood test *prueba de sangre* ①
  prwe-ba de *san*-gre
blue *azul* m&① a-*sool*
board (plane/ship) *abordar* a-bor-*dar*
boarding house *pensión* ① pen-*syon*
boarding pass *tiquete de abordaje* m
  tee-*ke*-te de a-bor-*da*-khe
boat *barco* m *bar*-ko
body *cuerpo* m *kwer*-po

C

boiled *hervido/a* ⓜ/ⓕ er·*vee*·do/a
bone *hueso* ⓜ *we*·so
book *libro* ⓜ *lee*·bro
book (make a booking) *reservar* re·ser·*var*
booked out *sin espacio* seen es·*pa*·syo
book shop *librería* ⓕ lee·bre·*ree*·a
boots *botas* ⓕ pl *bo*·tas
border (geographic) *frontera* ⓕ fron·*te*·ra
bored *aburrido/a* ⓜ/ⓕ a·boo·*ree*·do/a
boring *aburrido/a* ⓜ/ⓕ a·boo·*ree*·do/a
borrow *pedir prestado* pe·*deer* pres·*ta*·do
botanic garden *jardín botánico* ⓜ
   khar·*deen* bo·*ta*·nee·ko
both *ambos/as* ⓜ/ⓕ pl *am*·bos/as
bottle *botella* ⓕ bo·*te*·ya
bottle opener *abridor* ⓜ a·bree·*dor*
bottle shop *licorera* ⓕ lee·ko·*re*·ra
bottom (body) *trasero* ⓜ tra·*se*·ro
bottom (position) *fondo* ⓜ *fon*·do
bowl *plato hondo* ⓜ *pla*·to on·do
box *caja* ⓕ *ka*·kha
boxer shorts *bóxer* ⓜ *bok*·ser
boxing *boxeo* ⓜ *bok*·se·o
boy *chico* ⓜ *chee*·ko
boyfriend *novio* ⓜ *no*·vyo
bra *bracier* ⓜ bra·*syer*
brakes *frenos* ⓜ pl *fre*·nos
brave *valiente* ⓜ&ⓕ va·*lyen*·te
bread *pan* ⓜ pan
bread rolls *bollos de pan* ⓜ pl *bo*·yos de pan
break (in general) *quebrar* ke·*brar*
break (smash) *romper* rom·*per*
break down (car) *quedarse varado*
   ke·*dar*·se va·*ra*·do
breakfast *desayuno* ⓜ de·sa·*yoo*·no
breast (body) *pecho* ⓜ *pe*·cho
breast (poultry) *pechuga* ⓕ pe·*choo*·ga
breasts (body) *senos* ⓜ pl *se*·nos
bribe *soborno* ⓜ so·*bor*·no
bribe v *sobornar* so·bor·*nar*
bridge (structure) *puente* ⓜ *pwen*·te
briefcase *valija* ⓕ va·*lee*·kha
bring *traer* tra·*er*
brochure *panfleto* ⓜ pan·*fle*·to
broken *quebrado/a* ⓜ/ⓕ ke·*bra*·do/a
broken down (car) *descompuesto/a* ⓜ/ⓕ
   des·kom·*pwes*·to/a
bronchitis *bronquitis* ⓕ bron·*kee*·tees
brother *hermano* ⓜ er·*ma*·no
brown *café* ⓜ&ⓕ ka·*fe*

bruise *moretón* ⓜ mo·re·*ton*
brush *cepillo* ⓜ se·*pee*·yo
bucket *balde* ⓜ *bal*·de
Buddhist n&a *budista* ⓜ&ⓕ boo·*dees*·ta
budget *presupuesto* ⓜ pre·soo·*pwes*·to
buffet *buffet* ⓜ boo·*fe*
bug *bicho* ⓜ *bee*·cho
build *construir* kons·troo·*eer*
builder *constructor/constructora* ⓜ/ⓕ
   kons·trook·*tor*/kons·trook·*to*·ra
building *edificio* ⓜ e·dee·*fee*·syo
burn *quemadura* ⓕ ke·ma·*doo*·ra
burnt *quemado/a* ⓜ/ⓕ ke·*ma*·do/a
bus *bus* ⓜ boos
bus station *estación de bus* ⓕ
   es·ta·*syon* de boos
bus stop *parada de bus* ⓕ pa·*ra*·da de boos
business *negocio* ⓜ ne·*go*·syo
business class *clase ejecutiva* ⓕ
   kla·se e·khe·koo·*tee*·va
businessman *hombre de negocios* ⓜ
   om·bre de ne·*go*·syos
businesswoman *mujer de negocios* ⓕ
   moo·*kher* de ne·*go*·syos
busker *artista callejero* ⓜ&ⓕ
   ar·*tees*·ta ka·ye·*khe*·ro
busy *ocupado/a* ⓜ/ⓕ o·koo·*pa*·do/a
but *pero* *pe*·ro
butcher *carnicero* kar·nee·*se*·ro
butcher's shop *carnicería* ⓕ kar·nee·se·*ree*·a
butter *mantequilla* ⓕ man·te·*kee*·ya
butterfly *mariposa* ⓕ ma·ree·*po*·sa
button *botón* ⓜ bo·*ton*
buy *comprar* kom·*prar*

C

cabbage *repollo* ⓜ re·*po*·yo
cable car *teleférico* ⓜ te·le·*fe*·ree·ko
café *café* ⓜ ka·*fe*
cake *queque* ⓜ *ke*·ke
cake shop *pastelería* ⓕ pas·te·le·*ree*·a
calculator *calculadora* ⓕ kal·koo·la·*do*·ra
calendar *calendario* ⓜ ka·len·*da*·ryo
call (phone) *llamar* ya·*mar*
camera *cámara* ⓕ *ka*·ma·ra
camera shop *tienda de cámaras* ⓕ
   tyen·da de *ka*·ma·ras
camp *acampar* a·kam·*par*

camping ground *área de acampar* ⓕ
a·re·a de a·kam·par

camping store
tienda de artículos para acampar ⓕ
tyen·da de ar·tee·koo·los pa·ra a·kam·par

camp site *sitio para acampar* ⓜ
see·tyo pa·ra a·kam·par

can (be able/have permission) *poder* po·*der*

can (tin) *lata* ⓕ *la·*ta

Canada *Canadá* ⓕ ka·na·*da*

cancel *cancelar* kan·se·*lar*

cancer *cáncer* ⓜ *kan·*ser

candle *vela* ⓕ *ve·*la

candy *confite* ⓜ kon·*fee·*te

canoe *canoa* ⓕ ka·*no·*a

can opener *abrelatas* ⓜ a·bre·*la·*tas

cantaloupe *melón* ⓜ me·*lon*

capsicum *pimentón* ⓜ pee·men·*ton*

car *carro* ⓜ *ka·*ro

caravan *caravana* ⓕ ka·ra·*va·*na

cardiac arrest *ataque cardiaco* ⓜ
a·*ta·*ke kar·*dee·*a·ko

cards (playing) *naipes* ⓜ pl *nai·*pes

care (for someone) *cuidar de* kwee·*dar* de

car hire *alquiler de carros* ⓜ
al·kee·*ler* de *ka·*ros

Caribbean Sea *Mar Caribe* mar ka·*ree·*be

car owner's title *título de propiedad* ⓜ
*tee·*too·lo de pro·pee·e·*dad*

car park *parqueo* ⓜ par·*ke·*o

carpenter *carpintero* ⓜ kar·peen·*te·*ro

carrot *zanahoria* ⓕ sa·na·*o·*rya

carry *llevar* ye·*var*

carton *cartón* ⓜ kar·*ton*

cash *efectivo* ⓜ e·fek·*tee·*vo

cash (a cheque) *cambiar (un cheque)*
kam·*byar* (oon *che·*ke)

cash register *caja* ⓕ *ka·*kha

cashew *semilla de marañón* ⓕ
se·*mee·*ya de ma·ra·*nyon*

cashier *cajero/a* ⓜ/ⓕ ka·*khe·*ro/a

cash register *caja* ⓕ *ka·*kha

casino *casino* ⓜ ka·*see·*no

cassette *cassette* ⓜ ka·*se·*te

castle *castillo* ⓜ kas·*tee·*yo

casual work *trabajo temporal* ⓜ
tra·*ba·*kho tem·po·*ral*

cat *gato/a* ⓜ/ⓕ *ga·*to/a

cathedral *catedral* ⓕ ka·te·*dral*

Catholic n&a *católico/a* ⓜ/ⓕ ka·to·*lee·*ko/a

cave *cueva* ⓕ *kwe·*va

CD *CD* ⓜ se de

celebration *celebración* ⓕ se·le·bra·*syon*

cell phone *teléfono celular* ⓜ
te·*le·*fo·no se·loo·*lar*

cemetery *cementerio* ⓜ se·men·*te·*ryo

cent *centavo* ⓜ sen·*ta·*vo

centimetre *centímetro* ⓜ sen·*tee·*me·tro

centre *centro* ⓜ *sen·*tro

ceramics *cerámica* ⓕ se·*ra·*mee·ka

cereal (breakfast) *cereal* ⓜ se·re·*al*

certificate *certificado* ⓜ ser·tee·fee·*ka·*do

chain *cadena* ⓕ ka·*de·*na

chair *silla* ⓕ *see·*ya

champagne *champaña* ⓕ cham·*pa·*nya

championships *campeonatos* ⓜ pl
kam·pe·o·*na·*tos

chance *oportunidad* ⓕ o·por·too·nee·*dad*

change *cambio* ⓜ *kam·*byo

change (coins) *vuelto* ⓜ *vwel·*to

change (money) v *cambiar* kam·*byar*

changing room *vestidores* ⓜ pl
ves·tee·*do·*res

charming *encantador/encantadora* ⓜ/ⓕ
en·kan·ta·*dor*/en·kan·ta·*do·*ra

chat up (flirt) *ligar* lee·*gar*

cheap *barato/a* ⓜ/ⓕ ba·*ra·*to/a

cheat *tramposo/a* ⓜ/ⓕ tram·*po·*so/a

check v *revisar* re·vee·*sar*

check (banking) *cheque* ⓜ *che·*ke

check (bill) *cuenta* ⓕ *kwen·*ta

check-in (desk) *chequeo* ⓜ *che·*ke·o

checkpoint (border) *punto de control* ⓜ
*poon·*to de kon·*trol*

cheese *queso* ⓜ *ke·*so

chef *chef* ⓜ shef

chemist (pharmacist) *farmacéutico/a* ⓜ/ⓕ
far·ma·se·oo·*tee·*ko/a

chemist (pharmacy) *farmacia* ⓕ far·*ma·*sya

cheque (banking) *cheque* ⓜ *che·*ke

cherry *cereza* ⓕ se·*re·*sa

chess *ajedrez* ⓜ a·khe·*dres*

chest (body) *pecho* ⓜ *pe·*cho

chewing gum *chicle* ⓜ *chee·*kle

chicken *pollo* ⓜ *po·*yo

chicken pox *varicela* ⓕ va·ree·*se·*la

chickpea *garbanzo* ⓜ gar·*ban·*so

child *chiquito/a* ⓜ/ⓕ chee·*kee·*to/a

child-minding service *guardería* ①
gwar-de-*ree*-a
child seat *silla para niños* ①
see-ya pa-ra nee-nyos
children *niños/as* ⑩/① pl *nee*-nyos/as
chilli *chile* ⑩ *chee*-le
chilli sauce *salsa picante* ① *sal*-sa pee-*kan*-te
China *China* ① *chee*-na
chiropractor *qiropráctico* ⑩
kee-ro-*prak*-tee-ko
chocolate *chocolate* ⑩ cho-ko-*la*-te
choose *escoger* es-ko-*kher*
chopping board *tabla para picar* ①
ta-bla pa-ra pee-*kar*
chopsticks *palillos chinos* ⑩ pl
pa-*lee*-yos *chee*-nos
Christian n&a *cristiano/a* ⑩/①
krees-*tya*-no/a
Christian name *nombre cristiano* ⑩
nom-bre krees-*tya*-no
Christmas *Navidad* ① na-vee-*dad*
Christmas Day *día de Navidad* ⑩
dee-a de na-vee-*dad*
Christmas Eve *víspera de Navidad* ①
vees-pe-ra de na-vee-*dad*
church *iglesia* ① ee-*gle*-sya
cider *cidra* ① *see*-dra
cigar *cigarro* ⑩ see-*ga*-ro
cigarette *cigarrillo* ⑩ see-ga-*ree*-yo
cigarette lighter *encendedor* ⑩
en-sen-de-*dor*
cinema *cine* ⑩ *see*-ne
circus *circo* ⑩ *seer*-ko
citizenship *ciudadanía* ① syoo-da-da-*nee*-a
city *ciudad* ① syoo-*dad*
city centre *centro de la ciudad* ⑩
sen-tro de la syoo-*dad*
civil rights *derechos civiles* ⑩ pl
de-*re*-chos see-*vee*-les
clarinet *clarinete* ⑩ kla-ree-*ne*-te
class (category) *clase* ① *kla*-se
class system *escalas sociales* ① pl
es-*ka*-las so-*sya*-les
classical *clásico/a* ⑩/① *kla*-see-ko/a
clean *limpio/a* ⑩/① *leem*-pyo/a
clean v *limpiar* leem-*pyar*
cleaning *limpieza* ① leem-*pye*-sa
client *cliente* ⑩ klee-*en*-te
cliff *precipicio* ⑩ pre-see-*pee*-syo
climb v *escalar* es-ka-*lar*

cloakroom *guardaropa* ⑩ gwar-da-*ro*-pa
clock *reloj* ⑩ re-*lokh*
close (by) *cerca* *ser*-ka
close v *cerrar* se-*rar*
closed *cerrado/a* ⑩/① se-*ra*-do/a
clothesline *tendedero* ⑩ ten-de-*de*-ro
clothing *ropa* ① *ro*-pa
clothing store *tienda de ropa* ①
tyen-da de *ro*-pa
cloud *nube* ① *noo*-be
cloud forest *bosque nuboso* ⑩
bos-ke noo-*bo*-so
cloudy *nublado/a* ⑩/① noo-*bla*-do/a
clutch (car) *closh* klosh
coach (bus) *bus* ⑩ boos
coach (trainer) *entrenador/entrenadora*
⑩/① en-tre-na-*dor*/en-tre-na-*do*-ra
coach *entrenar* en-tre-*nar*
coast *costa* ① *kos*-ta
coat *abrigo* ① a-*bree*-go
cocaine *cocaína* ① ko-ka-*ee*-na
cockroach *cucaracha* ① koo-ka-*ra*-cha
cocktail *coctel* ⑩ kok-*tel*
cocoa *cacao* ⑩ ka-*kow*
coconut *coco* ⑩ *ko*-ko
coffee *café* ⑩ ka-*fe*
coins *monedas* ① pl mo-*ne*-das
cold *frío/a* ⑩/① *free*-o/a
cold (illness) *resfriado* ⑩ res-*free*-a-do
colleague *colega* ⑩&① ko-*le*-ga
collect call *llamada a cobrar* ①
ya-*ma*-da a ko-*brar*
college (university) *universidad* ①
oo-nee-ver-see-*dad*
colour *color* ⑩ ko-*lor*
comb *peine* ⑩ *pay*-ne
come *venir* ve-*neer*
comedy *comedia* ① ko-*me*-dya
comfortable *cómodo/a* ⑩/① *ko*-mo-do/a
commission *conmoción* ① kon-mo-*syon*
communications (profession)
comunicación ① ko-moo-nee-ka-*syon*
communion *comunión* ① ko-moo-*nyon*
communist n&a *comunista* ⑩&①
ko-moo-*nees*-ta
companion *compañero/a* ⑩/①
kom-pa-*nye*-ro/a
company (firm) *compañía* ① kom-pa-*nyee*-a
compass *brújula* ① *broo*-khoo-la
complain *quejarse* ke-*khar*-se

complaint *queja* ① ke-kha
complimentary (free) *gratis* ⑩&① gra-tees
computer *computadora* ①
  kom-poo-ta-do-ra
computer game *juego de computadora* ⑩
  khwe-go de kom-poo-ta-do-ra
concert *concierto* ⑩ kon-syer-to
concussion *contusión* ① kon-too-syon
conditioner (hair) *acondicionador* ⑩
  a-kon-dee-syo-na-dor
condom *preservativo* ⑩ pre-ser-va-tee-vo
conference (big) *congreso* ⑩ kon-gre-so
conference (small) *conferencia* ①
  kon-fe-ren-sya
confession (religious) *confesión* ①
  kon-fe-syon
confirm (a booking) *confirmar* kon-feer-mar
congratulations *felicidades* fe-lee-see-da-des
conjunctivitis *conjuntivitis* ①
  kon-khoon-tee-vee-tees
connection *conexión* ① ko-nek-syon
conservative n&a
  conservador/conservadora ⑩/①
  kon-ser-va-dor/kon-ser-va-do-ra
constipation *estreñimiento* ⑩
  es-tre-nyee-myen-to
consulate *consulado* ⑩ kon-soo-la-do
contact lenses *lentes de contacto* ⑩ pl
  len-tes de kon-tak-to
contact lens solution
  líquido para lentes de contacto ⑩
  lee-kee-do pa-ra len-tes de kon-tak-to
contraceptives *anticonceptivos* ⑩ pl
  an-tee-kon-sep-tee-vos
contract *contrato* ⑩ kon-tra-to
convenience store *súper* ⑩ soo-per
convent *convento* ⑩ kon-ven-to
cook *cocinero/a* ⑩/① ko-see-ne-ro/a
cook *cocinar* ko-see-nar
cookie *galleta* ① ga-ye-ta
cooking *cocina* ① ko-see-na
cool (temperature) *fresco/a* ⑩/① fres-ko/a
corkscrew *sacacorchos* ⑩ sa-ka-kor-chos
corn *maíz* ⑩ ma-ees
corner *esquina* ① es-kee-na
cornflakes *cornflakes* ⑩ pl korn-fleks
corrupt *corrupto/a* ⑩/① ko-roop-to/a
corruption *corrupción* ① ko-roop-syon
cost (price) *precio* ⑩ pre-syo
cost v *costar* kos-tar
cotton *algodón* ⑩ al-go-don

cotton balls *bolitas de algodón* ① pl
  bo-lee-tas de al-go-don
cotton buds (swabs) *aplicadores* ⑩ pl
  a-plee-ka-do-res
cough *tos* ① tos
cough v *toser* to-ser
cough medicine *jarabe para la tos* ⑩
  kha-ra-be pa-ra la tos
count *contar* kon-tar
counter (at bar) *barra* ① ba-ra
country *país* ⑩ pa-ees
countryside *campo* ⑩ kam-po
coupon *cupón* ⑩ koo-pon
court (legal) *corte* ① kor-te
court (tennis) *cancha de tenis* ①
  kan-cha de te-nees
cover charge *entrada* ① en-tra-da
cow *vaca* ① va-ka
cracker *galleta salada* ① ga-ye-ta sa-la-da
crafts *artesanías* ① pl ar-te-sa-nee-as
crash *choque* ⑩ cho-ke
crazy *loco/a* ⑩/① lo-ko/a
cream (food/lotion) *crema* ① kre-ma
crèche *cuna* ① koo-na
credit *crédito* ⑩ kre-dee-to
credit card *tarjeta de crédito* ①
  tar-khe-ta de kre-dee-to
cricket (sport) *cricket* ⑩ kree-ket
cross (religious) *cruz* ① kroos
crowded *lleno/a de gente* ⑩/①
  ye-no/a de khen-te
cucumber *pepino* ⑩ pe-pee-no
cup *taza* ① ta-sa
cupboard *armario* ⑩ ar-ma-ryo
currency exchange *cambio de moneda* ⑩
  kam-byo de mo-ne-da
current (electricity) *corriente* ① ko-ryen-te
current affairs *actualidad* ① ak-twa-lee-dad
custom *costumbre* ① kos-toom-bre
customs (immigration) *aduana* ①
  a-dwa-na
cut *cortada* ① kor-ta-da
cut v *cortar* kor-tar
cutlery *cubiertos* ⑩ pl koo-byer-tos
CV *currículum* ⑩ koo-ree-koo-loom
cycle (ride) *andar en bicicleta*
  an-dar en be-see-kle-ta
cycling *ciclismo* ⑩ see-klees-mo
cyclist *ciclista* ⑩&① see-klees-ta
cystitis *cistitis* ① sees-tee-tees

D

dad *papá* ⓜ pa·*pa*
daily adv *todos los días*
  to·dos los *dee*·as
dance *baile* ⓜ *bai*·le
dance v *bailar* bai·*lar*
dangerous *peligroso/a* ⓜ/ⓕ pe·lee·*gro*·so/a
dark (colour/night) *oscuro/a* ⓜ/ⓕ
  os·*koo*·ro/a
date (appointment) *cita* ⓕ *see*·ta
date (day) *fecha* ⓕ *fe*·cha
date (go out with) *salir con* sa·*leer* kon
date of birth *fecha de nacimiento* ⓕ
  fe·cha de na·see·*myen*·to
daughter *hija* ⓕ *ee*·kha
dawn *amanecer* ⓜ a·ma·ne·*ser*
day *día* ⓜ *dee*·a
day after tomorrow *pasado mañana* ⓜ
  pa·*sa*·do ma·*nya*·na
day before yesterday *anteayer* ⓜ
  an·te·a·*yer*
dead *muerto/a* ⓜ/ⓕ *mwer*·to/a
deaf *sordo/a* ⓜ/ⓕ *sor*·do/a
deal (cards) *repartir* re·par·*teer*
December *diciembre* ⓜ dee·*syem*·bre
decide *decidir* de·see·*deer*
deep *hondo/a* ⓜ/ⓕ *on*·do/a
deforestation *deforestación* ⓕ
  de·fo·res·ta·*syon*
degrees (temperature) *grados* ⓜ pl *gra*·dos
delay *atraso* ⓜ a·*tra*·so
delicatessen *delicatessen* ⓕ de·lee·ka·te·*sen*
deliver *enviar* en·*vyar*
democracy *democracia* ⓕ de·mo·*kra*·sya
demonstration (display) *demostración* ⓕ
  de·mos·tra·*syon*
demonstration (rally) *manifestación* ⓕ
  ma·nee·fes·ta·*syon*
Denmark *Dinamarca* ⓕ dee·na·*mar*·ka
dental floss *hilo dental* ⓜ *ee*·lo den·*tal*
dentist *dentista* ⓜ&ⓕ den·*tees*·ta
deodorant *desodorante* ⓜ de·so·do·*ran*·te
depart *partir* par·*teer*
department store *tienda por departamentos*
  ⓕ *tyen*·da por de·par·ta·*men*·tos
departure *salida* ⓕ sa·*lee*·da
departure gate *puerta de salida* ⓕ
  pwer·ta de sa·*lee*·da
deposit (bank) *depósito* ⓜ de·*po*·see·to
descendent *descendiente* ⓜ de·sen·*dyen*·te

desert *desierto* ⓜ de·*syer*·to
design *diseño* ⓜ dee·se·*nyo*
dessert *postre* ⓜ *pos*·tre
destination *destino* ⓜ des·*tee*·no
details *detalles* ⓜ pl de·*ta*·yes
diabetes *diabetes* ⓕ dee·a·*be*·tes
dial tone *tono* ⓜ *to*·no
diaper *pañal* ⓜ pa·*nyal*
diaphragm (contraceptive) *diafragma* ⓜ
  dya·*frag*·ma
diarrhoea *diarrea* ⓕ dee·a·*re*·a
diary *agenda* ⓕ a·*khen*·da
dice *dados* ⓜ pl *da*·dos
dictionary *diccionario* ⓜ deek·syo·*na*·ryo
die *morir* mo·*reer*
diet *dieta* ⓕ *dye*·ta
different *diferente* ⓜ&ⓕ dee·fe·*ren*·te
difficult *difícil* ⓜ&ⓕ dee·*fee*·seel
digital *digital* ⓜ&ⓕ dee·khee·*tal*
dinner *cena* ⓕ *se*·na
direct *directo/a* ⓜ/ⓕ dee·*rek*·to/a
direct-dial *marcación directa* ⓕ
  mar·ka·*syon* dee·*rek*·ta
direction *dirección* ⓕ dee·rek·*syon*
director *director/directora* ⓜ/ⓕ
  dee·rek·*tor*/dee·rek·*to*·ra
dirty *sucio/a* ⓜ/ⓕ *soo*·syo/a
disabled *discapacitado/a* ⓜ/ⓕ
  dees·ka·pa·see·*ta*·do/a
disco *discoteca* ⓕ dees·ko·*te*·ka
discount *descuento* ⓜ des·*kwen*·to
discrimination *discriminación* ⓕ
  dees·kree·mee·na·*syon*
disease *enfermedad* ⓕ en·fer·me·*dad*
dish *plato* ⓜ *pla*·to
disk (CD-ROM) *CD-ROM* ⓜ se de rom
disk (floppy) *disquete* ⓜ dees·*ke*·te
diving *buceo* ⓜ boo·*se*·o
diving equipment *equipo de buceo* ⓜ
  e·*kee*·po de boo·*se*·o
divorced *divorciado/a* ⓜ/ⓕ
  dee·vor·*sya*·do/a
dizzy *mareado/a* ⓜ/ⓕ ma·re·*a*·do/a
do *hacer* a·*ser*
doctor *doctor/doctora* ⓜ/ⓕ
  dok·*tor*/dok·*to*·ra
documentary *documental* ⓜ
  do·koo·men·*tal*
dog *perro/a* ⓜ/ⓕ *pe*·ro/a
doll *muñeca* ⓕ moo·*nye*·ka
dollar *dólar* ⓜ *do*·lar

door *puerta* ⓕ pwer·ta
dope (drugs) *hierba* ⓕ · *mota* ⓕ
  yer·ba · mo·ta
double *doble* ⓜ&ⓕ do·ble
double bed *cama matrimonial* ⓕ
  ka·ma ma·tree·mo·nyal
double room *cuarto doble* ⓜ kwar·to do·ble
down *abajo* a·ba·kho
downhill *cuesta abajo* kwes·ta a·ba·kho
dozen *docena* ⓕ do·se·na
drama *drama* ⓜ dra·ma
dream *sueño* ⓜ swe·nyo
dress *vestido* ⓜ ves·tee·do
dried *seco/a* ⓜ/ⓕ se·ko/a
dried fruit *frutas secas* ⓕ pl froo·tas se·kas
drink *bebida* ⓕ be·bee·da
drink v *beber* · *tomar* be·ber · to·mar
drink (alcoholic) *trago* ⓜ tra·go
drive *conducir* kon·doo·seer
driving licence *licencia de conductor* ⓕ
  lee·sen·sya de kon·dook·tor
drug (illicit) *droga* ⓕ dro·ga
drug (medicine) *medicamento* ⓜ
  me·dee·ka·men·to
drug addiction *drogadicción* ⓕ
  dro·ga·deek·syon
drug dealer *narcotraficante* ⓜ&ⓕ
  nar·ko·tra·fee·kan·te
drug trafficking *narcotráfico* ⓜ
  nar·ko·tra·fee·ko
drug user *drogadicto/a* ⓜ/ⓕ
  dro·ga·deek·to/a
drum (instrument) *tambor* ⓜ tam·bor
drums (kit) *batería* ⓕ ba·te·ree·a
drunk *borracho/a* ⓜ/ⓕ bo·ra·cho/a
dry *seco/a* ⓜ/ⓕ se·ko/a
dry (clothes, etc) *secar* se·kar
dry (onself) *secarse* se·kar·se
duck *pato* ⓜ pa·to
dummy (pacifier) *chupeta* ⓕ choo·pe·ta
DVD *DVD* ⓜ de ve de

E

each *cada* ka·da
ear *oreja* ⓕ o·re·kha
early adv *temprano* tem·pra·no
earn *ganar* ga·nar
earplugs *tapones para los oídos* ⓜ pl
  ta·po·nes pa·ra los o·ee·dos

earrings *aretes* ⓜ pl a·re·tes
Earth *tierra* ⓕ tye·ra
earthquake *terremoto* ⓜ te·re·mo·to
east *este* ⓜ es·te
Easter *Pascua* ⓕ pas·kwa
easy *fácil* ⓜ&ⓕ fa·seel
eat *comer* ko·mer
economy class *clase económica* ⓕ
  kla·se e·ko·no·mee·ka
ecstacy (drug) *éxtasis* ⓜ eks·ta·sees
eczema *eczema* ⓕ ek·se·ma
education *educación* ⓕ e·doo·ka·syon
egg *huevo* ⓜ we·vo
eggplant *berenjena* ⓕ be·ren·khe·na
election *elección* ⓕ e·lek·syon
electrical store *tienda de electrónicos* ⓕ
  tyen·da de e·lek·tro·nee·kos
electrician *electricista* ⓜ&ⓕ
  e·lek·tree·sees·ta
electricity *electricidad* ⓕ e·lek·tree·see·dad
elevator *ascensor* ⓜ a·sen·sor
email *correo electrónico* ⓜ
  ko·re·o e·lek·tro·nee·ko
embarrassed *avergonzado/a* ⓜ/ⓕ
  a·ver·gon·sa·do/a
embassy *embajada* ⓕ em·ba·kha·da
emergency *emergencia* ⓕ e·mer·khen·sya
emotional *emocional* ⓜ&ⓕ e·mo·syo·nal
employee *empleado/a* ⓜ/ⓕ em·ple·a·do/a
employer *empleador/empleadora* ⓜ/ⓕ
  em·ple·a·dor/em·ple·a·do·ra
empty *vacío/a* ⓜ/ⓕ va·see·o/a
end *fin* ⓜ feen
endangered species
  especie en peligro de extinción ⓕ
  es·pe·sye en pe·lee·gro de eks·teen·syon
engaged (phone) *ocupado* o·koo·pa·do
engaged (to marry) *comprometido/a* ⓜ/ⓕ
  kom·pro·me·tee·do/a
engagement (to marry) *compromiso* ⓜ
  kom·pro·mee·so
engine *motor* ⓜ mo·tor
engineer *ingeniero/a* ⓜ/ⓕ een·khe·nye·ro/a
engineering *ingeniería* ⓕ een·khe·nye·ree·a
England *Inglaterra* ⓕ een·gla·te·ra
English (language) *inglés* ⓜ een·gles
English a *inglés/inglesa* ⓜ/ⓕ
  een·gles/een·gle·sa
enjoy (oneself) *disfrutar* dees·froo·tar
enough *suficiente* soo·fee·syen·te

enter *entrar* en·*trar*
entertainment guide
 guía de entretenimiento ①
 gee·a de en·tre·te·nee·*myen*·to
entry *entrada* ① en·*tra*·da
envelope *sobre* ⓜ *so*·bre
environment *medio ambiente* ⓜ
 me·dyo am·*byen*·te
epilepsy *epilepsia* ① e·pee·*lep*·sya
equality *igualdad* ① ee·gwal·*dad*
equal opportunity
 igualdad de oportunidades ①
 ee·gwal·*dad* de o·por·too·nee·*da*·des
equipment *equipo* ⓜ e·*kee*·po
escalator *gradas* ① pl *gra*·das
estate agent *agente de bienes raíces* ⓜ
 a·*khen*·te de *bye*·nes ra·*ee*·ses
estuary *estuario* ⓜ es·*twa*·ryo
euro *euro* ⓜ e·oo·ro
Europe *Europa* ① e·oo·*ro*·pa
euthanasia *eutanasia* ① e·oo·ta·*na*·sya
evening *noche* ① *no*·che
every *todo/a* ⓜ/① *to*·do/a
everyone *todos/as* ⓜ/① pl *to*·dos/as
everything *todo* ⓜ *to*·do
exactly *exactamente* ek·sak·ta·*men*·te
example *ejemplo* ⓜ e·*khem*·plo
excellent *excelente* ⓜ&① ek·se·*len*·te
excess baggage *exceso de equipaje* ⓜ
 ek·*se*·so de e·kee·*pa*·khe
exchange *cambio* ⓜ *kam*·byo
exchange (money) *cambiar* kam·*byar*
exchange rate *tipo de cambio* ⓜ
 tee·po de *kam*·byo
excluded *excluido/a* ⓜ/① eks·kloo·*ee*·do/a
exhaust (car) *escape* ⓜ es·*ka*·pe
exhibition *exhibición* ① ek·see·bee·*syon*
exit *salida* ① sa·*lee*·da
expensive *caro/a* ⓜ/① *ka*·ro/a
experience *experiencia* ① eks·pe·*ryen*·sya
exploitation *explotación* ① eks·plo·ta·*syon*
express *directo/a* ⓜ/① dee·*rek*·to/a
express mail *correo express* ⓜ
 ko·*re*·o eks·*pres*
extension (visa) *extensión* ① eks·ten·*syon*
eyes *ojos* ⓜ pl o·khos
eye drops *gotas para los ojos* ① pl
 go·tas *pa*·ra los o·khos

F

fabric *tela* ① *te*·la
face *cara* ① *ka*·ra
face cloth *paño para la cara* ⓜ
 pa·nyo *pa*·ra la *ka*·ra
factory *fábrica* ① *fa*·bree·ka
fall (autumn) *otoño* ⓜ o·*to*·nyo
fall (down) v *caer* ka·*er*
family *familia* ① fa·*mee*·lya
family name *apellido* ⓜ a·pe·*yee*·do
famous *famoso/a* ⓜ/① fa·*mo*·so/a
fan (hand-held) *abanico* ⓜ a·ba·*nee*·ko
fan (machine) *ventilador* ⓜ ven·tee·la·*dor*
fan (sport, etc) *aficionado/a* ⓜ/①
 a·fee·syo·na·do/a
fanbelt *faja del abanico* ①
 fa·kha del a·ba·*nee*·ko
far (away) *lejos* le·khos
fare *tarifa* ① ta·*ree*·fa
farm *finca* ① *feen*·ka
farmer *finquero/a* ⓜ/① feen·*ke*·ro/a
fashion *moda* ① *mo*·da
fast *rápido/a* ⓜ/① *ra*·pee·do/a
fat *gordo/a* ⓜ/① *gor*·do/a
father *padre* ⓜ *pa*·dre
father-in-law *suegro* ⓜ *swe*·gro
faucet *tubo* ⓜ *too*·bo
fault (someone's) *culpa* ① *kool*·pa
faulty *defectuoso/a* ⓜ/① de·fek·*two*·so/a
fax machine *fax* ⓜ faks
February *febrero* ⓜ fe·*bre*·ro
feed *dar de comer* dar de ko·*mer*
feel (emotions) *sentir* sen·*teer*
feelings *sentimientos* ⓜ pl
 seen·tee·*myen*·tos
female *hembra* ① *em*·bra
fence *cerca* ① *ser*·ka
fencing (sport) *esgrima* ① es·*gree*·ma
ferry *ferry* ⓜ *fe*·ree
festival *fiesta* ① *fyes*·ta
fever *fiebre* ① *fye*·bre
few *poco/a* ⓜ/① *po*·ko/a
fiancé *prometido* ⓜ pro·me·*tee*·do
fiancée *prometida* ① pro·me·*tee*·da
fiction *ficción* ① feek·*syon*
fig *higo* ⓜ *ee*·go
fight *pelea* ① pe·*le*·a
fill *llenar* ye·*nar*
fillet *filete* ⓜ fee·*le*·te

film (cinema) *película* ① pe-*lee*-koo-la
film (for camera) *rollo* ⓜ *ro*-yo
film speed *asa* ⓜ *a*-sa
filtered *filtrado/a* ⓜ/① feel-*tra*-do/a
find *encontrar* en-kon-*trar*
fine adv *bien* byen
fine (payment) *multa* ① *mool*-ta
finger *dedo* ⓜ *de*-do
finish *meta* ① *me*-ta
finish v *terminar* ter-mee-*nar*
Finland *Finlandia* ① feen-*lan*-dya
fire *fuego* ⓜ *fwe*-go
firewood *leña* ① *le*-nya
first *primero/a* ⓜ/① pree-*me*-ro/a
first class *primera clase* ① pree-*me*-ra *kla*-se
first-aid kit *maletín de primeros auxilios* ⓜ
  ma-le-*teen* de pree-*me*-ros owk-*see*-lyos
first name *nombre cristiano* ⓜ
  nom-bre krees-*tya*-no
fish (animal) *pez* ⓜ pes
fish (meat) *pescado* ⓜ pes-*ka*-do
fishing *pesca* ① *pes*-ka
fishmonger *vendedor de pescado* ⓜ
  ven-de-*dor* de pes-*ka*-do
fish shop *tienda de pesca* ①
  tyen-da de *pes*-ka
flag *bandera* ① ban-*de*-ra
flannel (face cloth) *franela* ① fra-*ne*-la
flash (camera) *flash* ⓜ flash
flashlight (torch) *foco* ⓜ *fo*-ko
flat *plano/a* ⓜ/① *pla*-no/a
flat (apartment) *apartamento* ⓜ
  a-par-ta-*men*-to
flea *pulga* ① *pool*-ga
fleamarket *mercado de pulgas* ⓜ
  mer-*ka*-do de *pool*-gas
flight *vuelo* ⓜ *vwe*-lo
flood *inundación* ① ee-noon-da-*syon*
floor (ground) *suelo* ⓜ *swe*-lo
floor (storey) *piso* ⓜ *pee*-so
florist (shop) *floristería* ① flo-rees-te-*ree*-a
flour *harina* ① a-*ree*-na
flower *flor* ① flor
flu *gripe* ① *gree*-pe
flute *flauta* ① *flow*-ta
fly *mosca* ① *mos*-ka
fly v *volar* vo-*lar*
foggy *con neblina* kon ne-*blee*-na
follow *seguir* se-*geer*
food *comida* ① ko-*mee*-da

food supplies *provisiones* ① pl
  pro-vee-*syo*-nes
foot *pie* ⓜ pye
football (soccer) *fútbol* ⓜ *foot*-bol
footpath *sendero* ⓜ sen-*de*-ro
foreign *extranjero/a* ⓜ/① eks-tran-*khe*-ro/a
forest *bosque* ⓜ *bos*-ke
forever *para siempre* pa-ra syem-*pre*
forget *olvidar* ol-vee-*dar*
forgive *perdonar* per-do-*nar*
fork *tenedor* ⓜ te-ne-*dor*
fortnight *quincena* ① keen-*se*-na
fortune teller *adivino/a* ⓜ/①
  a-dee-*vee*-no/a
foul (soccer) *faul* ⓜ *fa*-ool
foyer *vestíbulo* ⓜ ves-*tee*-boo-lo
fragile *frágil* ⓜ&① *fra*-kheel
France *Francia* ① *fran*-sya
free (available) *disponible* ⓜ&①
  dees-po-*nee*-ble
free (gratis) *gratis* ⓜ&① *gra*-tees
free (not bound) *libre* ⓜ&① *lee*-bre
freeze *congelar* kon-khe-*lar*
French (language) *francés* fran-*ses*
fresh *fresco/a* ⓜ/① *fres*-ko/a
Friday *viernes* ⓜ *vyer*-nes
fridge *refri* ⓜ *re*-free
fried *frito/a* ⓜ/① *free*-to/a
friend *amigo/a* ⓜ/① a-*mee*-go/a
from *de* · *desde* de · *des*-de
frost *escarcha* ① es-*kar*-cha
frozen *congelado/a* ⓜ/① kon-khe-*la*-do/a
fruit *fruta* ① *froo*-ta
fry *freír* fre-*eer*
frying pan *sartén* ⓜ sar-*ten*
full *lleno/a* ⓜ/① *ye*-no/a
full time n *tiempo completo* ⓜ
  tyem-po kom-*ple*-to
fun *divertido/a* ⓜ/① dee-ver-*tee*-do/a
funeral *funeral* ⓜ foo-ne-*ral*
funny *vacilón/vacilona* ⓜ/①
  va-see-*lon*/va-see-*lo*-na
furniture *muebles* ⓜ pl *mwe*-bles
future *futuro* ⓜ foo-*too*-ro

G

game (sport) *partido* ⓜ par-*tee*-do
garage *garaje* ⓜ ga-*ra*-khe
garbage *basura* ① ba-*soo*-ra

garbage can *basurero* ⓜ ba-soo-*re*-ro
garden *jardín* ⓜ khar-*deen*
gardener *jardinero/a* ⓜ/① khar-dee-*ne*-ro/a
gardening *jardinería* ① khar-dee-ne-*ree*-a
garlic *ajo* ⓜ *a*-kho
gas (cooking) *gas* ⓜ gas
gas (petrol) *gasolina* ① ga-so-*lee*-na
gas cartridge *cilindro de gas* ⓜ
 see-*leen*-dro de gas
gas station *bomba* ① *bom*-ba
gastroenteritis *gastritis* ① gas-*tree*-tees
gate (airport, etc) *puerta* ① *pwer*-ta
gauze *gasa* ① *ga*-sa
gay n&a *gay* gay
gearbox *caja de cambios* ①
 ka-kha de *kam*-byos
German (language) *alemán* a-le-*man*
Germany *Alemania* ① a-le-*ma*-nya
get *obtener* ob-te-*ner*
get off (bus, train) *bajar* ba-*khar*
gift *regalo* ⓜ re-*ga*-lo
gig *chivo* ⓜ *chee*-vo
gin *ginebra* ① khee-*ne*-bra
girl *chiquita* ① chee-*kee*-ta
girlfriend *novia* ① *no*-vya
give *dar* dar
given name *nombre cristiano* ⓜ
 nom-bre krees-*tya*-no
glandular fever *mononucleosis* ①
 mo-no-noo-kle-o-*sees*
glass (drinking) *vaso* ⓜ *va*-so
glasses (spectacles) *anteojos* ⓜ pl
 an-te-o-khos
gloves *guantes* ⓜ pl *gwan*-tes
glue *pegamento* ⓜ pe-ga-*men*-to
go *ir* eer
go out (with) *salir (con)* sa-*leer* (kon)
go shopping *ir de compras* eer de *kom*-pras
goal (sport) *gol* ⓜ gol
goalkeeper *portero* ⓜ por-*te*-ro
goat *cabra* ① *ka*-bra
god *dios* ⓜ dee-os
goggles (diving) *mascara* ① mas-*ka*-ra
goggles (swimming) *mascarilla* ①
 mas-ka-*ree*-ya
gold *oro* ⓜ *o*-ro
golf ball *bola de golf* ① *bo*-la de golf
golf course *campo de golf* ⓜ *kam*-po de golf
good *bueno/a* ⓜ/① *bwe*-no/a
goodbye *adiós* a-*dyos*

government *gobierno* ⓜ go-*byer*-no
gram *gramo* ⓜ *gra*-mo
grandchild *nieto/a* ⓜ/① *nye*-to/a
grandfather *abuelo* ⓜ a-*bwe*-lo
grandmother *abuela* ① a-*bwe*-la
grapes *uvas* ① pl *oo*-vas
grass (lawn) *zacate* ⓜ sa-*ka*-te
grateful *agradecido/a* ⓜ/①
 a-gra-de-*see*-do/a
grave *tumba* ① *toom*-ba
great (fantastic) *fantástico/a* ⓜ/①
 fan-*tas*-tee-ko
green *verde* ⓜ&① *ver*-de
greengrocer *verdurería* ① ve-doo-re-*ree*-a
grey *gris* ⓜ&① grees
grocery store *súper* ⓜ *soo*-per
grow *crecer* kre-*ser*
guaranteed *garantizado/a* ⓜ/①
 ga-ran-tee-*sa*-do/a
guess *adivinar* a-dee-vee-*nar*
guesthouse *pensión* ① pen-*syon*
guide (audio) *guía* ① *gee*-a
guide (person) *guía* ⓜ&① *gee*-a
guidebook *guía turística* ①
 gee-a too-*rees*-tee-ka
guide dog *perro guía* ⓜ *pe*-ro *gee*-a
guided tour *tour con guía* ⓜ toor kon *gee*-a
guilty *culpable* ⓜ&① kool-*pa*-ble
guitar *guitarra* ① gee-*ta*-ra
gum (chewing) *chicle* ⓜ *chee*-kle
gums (mouth) *encías* ① pl en-*see*-as
gun *pistola* ① pees-*to*-la
gym (place) *gimnasio* ⓜ kheem-*na*-syo
gymnastics *gimnasia* ① kheem-*na*-sya
gynaecologist *ginecólogo/a* ⓜ/①
 khee-ne-ko-lo-go/a

H

hair *pelo* ⓜ *pe*-lo
hairbrush *cepillo* ⓜ se-*pee*-yo
haircut *corte de pelo* ⓜ *kor*-te de *pe*-lo
hairdresser *peluquero/a* ⓜ/① pe-loo-ke-ro/a
halal *halal* ⓜ&① a-*lal*
half *mitad* ① mee-*tad*
hallucination *alucinación* ①
 a-loo-see-na-*syon*
ham *jamón* ⓜ kha-*mon*
hammer *martillo* ⓜ mar-*tee*-yo

hammock *hamaca* ① a·*ma*·ka
hand *mano* ① *ma*·no
handbag *bolso* ⓜ *bol*·so
handball *balomano* ⓜ ba·lo·*ma*·no
handicraft *artesanías* ① pl ar·te·sa·*nee*·as
handkerchief *pañuelo* ⓜ pa·*nywe*·lo
handlebars *manillar* ⓜ ma·nee·*yar*
handmade *hecho/a a mano* ⓜ/①
e·cho/a a *ma*·no
handsome *guapo/a* ⓜ/① *gwa*·po/a
happy *feliz* ⓜ&① fe·*lees*
harassment *acoso* ⓜ a·*ko*·so
harbour *puerto* ⓜ *pwer*·to
hard (not soft) *duro/a* ⓜ/① *doo*·ro/a
hard-boiled (eggs) *duro/a* ⓜ/① *doo*·ro/a
hardware store *ferretería* ①
fe·re·te·*ree*·a
hashish *hachís* ⓜ a·*chees*
hat *sombrero* ⓜ som·*bre*·ro
have *tener* te·*ner*
have fun *divertirse* dee·ver·*teer*·se
hay fever *fiebre del heno* ① *fye*·bre del *e*·no
hazelnut *avellana* ① a·ve·*ya*·na
he *él* el
head *cabeza* ① ka·*be*·sa
headache *dolor de cabeza* ⓜ
do·*lor* de ka·*be*·sa
headlights *focos* ⓜ pl *fo*·kos
health *salud* ① sa·*lood*
health-food store *macrobiótica* ①
ma·kro·*byo*·tee·ka
hear *oír* o·*eer*
hearing aid *audífono* ⓜ ow·*dee*·fo·no
heart *corazón* ⓜ ko·ra·*son*
heart attack *ataque al corazón* ⓜ
a·*ta*·ke al ko·ra·*son*
heart condition *condición cardíaca* ①
kon·dee·*syon* kar·*dee*·a·ka
heat *calor* ⓜ ka·*lor*
heated *calentado/a* ⓜ/① ka·len·*ta*·do/a
heater *calentador* ⓜ ka·len·ta·*dor*
heating *calentamiento* ka·len·ta·*myen*·to
heavy (weight) *pesado/a* ⓜ/① pe·*sa*·do/a
helmet *casco* ⓜ *kas*·ko
help *ayuda* ① a·*yoo*·da
help v *ayudar* a·yoo·*dar*
hepatitis *hepatitis* ① e·pa·*tee*·tees
her *ella* *e*·ya
her (possessive) *su* soo
herb *hierba* ① *yer*·ba
herbalist *hierbero/a* ⓜ/① yer·*be*·ro/a

here *aquí* a·*kee*
heroin *heroína* ① e·ro·*ee*·na
herring *arenque* ⓜ a·*ren*·ke
high (height) *alto/a* ⓜ/① *al*·to/a
highchair *silla de comer para niños* ①
see·ya de ko·*mer* pa·ra *nee*·nyos
high school *colegio* ⓜ ko·*le*·khyo
highway *autopista* ① ow·to·*pees*·ta
hike *caminar* ka·mee·*nar*
hiking *caminata* ① ka·mee·*na*·ta
hiking boots *botas para caminata* ①
bo·tas pa·ra ka·mee·*na*·ta
hiking route *sendero* ⓜ sen·*de*·ro
hill *loma* ① *lo*·ma
him *él* el
Hindu n&a *hindú* ⓜ&① een·*doo*
hire (rent) *alquilar* al·kee·*lar*
his *su* soo
historical *histórico/a* ⓜ/① ees·to·*ree*·ko/a
history *historia* ① ees·*to*·rya
hitchhike *pedir un aventón*
pe·*deer* oon a·ven·*ton*
HIV *VIH* ⓓ ve ee *a*·che
hockey *hockey* ⓜ *o*·kee
holiday *feriado* ⓜ fe·*ree*·a·do
holidays *vacación* ① va·ka·*syon*
home *hogar* ⓜ o·*gar*
homeless n&a *indigente* ⓜ&①
een·dee·*khen*·te
homeopathy *homeopatía* ①
o·me·o·pa·*tee*·a
homesick *nostálgico/a* ⓜ/①
nos·*tal*·khee·ko/a
homosexual n&a *homosexual* ⓜ&①
o·mo·sek·*swal*
honey *miel* ① myel
honeymoon *luna de miel* ① *loo*·na de myel
horoscope *horóscopo* ⓜ o·*ros*·ko·po
horse *caballo* ⓜ ka·*ba*·yo
horse racing *carreras de caballo* ① pl
ka·*re*·ras de ka·*ba*·yo
horse riding *equitación* ① e·kee·ta·*syon*
hospital *hospital* ⓜ os·pee·*tal*
hospitality *hospitalidad* ① os·pee·ta·lee·*dad*
hot *caliente* ⓜ&① ka·*lyen*·te
hot water *agua caliente* ① *a*·gwa ka·*lyen*·te
hotel *hotel* ⓜ o·*tel*
hour *hora* ① *o*·ra
house *casa* ① *ka*·sa

housework *trabajo de la casa* ⓜ
tra-*ba*-kho de la *ka*-sa
how *cómo* *ko*-mo
how many *cuántos/as* ⓜ/ⓕ *kwan*-tos/as
how much *cuánto/a* ⓜ/ⓕ *kwan*-to/a
hug *abrazar* a-bra-*sar*
huge *enorme* ⓜ&ⓕ e-*nor*-me
humanities *humanidades* ⓕ pl
oo-ma-nee-*da*-des
human resources *recursos humanos* ⓜ pl
re-*koor*-sos oo-*ma*-nos
human rights *derechos humanos* ⓜ pl
de-*re*-chos oo-*ma*-nos
hundred *cien* syen
hungry *hambriento/a* ⓜ/ⓕ
am-bree-*yen*-to/a
hunting *caza* ⓕ *ka*-sa
hurt (be painful) *doler* do-*ler*
hurt (cause pain) *lastimar* las-tee-*mar*
husband *esposo* ⓜ es-*po*-so

I

I *yo* yo
ice *hielo* ⓜ *ye*-lo
ice cream *helado* ⓜ e-*la*-do
ice-cream parlour *heladería* ⓕ e-la-de-*ree*-a
ice hockey *hockey sobre hielo* ⓜ
o-kee *so*-bre *ye*-lo
identification *identificación* ⓕ
ee-den-tee-fee-ka-*syon*
identification card (ID)
cédula de identificación ⓕ
se-doo-la de ee-den-tee-fee-ka-*syon*
idiot *idiota* ⓜ&ⓕ ee-*dyo*-ta
if *si* see
ill *enfermo/a* ⓜ/ⓕ en-*fer*-mo/a
immigration *migración* ⓕ mee-gra-*syon*
important *importante* ⓜ&ⓕ eem-por-*tan*-te
impossible *imposible* ⓜ&ⓕ eem-po-*see*-ble
in *en* en
in a hurry *apurado/a* ⓜ/ⓕ a-poo-*ra*-do/a
included *incluido/a* ⓜ/ⓕ een-kloo-ee-do/a
income tax *impuesto* ⓜ eem-*pwes*-to
indicator *indicador* ⓜ een-dee-ka-*dor*
indigestion *indigestión* ⓕ
een-dee-khes-*tyon*
indoor *adentro* a-*den*-tro
industry *industria* ⓕ een-*doos*-tree-a
infection *infección* ⓕ een-fek-*syon*

inflammation *inflamación* ⓕ
een-fla-ma-*syon*
influenza *gripe* ⓕ *gree*-pe
information *información* ⓕ een-for-ma-*syon*
in front of *en frente de* en *fren*-te de
ingredient *ingrediente* ⓜ een-gre-*dyen*-te
inject *inyectar* een-yek-*tar*
injection *inyección* ⓕ een-yek-*syon*
injured *lastimado/a* ⓜ/ⓕ las-tee-*ma*-do/a
injury *herida* ⓕ e-*ree*-da
inner tube (tyre) *tubo interno* ⓜ
too-bo een-*ter*-no
innocent *inocente* ⓜ&ⓕ ee-no-*sen*-te
insect *insecto* ⓜ een-*sek*-to
insect repellent *repelente* ⓜ re-pe-*len*-te
inside *dentro de* *den*-tro de
instructor *instructor/instructora* ⓜ/ⓕ
eens-trook-*tor*/eens-trook-*to*-ra
insurance *seguro* ⓜ se-*goo*-ro
interesting *interesante* ⓜ&ⓕ
een-te-re-*san*-te
intermission *intermedio* ⓜ een-ter-*me*-dyo
international *internacional* ⓜ&ⓕ
een-ter-na-syo-*nal*
Internet *internet* ⓜ&ⓕ een-ter-*net*
Internet café *café internet* ⓜ
ka-*fe* een-ter-*net*
interpreter *intérprete* ⓜ&ⓕ een-*ter*-pre-te
interview *entrevista* ⓕ en-tre-*vees*-ta
invite *invitar* een-vee-*tar*
Ireland *Irlanda* ⓕ eer-*lan*-da
iron (for clothes) *plancha* ⓕ *plan*-cha
island *isla* ⓕ *ees*-la
IT (information technology)
informática ⓕ een-for-*ma*-tee-ka
Italy *Italia* ⓕ ee-*ta*-lya
itch *picazón* ⓕ pee-ka-*son*
itemized *detallado/a* ⓜ/ⓕ de-ta-*ya*-do/a
itinerary *itinerario* ⓜ ee-tee-ne-*ra*-ryo
IUD *DIU* ⓜ de ee oo

J

jacket *jacket* ⓕ *cha*-ket
jail *cárcel* ⓕ *kar*-sel
jam *jalea* ⓕ kha-*le*-a
January *enero* ⓜ e-*ne*-ro
Japan *Japón* ⓜ kha-*pon*
jar *frasco* ⓜ *fras*-ko
jaw *mandíbula* ⓕ man-*dee*-boo-la
jealous *celoso/a* ⓜ/ⓕ se-*lo*-so/a

jeans *jeans* ⓜ yeens
jeep *jeep* ⓜ yeep
jet lag *desfase de horario* ⓜ
des·fa·se de o·ra·ryo
jewellery *joyas* ⓕ pl *kho*·yas
Jewish *judío/a* ⓜ/ⓕ khoo·*dee*·o/a
job *trabajo* ⓜ tra·*ba*·kho
jogging *trotar* ⓜ tro·*tar*
joke *chiste* ⓜ *chees*·te
journalist *periodista* ⓜ&ⓕ pe·ree·o·*dees*·ta
journey *viaje* ⓜ *vya*·khe
judge *juez/jueza* ⓜ/ⓕ khwes/*khwe*·sa
juice *jugo* ⓜ *khoo*·go
July *julio* ⓜ *khoo*·lyo
jump *saltar* sal·*tar*
jumper (sweater) *suéter* ⓜ *swe*·ter
jumper leads *jumpers* ⓜ pl *chom*·pers
June *junio* ⓜ *khoo*·nyo

K

kayak *kayak* ⓜ ka·*yak*
ketchup *ketchup* ⓜ *ke*·choop
key (door etc) *llave* ⓕ *ya*·ve
keyboard *teclado* ⓜ te·*kla*·do
kick *patear* pa·te·*ar*
kidney *riñón* ⓜ ree·*nyon*
kilogram *kilogramo* ⓜ kee·lo·*gra*·mo
kilometre *kilómetro* ⓜ kee·*lo*·me·tro
kind (nice) *amable* ⓜ&ⓕ a·*ma*·ble
kindergarten *kínder* ⓜ *keen*·der
king *rey* ⓜ ray
kiosk *quiosco* ⓜ *kyos*·ko
kiss *beso* ⓜ *be*·so
kiss v *besar* be·*sar*
kitchen *cocina* ⓕ ko·*see*·na
knee *rodilla* ⓕ ro·*dee*·ya
knife *cuchillo* ⓜ koo·*chee*·yo
know (someone) *conocer* ko·no·*ser*
know (something) *saber* sa·*ber*
kosher *kosher* ⓜ&ⓕ ko·*sher*

L

labourer *trabajador/trabajadora* ⓜ/ⓕ
tra·ba·kha·*dor*/tra·ba·kha·*do*·ra
lake *lago* ⓜ *la*·go
lamb (meat) *cordero* ⓜ kor·*de*·ro
land *tierra* ⓕ *tye*·ra
landlady *dueña* ⓕ *dwe*·nya

landlord *dueño* ⓜ *dwe*·nyo
language *idioma* ⓜ ee·*dyo*·ma
laptop *laptop* ⓜ *lap*·top
large *grande* ⓜ&ⓕ *gran*·de
last (final) *último/a* ⓜ/ⓕ *ool*·tee·mo/a
last (previous) *pasado/a* ⓜ/ⓕ pa·*sa*·do/a
late adv *tarde* *tar*·de
later *más tarde* mas *tar*·de
laugh *reír* re·*eer*
launderette *lavandería* ⓕ la·van·de·*ree*·a
laundry (clothes) *ropa* ⓕ *ro*·pa
laundry (place) *lavandería* ⓕ la·van·de·*ree*·a
law (legislation) *ley* ⓕ lay
law (profession) *derecho* ⓜ de·*re*·cho
lawyer *abogado/a* ⓜ/ⓕ a·bo·*ga*·do/a
laxative *laxante* ⓜ lak·*san*·te
lazy *perezoso/a* ⓜ/ⓕ pe·re·*so*·so/a
leader *líder* ⓜ&ⓕ *lee*·der
leaf *hoja* ⓕ *o*·kha
learn *aprender* a·pren·*der*
leather *cuero* ⓜ *kwe*·ro
lecturer *presentador/presentadora* ⓜ/ⓕ
pre·sen·ta·*dor*/pre·sen·ta·*do*·ra
ledge *borde* ⓜ *bor*·de
left (direction) *izquierda* ⓕ ees·*kyer*·da
left-luggage office *consigna* ⓕ kon·*seeg*·na
left-wing *izquierdista* ⓜ&ⓕ ees·kyer·*dees*·ta
leg (body) *pierna* ⓕ *pyer*·na
legal *legal* ⓜ&ⓕ le·*gal*
legislation *legislación* ⓕ le·khee·sla·*syon*
legume *legumbre* ⓕ le·*goom*·bre
lemon *limón* ⓜ lee·*mon*
lemonade *limonada* ⓕ lee·mo·*na*·da
lens (camera) *objetivo* ⓜ ob·khe·*tee*·vo
lentil *lenteja* ⓕ len·*te*·kha
lesbian n&a *lesbiana* ⓕ les·*bya*·na
less *menos* *me*·nos
letter (mail) *carta* ⓕ *kar*·ta
lettuce *lechuga* ⓕ le·*choo*·ga
liar *mentiroso/a* ⓜ/ⓕ men·tee·*ro*·so/a
librarian *bibliotecario/a* ⓜ/ⓕ
bee·blee·o·te·*ka*·ryo/a
library *biblioteca* ⓕ bee·blee·o·*te*·ka
lice *piojos* ⓜ pl *pyo*·khos
licence *licencia* ⓕ lee·*sen*·sya
license plate number *número de placa* ⓜ
noo·me·ro de *pla*·ka
lie (not stand) *acostarse* a·kos·*tar*·se
lie (not tell the truth) *mentir* men·*teer*
life *vida* ⓕ *vee*·da

life jacket *chaleco salvavidas* ⓜ
cha-*le*-ko sal-va-*vee*-das
lift (elevator) *ascensor* ⓜ a-sen-*sor*
light *luz* ⓕ lus
light (colour) *claro/a* ⓜ/ⓕ *kla*-ro/a
light (weight) *liviano/a* ⓜ/ⓕ lee-*vya*-no/a
light bulb *bombillo* ⓜ bom-*bee*-yo
lighter (cigarette) *encendedor* ⓜ
en-sen-de-*dor*
light meter *medidor de luz* ⓜ
me-dee-*dor* de lus
like v *gustar* goos-*tar*
lime (fruit) *limón* ⓜ lee-*mon*
linen (material) *lino* ⓜ *lee*-no
linen (sheets) *sábanas* ⓕ pl *sa*-ba-nas
linguist *lingüista* ⓜ&ⓕ leen-*gwees*-ta
lip balm *brillo* ⓜ *bree*-yo
lips *labios* ⓜ pl *la*-byos
lipstick *pintura de labios* ⓕ
peen-*too*-ra de *la*-byos
liquor store *licorera* ⓕ lee-ko-*re*-ra
listen *escuchar* es-koo-*char*
little (quantity) *poco/a* ⓜ/ⓕ *po*-ko/a
little (size) *pequeño/a* ⓜ/ⓕ pe-*ke*-nyo/a
live *vivir* vee-*veer*
liver *hígado* ⓜ *ee*-ga-do
lizard *lagartija* ⓕ la-gar-*tee*-kha
local *local* ⓜ&ⓕ lo-*kal*
lock *candado* ⓜ kan-*da*-do
lock v *cerrar con llave* se-*rar* kon ya-ve
locked *cerrado/a con llave* ⓜ/ⓕ
se-*ra*-do/a kon *ya*-ve
long *largo/a* ⓜ/ⓕ *lar*-go/a
look *ver* ver
look after *cuidar* kwee-*dar*
look for *buscar* boos-*kar*
lookout *mirador* ⓜ mee-ra-*dor*
loose *flojo/a* ⓜ/ⓕ *flo*-kho/a
loose change *menudo* ⓜ me-*noo*-do
lose *perder* per-*der*
lost *perdido/a* ⓜ/ⓕ per-*dee*-do/a
lost property office
oficina de objetos perdidos ⓕ
o-fee-*see*-na de ob-*khe*-tos per-*dee*-dos
(a) lot *mucho/a* ⓜ/ⓕ *moo*-cho/a
loud *ruidoso/a* ⓜ/ⓕ rwee-*do*-so/a
love *amor* ⓜ a-*mor*
love v *amar* a-*mar*
lover *amante* ⓜ&ⓕ a-*man*-te
low *bajo/a* ⓜ/ⓕ *ba*-kho/a

lubricant *lubricante* ⓜ loo-bree-*kan*-te
luck *suerte* ⓕ *swer*-te
lucky *afortunado/a* ⓜ/ⓕ a-for-too-na-do/a
luggage *equipaje* ⓜ e-kee-*pa*-khe
luggage tag *etiqueta del equipaje* ⓕ
e-tee-*ke*-ta del e-kee-*pa*-khe
lump *bulto* ⓜ *bool*-to
lunch *almuerzo* ⓜ al-*mwer*-so
lung *pulmón* ⓜ pool-*mon*
luxury *lujoso/a* ⓜ/ⓕ loo-*kho*-so/a

M

machine *máquina* ⓕ *ma*-kee-na
magazine *revista* ⓕ re-*vees*-ta
mail *correo* ⓜ ko-*re*-o
mail *enviar* en-*vyar*
mailbox *buzón* ⓜ boo-*son*
main *principal* ⓜ&ⓕ preen-see-*pal*
main road *calle principal* ⓕ
ka-ye preen-se-*pal*
make *hacer* a-*ser*
make-up *maquillaje* ⓜ ma-kee-*ya*-khe
malaria *malaria* ⓕ ma-*la*-rya
mammogram *mamografía* ⓕ
ma-mo-gra-*fee*-a
man *hombre* ⓜ *om*-bre
manager (business) *gerente* ⓜ&ⓕ
khe-*ren*-te
manager (sport) *director/directora* ⓜ/ⓕ
dee-rek-*tor*/dee-rek-*to*-ra
mandarin *mandarina* ⓕ man-da-*ree*-na
mango *mango* ⓜ *man*-go
mangrove *manglar* ⓜ man-*glar*
many *muchos/as* ⓜ/ⓕ pl *moo*-chos/as
map *mapa* ⓜ *ma*-pa
March *marzo* ⓜ *mar*-so
margarine *margarina* ⓕ mar-ga-*ree*-na
marijuana *marihuana* ⓕ ma-ree-*wa*-na
marital status *estado civil* ⓜ
es-*ta*-do see-*veel*
market *mercado* ⓜ mer-*ka*-do
marriage *matrimonio* ⓜ ma-tree-*mo*-nyo
married *casado/a* ⓜ/ⓕ ka-*sa*-do/a
marry *casarse* ka-*sar*-se
martial arts *artes marciales* ⓕ
ar-tes mar-*sya*-les
mass (Catholic) *misa* ⓕ *mee*-sa
massage *masaje* ⓜ ma-*sa*-khe

masseur *masajeador* ⓜ ma·sa·khe·a·*dor*
masseuse *masajeadora* ⓕ ma·sa·khe·a·*do*·ra
mat *colchoneta* ⓕ kol·cho·*ne*·ta
match (sports) *partido* ⓜ par·*tee*·do
matches (lighting) *fósforos* ⓜ pl *fos*·fo·ros
mattress *colchón* ⓜ kol·*chon*
May *mayo* ⓜ *ma*·yo
maybe *tal vez* tal ves
mayonnaise *mayonesa* ⓕ ma·yo·*ne*·sa
mayor *alcalde/alcaldesa* ⓜ/ⓕ
  al·*kal*·de/al·kal·*de*·sa
me *mí* mee
meal *comida* ⓕ ko·*mee*·da
measles *sarampión* ⓜ sa·ram·*pyon*
meat *carne* ⓕ *kar*·ne
mechanic *mecánico/a* ⓜ/ⓕ me·*ka*·nee·ko/a
media *medios* ⓜ pl *me*·dyos
medicine (medication) *medicamento* ⓜ
  me·dee·ka·*men*·to
medicine (profession) *medicina* ⓕ
  me·dee·*see*·na
meditation *meditación* ⓕ me·dee·ta·*syon*
meet (first time) *conocerse* ko·no·*ser*·se
meet (get together) *encontrarse*
  en·kon·*trar*·se
melon *melón* ⓜ me·*lon*
member *miembro/a* ⓜ/ⓕ *myem*·bro/a
memory card *tarjeta de memoria* ⓕ
  tar·*khe*·ta de me·*mo*·rya
menstruation *regla* ⓕ *re*·gla
menu *menú* ⓜ me·*noo*
message *mensaje* ⓜ men·*sa*·khe
metal *metal* ⓜ me·*tal*
metre *metro* ⓜ *me*·tro
microwave oven *horno microondas* ⓜ
  or·no mee·kro·on·das
midday *mediodía* ⓜ me·dyo·*dee*·a
midnight *medianoche* ⓕ me·dya·no·che
migraine *migraña* ⓕ mee·*gra*·nya
military *ejército* ⓜ e·*kher*·see·to
military service *servicio militar* ⓜ
  ser·*vee*·syo mee·lee·*tar*
milk *leche* ⓕ *le*·che
millimetre *milímetro* ⓜ mee·*lee*·me·tro
million *millón* ⓜ mee·*yon*
mince *picadillo* ⓜ pee·ka·*dee*·yo
mineral water *agua mineral* ⓕ
  a·gwa mee·ne·*ral*
minute *minuto* ⓜ mee·*noo*·to
mirror *espejo* ⓜ es·*pe*·kho

miscarriage *aborto natural* ⓜ
  a·*bor*·to na·too·*ral*
miss (feel absence of) *extrañar* eks·tra·*nyar*
miss (lose) *perder* per·*der*
mistake *error* ⓜ e·*ror*
mix *mezclar* mes·*klar*
mobile phone *teléfono celular* ⓜ
  te·*le*·fo·no se·loo·*lar*
modem *módem* ⓜ *mo*·dem
modern *moderno/a* ⓜ/ⓕ mo·*der*·no/a
moisturiser *humectante* ⓜ oo·mek·*tan*·te
monastery *monasterio* ⓜ mo·nas·*te*·ryo
Monday *lunes* ⓜ *loo*·nes
money *dinero* ⓜ dee·*ne*·ro
monk *monje* ⓜ *mon*·khe
monkey *mono* ⓜ *mo*·no
month *mes* ⓜ mes
monument *monumento* ⓜ mo·noo·*men*·to
moon *luna* ⓕ *loo*·na
more *más* mas
morning *mañana* ⓕ ma·*nya*·na
morning sickness *achaques* ⓜ pl a·*cha*·kes
mosque *mezquita* ⓕ mes·*kee*·ta
mosquito *zancudo* ⓜ san·*koo*·do
mosquito coil *espiral para mosquitos* ⓕ
  es·pee·*ral* pa·ra mos·*kee*·tos
mosquito net *mosquitero* ⓜ mos·kee·*te*·ro
motel *motel* ⓜ mo·*tel*
mother *madre* ⓕ *ma*·dre
mother-in-law *suegra* ⓕ *swe*·gra
motorbike *moto* ⓕ *mo*·to
motorboat *lancha* ⓕ *lan*·cha
motorcycle *moto* ⓕ *mo*·to
motorway (tollway) *autopista* ⓕ
  ow·to·*pees*·ta
mountain *montaña* ⓕ mon·*ta*·nya
mountain bike *bicicleta montañera* ⓕ
  bee·see·*kle*·ta mon·ta·*nye*·ra
mountaineering *montañismo* ⓜ
  mon·ta·*nyees*·mo
mountain path *camino de montaña* ⓜ
  ka·*mee*·no de mon·*ta*·nya
mountain range *cordillera* ⓕ kor·dee·*ye*·ra
mouse (animal) *ratón* ⓜ ra·*ton*
mouse (computer) *mouse* ⓜ mows
mouth *boca* ⓕ *bo*·ka
movie *película* ⓕ pe·*lee*·koo·la
mud *barro* ⓜ *ba*·ro
muesli *granola* ⓕ gra·*no*·la
mumps *paperas* ⓕ pl pa·*pe*·ras

murder *asesinato* ⓜ a-se-see-*na*-to
murder v *asesinar* a-se-see-*nar*
muscle *músculo* ⓜ *moos*-koo-lo
museum *museo* ⓜ moo-*se*-o
mushroom *hongo* ⓜ *on*-go
music *música* ⓕ *moo*-see-ka
music shop *tienda de música* ⓕ
  tyen-da de *moo*-see-ka
musician *músico/a* ⓜ/ⓕ *moo*-see-ko/a
Muslim *musulmán/musulmana* ⓜ/ⓕ
  moo-sool-*man*/moo-sool-*ma*-na
mussel *mejillón* ⓜ me-khee-*yon*
mustard *mostaza* ⓕ mos-*ta*-sa
mute *mudo/a* ⓜ/ⓕ *moo*-do/a
my *mi* mee

N

nail clippers *cortaúñas* ⓜ kor-ta-*oo*-nyas
name *nombre* ⓜ *nom*-bre
napkin *servilleta* ⓕ ser-vee-*ye*-ta
nappy *pañal* ⓜ pa-*nyal*
nappy rash *salpullido* ⓜ sal-poo-*yee*-do
nationality *nacionalidad* ⓕ
  na-syo-na-lee-*dad*
national park *parque nacional* ⓜ
  par-ke na-syo-*nal*
nature *naturaleza* ⓕ na-too-ra-*le*-sa
naturopathy *neuropatía* ⓕ ne-oo-ro-pa-*tee*-a
nausea *náuseas* ⓕ pl *now*-se-as
near *cerca de* ser-ka de
nearby *cerca* ser-ka
nearest *más cerca* mas *ser*-ka
necessary *necesario/a* ⓜ/ⓕ ne-se-*sa*-ryo/a
neck *cuello* ⓜ *kwe*-yo
necklace *cadena* ⓕ ka-*de*-na
nectarine *nectarina* ⓕ nek-ta-*ree*-na
need *necesitar* ne-se-see-*tar*
needle (sewing) *aguja* ⓕ a-*goo*-kha
needle (syringe) *jeringa* ⓕ khe-*reen*-ga
negative *negativo/a* ⓜ/ⓕ ne-ga-*tee*-vo/a
negatives (photos) *negativos* ⓜ pl
  ne-ga-*tee*-vos
neither *ninguno/a* ⓜ/ⓕ neen-*goo*-no/a
net *red* ⓕ red
Netherlands *Holanda* ⓕ o-*lan*-da
network (phone/Internet) *red* ⓕ red
never *nunca* *noon*-ka
new *nuevo/a* ⓜ/ⓕ *nwe*-vo/a

news *noticias* ⓕ pl no-*tee*-syas
newsagency *agencia de noticias* ⓕ
  a-*khen*-sya de no-*tee*-syas
newspaper *periódico* ⓜ pe-*ryo*-dee-ko
newsstand *venta de periódicos* ⓕ
  ven-ta de pe-*ryo*-dee-kos
New Year's Day *día de Año Nuevo* ⓜ
  dee-a de *a*-nyo *nwe*-vo
New Year's Eve *víspera de Año Nuevo* ⓕ
  vees-pe-ra de *a*-nyo *nwe*-vo
New Zealand *Nueva Zelanda* ⓕ
  nwe-va se-*lan*-da
next (following) *próximo/a* ⓜ/ⓕ
  prok-see-mo/a
next to *junto a khoon*-to a
nice *bueno/a* ⓜ/ⓕ *bwe*-no/a
Nicaragua *Nicaragua* ⓕ nee-ka-*ra*-gwa
nickname *apodo* ⓜ a-*po*-do
night *noche* ⓕ *no*-che
nightclub *club nocturno* ⓜ
  kloob nok-*toor*-no
night out *salida de noche* ⓕ
  sa-*lee*-da de *no*-che
no *no* no
noisy *ruidoso/a* ⓜ/ⓕ rwee-*do*-so/a
none *ninguno/a* ⓜ/ⓕ neen-*goo*-no/a
nonsmoking *no fumado* no foo-*ma*-do
noodles *fideos* ⓜ pl fee-*de*-os
noon *mediodía* ⓜ me-dyo-*dee*-a
north *norte* ⓜ *nor*-te
Norway *Noruega* ⓕ no-*rwe*-ga
nose *nariz* ⓕ na-*rees*
not *no* no
notebook *cuaderno* ⓜ kwa-*der*-no
nothing *nada na*-da
November *noviembre* ⓜ no-*vyem*-bre
now *ahora* a-*o*-ra
nuclear energy *energía nuclear* ⓕ
  e-ner-*khee*-a noo-kle-*ar*
nuclear testing *pruebas nucleares* ⓕ pl
  prwe-bas noo-kle-*a*-res
nuclear waste *desechos nucleares* ⓜ pl
  de-*se*-chos noo-kle-*a*-res
number *número* ⓜ *noo*-me-ro
numberplate *placa* ⓕ *pla*-ka
nun *monja* ⓕ *mon*-kha
nurse *enfermero/a* ⓜ/ⓕ en-fer-*me*-ro/a
nut (food) *nuez* ⓕ nwes

O

oats *avena* ① a·ve·na
ocean *océano* ⓜ o·se·a·no
October *octubre* ⓜ ok·too·bre
off (power) *apagado/a* ⓜ/① a·pa·*ga*·do/a
off (spoilt) *malo/a* ⓜ/① *ma*·lo/a
office *oficina* ① o·fee·*see*·na
office worker *trabajador de oficina* ⓜ
  tra·ba·kha·*dor* de o·fee·*see*·na
often *a menudo* a me·*noo*·do
oil (cooking) *aceite* ⓜ a·*say*·te
oil (petrol) *petróleo* ⓜ pe·tro·le·o
old (age) *viejo/a* ⓜ/① *vye*·kho/a
olive *aceituna* ① a·say·*too*·na
olive oil *aceite de oliva* ⓜ a·*say*·te de o·*lee*·va
Olympic Games *Juegos Olímpicos* ⓜ pl
  khwe·gos o·*leem*·pee·kos
omelette *omelet* ① o·me·*let*
on *sobre* so·bre
on (power) *encendido/a* ⓜ/①
  en·sen·*dee*·do/a
once *una vez* oo·na ves
one *uno/a* ⓜ/① *oo*·no/a
one-way ticket *tiquete de ida* ①
  tee·*ke*·te de *ee*·da
onion *cebolla* ① se·*bo*·ya
only *sólo* so·lo
on time *a tiempo* a *tyem*·po
open *abrir* a·*breer*
open (business) *abierto/a* ⓜ/① a·*byer*·to/a
opening hours *horario* ⓜ o·*ra*·ryo
opera *ópera* ① o·pe·ra
operation (medical) *operación* ①
  o·pe·ra·*syon*
operator (telephone) *operador/operadora*
  ⓜ/① o·pe·ra·*dor*/o·pe·ra·*do*·ra
opinion *opinión* ① o·pee·*nyon*
opposite *opuesto* o·*pwes*·to
optometrist *optometrista* ⓜ&①
  op·to·me·*trees*·ta
or *o* o
orange (colour) *anaranjado/a* ⓜ/①
  a·na·ran·*kha*·do/a
orange (fruit) *naranja* ① na·*ran*·kha
orange juice *jugo de naranja* ⓜ
  khoo·go de na·*ran*·kha
orchestra *orquesta* ① or·*kes*·ta
order (food) *pedido* ⓜ pe·*dee*·do

order *orden* ⓜ or·den
order v *ordenar* or·de·*nar*
ordinary *ordinario/a* ⓜ/① or·dee·*na*·ryo/a
orgasm *orgasmo* ⓜ or·*gas*·mo
original *original* ⓜ&① o·ree·khee·*nal*
other *otro/a* ⓜ/① o·tro/a
our *nuestro/a* ⓜ/① *nwes*·tro/a
out of order *fuera de servicio*
  fwe·ra de ser·*vee*·syo
outside *fuera de* *fwe*·ra de
ovarian cyst *quiste en los ovarios* ⓜ
  kees·te en los o·*va*·ryos
ovary *ovario* ⓜ o·*va*·ryo
oven *horno* ⓜ or·no
overcoat *abrigo* ⓜ a·*bree*·go
overdose *sobredosis* ① so·bre·do·sees
overnight *por a noche* por a *no*·che
overseas *extranjero/a* ⓜ/①
  eks·tran·*khe*·ro/a
owe *deber* de·*ber*
owner *dueño/a* ⓜ/① *dwe*·nyo/a
oxygen *oxígeno* ⓜ ok·*see*·khe·no
oyster *ostra* ① os·tra
ozone layer *capa de ozono* ①
  ka·pa de o·*so*·no

P

pacemaker *marcapasos* ⓜ mar·ka·*pa*·sos
Pacific Ocean *Océano Pacífico* ⓜ
  o·se·a·no pa·*see*·fee·ko
pacifier (dummy) *chupeta* ① choo·*pe*·ta
package *paquete* ⓜ pa·*ke*·te
packet *paquete* ⓜ pa·*ke*·te
padlock *candado* ⓜ kan·*da*·do
page *página* ① *pa*·khee·na
pain *dolor* ⓜ do·*lor*
painful *doloroso/a* ⓜ/① do·lo·ro·so/a
painkiller *pastilla para el dolor* ①
  pas·*tee*·ya pa·ra el do·*lor*
painter *pintor/pintora* ⓜ/①
  peen·*tor*/peen·*to*·ra
painting (artwork) *cuadro* ① *kwa*·dro
painting (technique) *pintura* ① peen·*too*·ra
pair (couple) *pareja* ① pa·*re*·kha
palace *palacio* ① pa·*la*·syo
pan *sartén* ⓜ sar·*ten*
Panama *Panamá* ① pa·na·*ma*

pants (trousers) *pantalones* ⓜ pl
pan·ta·*lo*·nes
pantyhose *pantys* ① pl *pan*·tees
panty liners *protectores* ⓜ pl pro·tek·*to*·res
paper *papel* ⓜ pa·*pel*
paperwork *papeleo* ⓜ pa·pe·*le*·o
pap smear *papanicolau* ① pa·pa·nee·ko·*low*
paraplegic *parapléjico/a* ⓜ/① pa·ra·*ple*·khee·ko/a
parcel *parcela* ① par·*se*·la
parents *papás* ⓜ pl pa·*pas*
park *parque* ⓜ *par*·ke
park (vehicle) *parquear* par·ke·*ar*
parliament *parlamento* ⓜ par·la·*men*·to
parrot *loro/a* ⓜ/① *lo*·ro/a
part (component) *parte* ① *par*·te
part-time *tiempo parcial* ⓜ *tyem*·po par·*syal*
party (night out) *fiesta* ① *fyes*·ta
party (politics) *partido* ⓜ par·*tee*·do
pass *pasar* pa·*sar*
passenger *pasajero/a* ⓜ/① pa·sa·*khe*·ro/a
passionfruit *maracuyá* ① ma·ra·koo·*ya*
passport *pasaporte* ⓜ pa·sa·*por*·te
passport number *número de pasaporte* ⓜ *noo*·me·ro de pa·sa·*por*·te
past *pasado* ⓜ pa·*sa*·do
pasta *pasta* ① *pas*·ta
pastry *pastel* ⓜ pas·*tel*
path *camino* ⓜ ka·*mee*·no
pay *pagar* pa·*gar*
payment *pago* ⓜ *pa*·go
pea *petipoa* ① pe·tee·*po*·a
peace *paz* ① pas
peach *melocotón* ⓜ me·lo·ko·*ton*
peak (mountain) *cima* ① *see*·ma
peanut *maní* ① ma·*nee*
pear *pera* ① *pe*·ra
pedal *pedal* ⓜ pe·*dal*
pedestrian *peatón* ⓜ pe·a·*ton*
pen (ballpoint) *lapicero* ⓜ la·pee·*se*·ro
pencil *lápiz* ⓜ *la*·pees
penis *pene* ⓜ *pe*·ne
penknife *navaja* ① na·*va*·kha
pensioner *pensionado/a* ⓜ/① pen·syo·*na*·do/a
people *gente* ① *khen*·te
pepper (bell) *pimentón* ⓜ pee·men·*ton*
pepper (spice) *pimienta* ① pee·*myen*·ta
per (day) *por (día)* por (*dee*·a)
per cent *porcentaje* ⓜ por·sen·*ta*·khe

perfect *perfecto/a* ⓜ/① per·*fek*·to/a
performance *presentación* ① pre·sen·ta·*syon*
perfume *perfume* ⓜ per·*foo*·me
period pain *dolores menstruales* ⓜ pl do·*lo*·res mens·*trwa*·les
permission *permiso* ⓜ per·*mee*·so
permit *permiso* ⓜ per·*mee*·so
person *persona* ① per·*so*·na
petition *petición* ① pe·tee·*syon*
petrol *gasolina* ① ga·so·*lee*·na
petrol station *bomba* ① *bom*·ba
pharmacist *farmacéutico/a* ⓜ/① far·ma·*se*·oo·tee·ko/a
pharmacy *farmacia* ① far·*ma*·sya
phone book *guía telefónica* ① *gee*·a te·le·*fo*·nee·ka
phone box *casetilla de teléfono* ① ka·se·*tee*·ya de te·*le*·fo·no
phone card *tarjeta de teléfono* ① tar·*khe*·ta de te·*le*·fo·no
photo *foto* ① *fo*·to
photograph v *fotografiar* fo·to·gra·*fyar*
photographer *fotógrafo/a* ⓜ/① fo·*to*·gra·fo/a
photography *fotografía* ① fo·to·gra·*fee*·a
phrasebook *libro de frases* ⓜ *lee*·bro de *fra*·ses
piano *piano* ⓜ pee·*a*·no
pickaxe *pico* ⓜ *pee*·ko
pickles *pepinillos* ⓜ pl pe·pee·*nee*·yos
picnic *picnic* ⓜ *peek*·neek
pie *pastel* ⓜ pas·*tel*
piece *pedazo* ⓜ pe·*da*·so
pig *cerdo* ⓜ • *chancho* *ser*·do • *chan*·cho
pill *pastilla* ① pas·*tee*·ya
the pill *pastilla anticonceptiva* ① pas·*tee*·ya an·tee·kon·sep·*tee*·va
pillow *almohada* ① al·mo·*a*·da
pillowcase *funda* ① *foon*·da
pineapple *piña* ① *pee*·nya
pink *rosado/a* ⓜ/① ro·*sa*·do/a
pistachio *pistacho* ⓜ pees·*ta*·cho
place *lugar* ⓜ loo·*gar*
place of birth *lugar de nacimiento* ⓜ loo·*gar* de na·see·*myen*·to
plane *avión* ⓜ a·*vyon*
planet *planeta* ⓜ pla·*ne*·ta
plant *mata* ① *ma*·ta
plastic *plástico* ⓜ *plas*·tee·ko

plate *plato* ⓜ pla-to
plateau *meseta* ⓕ me-se-ta
platform *plataforma* ⓕ pla-ta-for-ma
play (cards, etc) *jugar* khoo-*gar*
play (instrument) *tocar* to-*kar*
play (theatre) *obra de teatro* ⓕ o-bra de te-a-tro
plug (bath) *tapón* ⓜ ta-pon
plug (electricity) *enchufe* ⓜ en-choo-fe
plum *ciruela* ⓕ see-rwe-la
plumber *plomero* ⓜ plo-me-ro
pocket *bolsillo* ⓜ bol-see-yo
pocketknife *cuchilla* ⓕ koo-chee-ya
poetry *poesía* ⓕ po-e-see-a
point *señalar* se-nya-lar
poisonous *venenoso/a* ⓜ/ⓕ ve-ne-no-so/a
police *policía* ⓕ po-lee-see-a
police officer (city) *policía* ⓜ&ⓕ po-lee-see-a
police officer (country) *guarda rural* ⓜ&ⓕ gwar-da roo-ral
police station *estación de policía* ⓕ es-ta-syon de po-lee-see-a
policy *política* ⓕ po-lee-tee-ka
politician *político* ⓜ po-lee-tee-ko
politics *política* ⓕ po-lee-tee-ka
pollen *polen* ⓜ po-len
pollution *contaminación* ⓕ kon-ta-mee-na-syon
pool (game) *pool* ⓜ pool
pool (swimming) *piscina* ⓕ pee-see-na
poor *pobre* ⓜ&ⓕ po-bre
popular *popular* ⓜ&ⓕ po-poo-lar
pork *cerdo* ⓜ • *chancho* ⓜ ser-do • chan-cho
port (harbour) *puerto* ⓜ pwer-to
positive *positivo/a* ⓜ/ⓕ po-see-tee-vo/a
possible *posible* ⓜ&ⓕ po-see-ble
post *mandar* man-dar
postage *franqueo* ⓜ fran-ke-o
postcard *postal* ⓕ pos-tal
poster *póster* ⓜ pos-ter
postcode *código postal* ⓜ ko-dee-go pos-tal
post office *correo* ⓜ ko-re-o
pot (ceramics) *vasija* ⓕ va-see-kha
pot (cooking) *olla* ⓕ o-ya
potato *papa* ⓕ pa-pa
pottery *alfarería* ⓕ al-fa-re-ree-a
pound (currency/weight) *libra* ⓕ lee-bra
poverty *pobreza* ⓕ po-bre-sa
powder *polvo* ⓜ pol-vo

power *poder* ⓜ po-der
prawn *gamba* ⓕ gam-ba
prayer *oración* ⓕ o-ra-syon
prayer book *libro de oraciones* ⓜ lee-bro de o-ra-syo-nes
prefer *preferir* pre-fe-reer
pregnancy test kit *prueba de embarazo* ⓕ prwe-ba de em-ba-ra-so
pregnant *embarazada* ⓕ em-ba-ra-sa-da
premenstrual tension *tensión premenstrual* ⓕ ten-syon pre-mens-trwal
prepare *preparar* pre-pa-rar
prescription (medical) *receta* ⓕ re-se-ta
present (gift) *regalo* ⓜ re-ga-lo
present (time) *presente* ⓜ pre-sen-te
president *presidente* ⓜ&ⓕ pre-see-den-te
pressure (tyre) *presión* ⓕ pre-syon
pretty *bonito/a* ⓜ/ⓕ bo-nee-to/a
price *precio* ⓜ pre-syo
priest *cura* ⓜ koo-ra
prime minister *primer ministro/primera ministra* ⓜ/ⓕ pree-mer mee-nees-tro/ pree-me-ra mee-nees-tra
printer (computer) *impresora* ⓕ eem-pre-so-ra
prison *cárcel* ⓜ kar-sel
prisoner *reo/a* ⓜ/ⓕ re-o/a
private *privado/a* ⓜ/ⓕ pree-va-do/a
produce *producir* pro-doo-seer
profit *lucrar* loo-krar
program *programa* ⓜ pro-gra-ma
projector *proyector* ⓜ pro-yek-tor
promise *prometer* pro-me-ter
prostitute *prostituto/a* ⓜ/ⓕ pros-tee-too-to/a
protect *proteger* pro-te-kher
protected *protegido/a* ⓜ/ⓕ pro-te-khee-do/a
protest *protesta* ⓕ pro-tes-ta
protest v *protestar* pro-tes-tar
provisions *provisiones* ⓕ pl pro-vee-syo-nes
public gardens *jardines públicos* ⓜ pl khar-dee-nes poo-blee-kos
public phone *teléfono público* ⓜ te-le-fo-no poo-blee-ko
public relations *relaciones públicas* ⓕ pl re-la-syo-nes poo-blee-kas
public toilet *baño público* ⓜ ba-nyo poo-blee-ko
pull *halar* a-lar

pump *bomba* ① bom·ba
pumpkin *calabaza* ① ka·la·ba·sa
puncture v *estallar* es·ta·yar
pure *puro/a* ⊕/① poo·ro/a
purple *morado/a* ⊕/① mo·ra·do/a
purse *cartera* ① kar·te·ra
push *empujar* em·poo·khar
put *poner* po·ner

Q

quadriplegic *cuadrapléjico/a* ⊕/①
 kwa·dra·ple·khee·ko/a
qualifications *cualidades* ① pl
 kwa·lee·da·des
quality *calidad* ① ka·lee·dad
quarantine *cuarentena* ① kwa·ren·te·na
quarter *cuarto* ⊕ kwar·to
queen *reina* ① ray·na
question *pregunta* ① pre·goon·ta
queue *fila* ① fee·la
quick *rápido/a* ⊕/① ra·pee·do/a
quiet *callado/a* ⊕/① ka·ya·do/a
quit *darse por vencido/a* ⊕/①
 dar·se por ven·see·do/a

R

rabbit *conejo* ⊕ ko·ne·kho
rabies *rabia* ① ra·bya
race (sport) *carrera* ① ka·re·ra
racetrack *pista* ① pees·ta
racing bike *bicicleta de carreras* ①
 bee·see·kle·ta de ka·re·ras
racism *racismo* ⊕ ra·sees·mo
racquet *raqueta* ① ra·ke·ta
radiator *radiador* ⊕ ra·dya·dor
radio *radio* ① ra·dyo
radish *rábano* ⊕ ra·ba·no
railway station *estación de tren* ①
 es·ta·syon de tren
rain *lluvia* ① yoo·vya
raincoat *capa* ① ka·pa
rainforest *bosque lluvioso* ⊕
 bos·ke yoo·vyo·so
raisin *pasa* ① pa·sa
rally (protest) *protesta* ① pro·tes·ta
rape *violación* ① vyo·la·syon
rape v *violar* vyo·lar

rare (steak) *poco cocido/a* po·ko ko·see·do/a
rare (uncommon) *raro/a* ⊕/① ra·ro/a
rash *salpullido* sal·poo·yee·do
raspberry *frambuesa* ① fram·bwe·sa
rat *rata* ① ra·ta
rave (party) *rave* ra·ve
raw *crudo/a* ⊕/① kroo·do/a
razor *rasuradora* ① ra·soo·ra·do·ra
razor blade *navajilla* ① na·va·khee·ya
read *leer* le·er
reading *lectura* ① lek·too·ra
ready *listo/a* ⊕/① lees·to/a
real estate agent *agente de bienes raíces* ⊕
 a·khen·te de bye·nes ra·ee·ses
realistic *realista* ⊕&① re·a·lees·ta
rear (location) *atrás* a·tras
reason *razón* ① ra·son
receipt *recibo* ⊕ re·see·bo
recently *recientemente* re·syen·te·men·te
recommend *recomendar* re·ko·men·dar
record *grabar* gra·bar
recording *grabación* ① gra·ba·syon
recyclable *reciclable* ⊕&① re·see·kla·ble
recycle *reciclar* re·see·klar
red *rojo/a* ⊕/① ro·kho/a
red wine *vino tinto* vee·no teen·to
referee *árbitro* ⊕ ar·bee·tro
reference *referencia* ① re·fe·ren·sya
reflexology *reflexología* ①
 re·flek·so·lo·khee·a
refrigerator *refri* ⊕ re·free
refugee *refugiado/a* ⊕/① re·foo·khya·do/a
refund *reintegro* ⊕ re·een·te·gro
refuse *negar* ne·gar
regional *regional* ⊕&① re·khyo·nal
registered mail *correo certificado* ⊕
 ko·re·o ser·tee·fee·ka·do
rehydration salts *sales para rehidratación*
 ① pl sa·les pa·ra re·ee·dra·ta·syon
relationship *relación* ① re·la·syon
relax *relajarse* re·la·khar·se
relic *reliquia* ① re·lee·kya
religion *religión* ① re·lee·khyon
religious *religioso/a* ⊕/① re·lee·khyo·so/a
remote *remoto/a* ⊕/① re·mo·to/a
remote control *control remoto* ⊕
 kon·trol re·mo·to
rent *alquilar* al·kee·lar
repair *reparar* re·pa·rar
republic *república* ① re·poo·blee·ka

reservation (booking) *reservación* ① re·ser·va·syon

rest *descansar* des·kan·sar

restaurant *restaurante* ⑩ re·stow·ran·te

résumé (CV) *currículum* ⑩ koo·ree·koo·loom

retired *retirado/a* ⑩/① re·tee·ra·do/a

return *volver* vol·ver

return ticket *tiquete de ida y vuelta* ⑩ tee·ke·te de ee·da ee vwel·ta

review *revisión* ① re·vee·syon

rhythm *ritmo* ⑩ reet·mo

rib (body) *costilla* ① kos·tee·ya

rice *arroz* ⑩ a·ros

rich *rico/a* ⑩/① ree·ko/a

ride *aventón* a·ven·ton

ride (bike, horse) *andar* an·dar

right (correct) *correcto/a* ⑩/① ko·rek·to/a

right (direction) *derecha* ① de·re·cha

right-wing *derechista* ⑩&① de·re·chees·ta

ring (jewellry) *anillo* ⑩ a·nee·yo

ring (phone) *timbre* ⑩ teem·bre

rip-off *robo* ⑩ ro·bo

risk *riesgo* ⑩ ryes·go

river *río* ⑩ ree·o

road *calle* ① ka·ye

road map *mapa de calles* ⑩ ma·pa de ka·yes

rob *robar* ro·bar

rock (music) *rock* ⑩ rok

rock (stone) *piedra* ① pye·dra

rock climbing *escalada* ① es·ka·la·da

rock group *grupo de rock* ⑩ groo·po de rok

roll (bread) *bollo (de pan)* ⑩ bo·yo (de pan)

rollerblading *patinaje sobre ruedas* ⑩ pa·tee·na·khe so·bre rwe·das

romantic n&a *romántico/a* ⑩/① ro·man·tee·ko/a

room *habitación* ① a·bee·ta·syon

room number *número de habitación* ⑩ noo·me·ro de a·bee·ta·syon

rope *cuerda* ① kwer·da

round (drinks) *ronda* ① ron·da

round (shape) *redondo/a* ⑩/① re·don·do/a

roundabout *rotonda* ① ro·ton·da

route *ruta* ① roo·ta

rowing *remo* ⑩ re·mo

rubbish *basura* ① ba·soo·ra

rubella *rubéola* ① roo·be·o·la

rug *alfombra* ① al·fom·bra

ruins *ruinas* ① pl rwee·nas

rule *regla* ① re·gla

rum *ron* ⑩ ron

run *correr* ko·rer

running *corriendo* ⑩ ko·ryen·do

runny nose *moquera* ① mo·ke·ra

S

S

sad *triste* ⑩&① trees·te

saddle *montura* ① mon·too·ra

safe *seguro/a* ⑩/① se·goo·ro/a

safe (for valuables) *caja fuerte* ① ka·kha fwer·te

safe sex *sexo seguro* ⑩ sek·so se·goo·ro

sailboarding *windsurf* ⑩ weend·soorf

saint *santo/a* ⑩/① san·to/a

salad *ensalada* ① en·sa·la·da

salami *salami* ⑩ sa·la·mee

salary *salario* ⑩ sa·la·ryo

sale *promoción* ① pro·mo·syon

sales assistant *asistente de ventas* ⑩&① a·sees·ten·te de ven·tas

sales tax *impuesto de ventas* ⑩ eem·pwes·to de ven·tas

salmon *salmón* ⑩ sal·mon

salt *sal* ① sal

same *mismo/a* ⑩/① mees·mo/a

sand *arena* ① a·re·na

sandals *chancletas* ① pl chan·kle·tas

sanitary napkin *toalla sanitaria* ① to·a·ya sa·nee·ta·rya

sardine *sardina* ① sar·dee·na

Saturday *sábado* ⑩ sa·ba·do

sauce *salsa* ① sal·sa

saucepan *olla* ① o·ya

sauna *sauna* ① sow·na

sausage *chorizo* ⑩ cho·ree·so

saxophone *saxofón* ⑩ sak·so·fon

say *decir* de·seer

scalp *cuero cabelludo* ⑩ kwe·ro ka·be·yoo·do

scarf *bufanda* ① boo·fan·da

school *escuela* ① es·kwe·la

science *ciencia* ① syen·sya

scientist *científico/a* ⑩/① syen·tee·fee·ko/a

scissors *tijeras* ① pl tee·khe·ras

score *anotar* a·no·tar

scoreboard *marcador* ⑩ mar·ka·dor

Scotland *Escocia* ① es·ko·sya

scrambled (eggs) *revuelto/a* ⓜ/ⓕ re·vwel·to/a

sculpture *escultura* ⓕ es·kool·too·ra

sea *mar* ⓜ mar

seasick *mareado/a* ⓜ/ⓕ ma·re·a·do/a

seaside *costa* ⓕ kos·ta

season *temporada* ⓕ tem·po·ra·da

seat (place) *asiento* ⓜ a·syen·to

seatbelt *cinturón* ⓜ seen·too·ron

second (time unit) *segundo* ⓜ se·goon·do

second (number) *segundo/a* ⓜ/ⓕ se·goon·do/a

second class *segunda clase* ⓕ se·goon·da kla·se

secondhand *usado/a* ⓜ/ⓕ oo·sa·do/a

secondhand shop *tienda de artículos usados* ⓕ tyen·da de ar·tee·koo·los oo·sa·dos

secretary *secretario/a* ⓜ/ⓕ se·kre·ta·ryo/a

see *ver* ver

self-employed *tener su propio negocio* te·ner soo pro·pyo ne·go·syo

selfish *egoísta* ⓜ&ⓕ e·go·ees·ta

self-service ⓜ *auto servicio* ow·to ser·vee·syo

sell *vender* ven·der

send *enviar* en·vyar

sensible *sensible* ⓜ&ⓕ sen·see·ble

sensual *sensual* ⓜ&ⓕ sen·swal

separate *separado/a* ⓜ/ⓕ se·pa·ra·do/a

September *septiembre* ⓜ sep·tyem·bre

serious *serio/a* ⓜ/ⓕ se·ryo/a

service *servicio* ⓜ ser·vee·syo

service charge *servicio* ⓜ ser·vee·syo

service station *bomba* ⓕ bom·ba

serviette *servilleta* ⓕ ser·vee·ye·ta

several *varios/as* ⓜ/ⓕ pl va·ryos/as

sew *coser* ko·ser

sex *sexo* ⓜ sek·so

sexism *sexismo* ⓜ sek·sees·mo

shade *sombra* ⓕ som·bra

shadow *sombra* ⓕ som·bra

shampoo *champú* ⓜ cham·poo

shape *forma* ⓕ for·ma

share (with) *compartir (con)* kom·par·teer (kon)

shave *rasurar* ra·soo·rar

shaving cream *espuma de afeitar* ⓕ es·poo·ma de a·fay·tar

she *ella* e·ya

sheep *oveja* ⓕ o·ve·kha

sheet (bed) *sábana* ⓕ sa·ba·na

shelf *repisa* ⓕ re·pee·sa

shingles (illness) *herpes* ⓜ er·pes

ship *barco* ⓜ bar·ko

shirt *camisa* ⓕ ka·mee·sa

shoe *zapato* ⓜ sa·pa·to

shoelace *cordón de zapato* ⓜ kor·don de sa·pa·to

shoe shop *zapatería* ⓕ sa·pa·te·ree·a

shoot *disparar* dees·pa·rar

shop *tienda* ⓕ tyen·da

shop v *ir de compras* eer de kom·pras

shopping *compras* ⓕ pl kom·pras

shopping centre *centro comercial* ⓜ sen·tro ko·mer·syal

short (height) *bajo/a* ⓜ/ⓕ ba·kho/a

short (length) *corto/a* ⓜ/ⓕ kor·to/a

shortage *escasez* ⓕ es·ka·ses

shorts *chores* ⓜ pl cho·res

shoulder *hombro* ⓜ om·bro

shout *gritar* gree·tar

show *espectáculo* ⓜ es·pek·ta·koo·lo

show v *enseñar* en·se·nyar

shower (bath) *ducha* ⓕ doo·cha

shrine *santuario* ⓜ san·too·a·ryo

shut *cerrado/a* ⓜ/ⓕ se·ra·do/a

shy *tímido/a* ⓜ/ⓕ tee·mee·do/a

sick *enfermo/a* ⓜ/ⓕ en·fer·mo/a

side *lado* ⓜ la·do

sign *señal* ⓕ se·nyal

sign (one's name) v *firmar* feer·mar

signature *firma* ⓕ feer·ma

silk *seda* ⓕ se·da

silver *plata* ⓕ pla·ta

SIM card *tarjeta SIM* ⓕ tar·khe·ta seem

similar *similar* ⓜ&ⓕ see·mee·lar

simple *sencillo/a* ⓜ/ⓕ sen·see·yo/a

since (time) *desde* des·de

sing *cantar* kan·tar

singer *cantante* ⓜ&ⓕ kan·tan·te

single (person) *soltero/a* ⓜ/ⓕ sol·te·ro/a

single room *habitación sencilla* ⓕ a·bee·ta·syon sen·see·ya

sister *hermana* ⓕ er·ma·na

sit *sentarse* sen·tar·se

size (clothes) *talla* ⓕ ta·ya

size (general) *tamaño* ⓜ ta·ma·nyo

skate *patinar* pa·tee·nar

skateboarding *andar en patineta* ⓜ an·dar en pa·tee·ne·ta

ski *esquiar* es·kyar

218

skiing *esquí* ⓜ es·kee
skim milk *leche descremada* ⓕ le·che des·kre·ma·da
skin *piel* ⓕ pyel
skirt *enagua* ⓕ e·na·gwa
skull *cráneo* ⓜ kra·ne·o
sky *cielo* ⓜ sye·lo
sleep *sueño* ⓜ swe·nyo
sleep *dormir* dor·meer
sleeping bag *saco de dormir* ⓜ sa·ko de dor·meer
sleeping berth *litera* ⓕ lee·te·ra
sleeping pills *pastillas para dormir* ⓕ pl pas·tee·yas pa·ra dor·meer
slice *tajada* ⓕ ta·kha·da
slide (film) *diapositivas* ⓕ pl dya·po·see·tee·vas
slow *lento/a* ⓜ/ⓕ len·to/a
slowly *despacio* des·pa·syo
small *pequeño/a* ⓜ/ⓕ pe·ke·nyo/a
smaller *más pequeño/a* ⓜ/ⓕ mas pe·ke·nyo/a
(the) smallest *el/la más pequeño/a* ⓜ/ⓕ el/la mas pe·ke·nyo/a
smell *olor* ⓜ o·lor
smile *sonreír* son·re·eer
smoke (cigarettes) *fumar* foo·mar
snack *merienda* ⓕ me·ryen·da
snail *caracol* ⓜ ka·ra·kol
snake *culebra* ⓕ koo·le·bra
snorkelling *esnorclear* ⓜ es·nor·kle·ar
snow *nieve* ⓕ nye·ve
snowboarding *snowboarding* ⓜ es·no·bor·deen
snow pea *vainica china* ⓕ vai·nee·ka chee·na
soap *jabón* ⓜ kha·bon
soap opera *novela* ⓕ no·ve·la
soccer *fútbol* ⓜ foot·bol
socialist n&a *socialista* ⓜ&ⓕ so·sya·lees·ta
social welfare *bienestar social* ⓜ byen·es·tar so·syal
socks *medias* ⓕ pl me·dyas
soft-boiled (eggs) *tierno/a* ⓜ/ⓕ tyer·no/a
soft drink *refresco* ⓜ re·fres·ko
soldier *soldado* ⓜ sol·da·do
some *algún/alguna* ⓜ/ⓕ al·goon/al·goo·na
someone *alguien* al·gyen
something *algo* al·go
sometimes *a veces* a ve·ses

son *hijo* ⓜ ee·kho
song *canción* ⓕ kan·syon
soon *pronto* ⓜ pron·to
sore *adolorido/a* ⓜ/ⓕ a·do·lo·ree·do/a
soup *sopa* ⓕ so·pa
sour cream *natilla* ⓕ na·tee·ya
south *sur* ⓜ soor
souvenir *recuerdo* ⓜ re·kwer·do
souvenir shop *tienda de recuerdos* ⓕ tyen·da de re·kwer·dos
soy milk *leche de soya* ⓕ le·che de so·ya
soy sauce *salsa de soya* ⓕ sal·sa de so·ya
space (room) *campo* ⓜ kam·po
Spain *España* ⓕ es·pa·nya
Spanish (language) *castellano* • *español* ka·ste·ya·no • es·pa·nyol
sparkling wine *vino espumante* ⓜ vee·no es·poo·man·te
speak *hablar* a·blar
special *especial* ⓜ&ⓕ es·pe·syal
specialist *especialista* ⓜ&ⓕ es·pe·sya·lees·ta
speed (drug) *anfetamina* ⓕ an·fe·ta·mee·na
speed (travel) *velocidad* ⓕ ve·lo·see·dad
speed limit *límite de velocidad* ⓜ lee·mee·te de ve·lo·see·dad
speedometer *velocímetro* ⓜ ve·lo·see·me·tro
spider *araña* ⓕ a·ra·nya
spinach *espinaca* ⓕ es·pee·na·ka
spoilt (food) *podrido/a* ⓜ/ⓕ po·dree·do/a
spoilt (person) *chineado/a* ⓜ/ⓕ chee·ne·a·do/a
spoke (wheel) *radio* ⓜ ra·dyo
spoon *cuchara* ⓕ koo·cha·ra
sport *deporte* ⓜ de·por·te
sportsperson *deportista* ⓜ&ⓕ de·por·tees·ta
sports store *tienda deportiva* ⓕ tyen·da de·por·tee·va
sprain *esguince* ⓜ es·geen·se
spring (coil) *resorte* ⓜ re·sor·te
spring (season) *primavera* ⓕ pree·ma·ve·ra
square (town) *plaza* ⓕ pla·sa
stadium *estadio* ⓜ es·ta·dyo
stairway *escaleras* ⓕ pl es·ka·le·ras
stale *rancio/a* ⓜ/ⓕ ran·syo/a
stamp (postage) *estampilla* ⓕ es·tam·pee·ya
stand-by ticket *tiquete de stand-by* ⓜ tee·ke·te de stan·bai

star *estrella* ① es·tre·ya

(four-)star *(cuatro) estrellas*
(kwa·tro) es·tre·yas

start *inicio* ⓜ ee·nee·syo

start *empezar* em·pe·sar

station *estación* ① es·ta·syon

stationer *librería* ① lee·bre·ree·a

statue *estatua* ① es·ta·twa

stay *quedarse* ke·dar·se

steak (beef) *bistec* ⓜ bee·stek

steal *robar* ro·bar

steep *empinado/a* ⓜ/① em·pee·na·do/a

step *grada* ① gra·da

stereo *equipo de sonido* ⓜ
e·kee·po de so·nee·do

still water *agua sin gas* ① a·gwa seen gas

stockings *calcetines* ① pl kal·se·tee·nes

stolen *robado/a* ⓜ/① ro·ba·do/a

stomach *estómago* ⓜ es·to·ma·go

stomachache *dolor de estómago* ⓜ
do·lor de es·to·ma·go

stone *piedra* ① pye·dra

stoned (drugged) *pijiado/a* ⓜ/①
pee·khya·do/a

stop (bus, tram) *parada* ① pa·ra·da

stop (cease) *parar* pa·rar

stop (prevent) *prevenir* pre·ve·neer

storm *tormenta* ① tor·men·ta

story *cuento* ⓜ kwen·to

stove *cocina* ① ko·see·na

straight *recto/a* ⓜ/① rek·to/a

strange *raro/a* ⓜ/① ra·ro/a

stranger *desconocido/a* ⓜ/①
des·ko·no·see·do/a

strawberry *fresa* ① fre·sa

stream *arrollo* ⓜ a·ro·yo

street *calle* ① ka·ye

street market *mercado callejero* ⓜ
mer·ka·do ka·ye·khe·ro

strike (hit) *golpe* ⓜ gol·pe

strike (stoppage) *huelga* ① wel·ga

string *hilo* ⓜ ee·lo

stroke (health) *derrame* ⓜ de·ra·me

stroller *coche* ⓜ ko·che

strong *fuerte* ⓜ&① fwer·te

stubborn *terco/a* ⓜ/① ter·ko/a

student *estudiante* ⓜ&① es·too·dyan·te

studio *estudio* ⓜ es·too·dyo

stupid *estúpido/a* ⓜ/① es·too·pee·do/a

style *estilo* ⓜ es·tee·lo

subtitles *subtítulos* ⓜ pl soob·tee·too·los

suburb *suburbio* ⓜ soo·boor·byo

sugar *azúcar* ⓜ a·soo·kar

suitcase *maleta* ① ma·le·ta

summer *verano* ⓜ ve·ra·no

sun *sol* ⓜ sol

sunblock *bloqueador* ⓜ blo·ke·a·dor

sunburn *quemadura de sol* ①
ke·ma·doo·ra de sol

Sunday *domingo* ⓜ do·meen·go

sunglasses *anteojos de sol* ⓜ pl
an·te·o·khos de sol

sunny *soleado/a* ⓜ/① so·le·a·do/a

sunrise *amanecer* ⓜ a·ma·ne·ser

sunset *atardecer* ⓜ a·tar·de·ser

sunstroke *insolación* ① een·so·la·syon

supermarket *supermercado* ⓜ
soo·per·mer·ka·do

superstition *superstición* ①
soo·pers·tee·syon

supporter (politics) *partidario/a* ⓜ/①
par·tee·da·ryo/a

supporter (sport) *aficionado/a* ⓜ/①
a·fee·syo·na·do/a

surfing *surf* ⓜ soorf

surf v *surfear* soor·fe·ar

surface mail (land) *correo por tierra* ⓜ
ko·re·o por tye·ra

surface mail (sea) *correo por mar* ⓜ
ko·re·o por mar

surfboard *tabla de surf* ① ta·bla de soorf

surfing *surf* ⓜ soorf

surname *apellido* ⓜ a·pe·yee·do

surprise *sorpresa* ① sor·pre·sa

sweater *suéter* ⓜ swe·ter

Sweden *Suecia* ① swe·sya

sweet *dulce* ⓜ&① dool·se

sweets *dulces* ⓜ pl dool·ses

swelling *hinchazón* ① een·cha·son

swim *nadar* na·dar

swimming *nado* ⓜ na·do

swimming pool *piscina* ① pee·see·na

swimsuit *vestido de baño* ⓜ
ves·tee·do de ba·nyo

Switzerland *Suiza* ① swee·sa

synagogue *sinagoga* ① see·na·go·ga

synthetic *sintético/a* ⓜ/① seen·te·tee·ko/a

syringe *jeringa* ① khe·reen·ga

T

table *mesa* ① me·sa
tablecloth *mantel* ⓜ man·tel
table tennis *tenis de mesa* ⓜ
    te·nees de me·sa
tail *cola* ① ko·la
tailor *sastre* ⓜ sas·tre
take *llevar* ye·var
take a photo *tomar una foto*
    to·mar oo·na fo·to
talk *hablar* a·blar
tall *alto/a* ⓜ/① al·to/a
tampon *tampón* ⓜ tam·pon
tanning lotion *bronceador* ⓜ bron·se·a·dor
tap (sink) *tubo* ⓜ too·bo
tap water *agua de tubo* ① a·gwa de too·bo
tasty *rico/a* ⓜ/① ree·ko/a
tax *impuesto* ⓜ eem·pwes·to
taxi *taxi* ⓜ tak·see
taxi stand *parada de taxis* ①
    pa·ra·da de tak·sees
tea *té* ⓜ te
teacher *maestro/a* ⓜ/① ma·es·tro/a
team *equipo* ⓜ e·kee·po
teaspoon *cucharita* ① koo·cha·ree·ta
technique *técnica* ① tek·nee·ka
teeth *dientes* ⓜ pl dyen·tes
telegram *telegrama* ⓜ te·le·gra·ma
telephone *teléfono* ⓜ te·le·fo·no
telephone *llamar* ya·mar
telephone centre *central telefónica* ①
    sen·tral te·le·fo·nee·ka
telescope *telescopio* ⓜ te·les·ko·pyo
television *televisión* ① te·le·vee·syon
tell *decir* de·seer
temperature (fever) *fiebre* ① fye·bre
temperature (weather) *temperatura* ①
    tem·pe·ra·too·ra
temple (building) *templo* ⓜ tem·plo
tennis *tenis* ⓜ te·nees
tennis court *cancha de tenis* ①
    kan·cha de te·nees
tent *tienda de campaña* ①
    tyen·da de kam·pa·nya
tent peg *clavija* ① kla·vee·kha
terrible *terrible* ⓜ&① te·ree·ble
terrorism *terrorismo* ⓜ te·ro·rees·mo
test *prueba* ① prwe·ba

thank *agradecer* a·gra·de·ser
that *a ese/a* ⓜ/① e·se/a
theatre *teatro* ⓜ te·a·tro
their *su* soo
there *ahí* a·ee
they *ellos/as* ⓜ/① pl e·yos/as
thick *grueso/a* ⓜ/① grwe·so/a
thief *ladrón/ladrona* ⓜ/① la·dron/la·dro·na
thin *delgado/a* ⓜ/① del·ga·do/a
think *pensar* pen·sar
third *tercero/a* ⓜ/① ter·se·ro/a
this *a este/a* ⓜ/① es·te/a
thread *hilo* ⓜ ee·lo
throat *garganta* ① gar·gan·ta
thrush (health) *zorzal* ⓜ sor·sal
thunderstorm *tormenta eléctrica* ①
    tor·men·ta e·lek·tree·ka
Thursday *jueves* ⓜ khwe·ves
ticket *tiquete* ⓜ tee·ke·te
ticket collector *colector de tiquetes* ⓜ
    ko·lek·tor de tee·ke·tes
ticket machine *máquina de tiquetes* ①
    ma·kee·na de tee·ke·tes
ticket office *ventanilla* ① ven·ta·nee·ya
tide *marea* ① ma·re·a
tight *socado/a* ⓜ/① so·ka·do/a
time *tiempo* ⓜ tyem·po
time difference *diferencia de hora* ①
    dee·fe·ren·sya de o·ra
timetable *itinerario* ⓜ ee·tee·ne·ra·ryo
tin (can) *lata* ① la·ta
tin opener *abrelatas* ⓜ a·bre·la·tas
tiny *diminuto/a* ⓜ/① dee·mee·noo·to/a
tip (gratuity) *propina* ① pro·pee·na
tire *llanta* ① yan·ta
tired *cansado/a* ⓜ/① kan·sa·do/a
tissues *klíneks* ⓜ pl klee·neks
to *a* a
toast (food) *tostada* ① tos·ta·da
toaster *tostador* ⓜ tos·ta·dor
tobacco *tabaco* ⓜ ta·ba·ko
tobacconist *tabaquería* ① ta·ba·ke·ree·a
today *hoy* oi
toe *dedo del pie* ⓜ de·do del pye
together *juntos/as* ⓜ/① pl khoon·tos/as
toilet *baño* ⓜ ba·nyo
toilet paper *papel higiénico* ⓜ
    pa·pel pa·khye·nee·ko
tomato *tomate* ⓜ to·ma·te

tomato sauce *salsa de tomate* ①
 sal·sa de to·*ma*·te

tomorrow *mañana* ma·*nya*·na

tonight *esta noche* es·ta *no*·che

too (much) *demasiado* de·ma·*sya*·do

too (also) *también* tam·*byen*

tooth *diente* ⓜ *dyen*·te

toothache *dolor de diente* ⓜ
 do·*lor* de *dyen*·te

toothbrush *cepillo de dientes* ⓜ
 se·*pee*·yo de *dyen*·tes

toothpaste *pasta de dientes* ①
 pas·ta de *dyen*·tes

toothpick *palillo de dientes* ⓜ
 pa·*lee*·yo de *dyen*·tes

torch (flashlight) *foco* ⓜ *fo*·ko

touch *tocar* to·*kar*

tour *tour* ⓜ toor

tourist *turista* ⓜ&① too·*rees*·ta

tourist office *oficina de turismo* ①
 o·fee·*see*·na de too·*rees*·mo

towards *hacia* a·*see*·a

towel *paño* ⓜ *pa*·nyo

tower *torre* ① *to*·re

toxic waste *desecho tóxico* ⓜ
 de·*se*·cho *tok*·see·ko

toy shop *juguetería* ① khoo·ge·te·*ree*·a

track (path) *camino* ⓜ ka·*mee*·no

track (sport) *pista* ① *pees*·ta

trade *comercio* ⓜ ko·*mer*·syo

tradesperson *comerciante* ⓜ&①
 ko·mer·*syan*·te

traffic *tránsito* ⓜ *tran*·see·to

traffic light *semáforo* ⓜ se·*ma*·fo·ro

trail *camino* ⓜ ka·*mee*·no

train *tren* ⓜ tren

train station *estación de tren* ①
 es·ta·*syon* de tren

tram *tranvía* ① tran·*vee*·a

translate *traducir* tra·doo·*seer*

translator *traductor/traductora* ⓜ/①
 tra·dook·*tor*/tra·dook·*to*·ra

transport *transporte* ⓜ trans·*por*·te

travel *viajar* vya·*khar*

travel agency *agencia de viajes* ①
 a·*khen*·sya de *vya*·khes

travellers cheque *cheque de viajero* ⓜ
 che·ke de vya·*khe*·ro

travel sickness *enfermedad del viajero* ①
 en·fer·me·*dad* del vya·*khe*·ro

tree *árbol* ⓜ *ar*·bol

trip (journey) *viaje* ⓜ *vya*·khe

tropical plains *llanuras* ① pl ya·*noo*·ras

trousers *pantalones* ⓜ pl pan·ta·*lo*·nes

truck *camión* ⓜ ka·*myon*

trumpet *trompeta* ① trom·*pe*·ta

trust *confiar* kon·*fyar*

try (attempt) *tratar* tra·*tar*

T-shirt *camiseta* ① ka·mee·*se*·ta

tube (tyre) *neumático* ⓜ ne·oo·*ma*·tee·ko

Tuesday *martes* ⓜ *mar*·tes

tumour *tumor* ⓜ too·*mor*

tuna *atún* ⓜ a·*toon*

tune *melodía* ① me·lo·*dee*·a

turkey *pavo* ⓜ *pa*·vo

turn *dar vuelta* dar *vwel*·ta

TV *televisor* ⓜ te·le·vee·*sor*

tweezers *pinzas* ① pl *peen*·sas

twice *dos veces* dos *ve*·ses

twin beds *camas sencillas* ① pl
 ka·mas sen·*see*·yas

twins *gemelos/as* ⓜ/① pl khe·*me*·los/as

two *dos* dos

type *tipo* ⓜ *tee*·po

typhoid *tifoidea* ① tee·foy·*de*·a

typical *típico/a* ⓜ/① *tee*·pee·ko/a

tyre *llanta* ① *yan*·ta

U

ultrasound *ultrasonido* ⓜ ool·tra·so·*nee*·do

umbrella *sombrilla* ① som·*bree*·ya

uncomfortable *incómodo/a* ⓜ/①
 een·*ko*·mo·do/a

understand *entender* en·ten·*der*

underwear *ropa interior* ① *ro*·pa een·te·*ryor*

unemployed *desempleado/a* ⓜ/①
 de·sem·ple·a·do/a

unfair *injusto/a* ⓜ/① een·*khoos*·to/a

uniform *uniforme* ⓜ oo·nee·*for*·me

universe *universo* ⓜ oo·nee·*ver*·so

university *universidad* ① oo·nee·ver·see·*dad*

unleaded (petrol) *sin plomo* seen *plo*·mo

unsafe *inseguro/a* ⓜ/① een·se·*goo*·ro/a

until *hasta* as·ta

unusual *raro/a* ⓜ/① *ra*·ro/a

up *arriba* a·*ree*·ba

uphill *cuesta arriba* kwes·ta a·*ree*·ba

urgent *urgente* ⓜ&① oor·*khen*·te

222

urinary infection *infección urinaria* ①
een·fek·*syon* oo·ree·*na*·rya
USA *Estados Unidos* ⓜ pl
es·*ta*·dos oo·*nee*·dos
useful *útil* ⓜ&① *oo*·teel

V

vacancy *espacio disponible* ⓜ
es·*pa*·syo dees·po·*nee*·ble
vacant *vacío/a* ⓜ/① va·*see*·o/a
vacation *vacación* ① va·ka·*syon*
vaccination *vacunación* ① va·koo·na·*syon*
vagina *vagina* ① va·*khee*·na
validate *validar* va·lee·*dar*
valley *valle* ⓜ *va*·ye
valuable *valioso/a* ⓜ/① va·*lyo*·so/a
value (price) *valor* ⓜ va·*lor*
van *van* ① van
veal *ternera* ① ter·*ne*·ra
vegetable *vegetal* ⓜ ve·khe·*tal*
vegetarian n&a *vegetariano/a* ⓜ/①
ve·khe·ta·*rya*·no/a
vein *vena* ① *ve*·na
venereal disease *enfermedad venérea* ①
en·fer·me·*dad* ve·*ne*·re·a
venue *lugar* ⓜ loo·*gar*
very *muy* mooy
video camera *cámara de video* ①
ka·ma·ra de vee·*de*·o
video recorder *video* ⓜ vee·*de*·o
video tape *cinta de video* ①
seen·ta de vee·*de*·o
view *vista* ① *vees*·ta
village *pueblo* ⓜ *pwe*·blo
vine *vid* ① veed
vinegar *vinagre* ⓜ vee·*na*·gre
vineyard *viñedo* ⓜ vee·*nye*·do
violin *violín* ⓜ vee·o·*leen*
virus *virus* ⓜ *vee*·roos
visa *visa* ① *vee*·sa
visit *visita* ① vee·*see*·ta
vitamins *vitaminas* ① pl vee·ta·*mee*·nas
visually impaired *discapacitado/a visual*
ⓜ/① dees·ka·pa·see·*ta*·do/a vee·*swal*
voice *voz* ① vos
volcano *volcán* ⓜ vol·*kan*
volleyball *volibol* ⓜ vo·lee·*bol*
volume *volumen* ⓜ vo·loo·*men*
vote *votar* vo·*tar*

W

wage *salario* ⓜ sa·*la*·ryo
wait *esperar* es·pe·*rar*
waiter *mesero/a* ⓜ/① me·*se*·ro/a
waiting room *sala de espera* ①
sa·la de es·*pe*·ra
wake (someone) up *despertar* des·per·*tar*
walk *caminar* ka·mee·*nar*
wall *pared* ① pa·*red*
want *querer* ke·*rer*
war *guerra* ① *ge*·ra
wardrobe *armario* ⓜ ar·*ma*·ryo
warm *caliente* ⓜ&① ka·*lyen*·te
warn *advertir* ad·ver·*teer*
wash (oneself) *lavarse* la·*var*·se
wash (something) *lavar* la·*var*
wash cloth (flannel) *toallita* ① to·a·*yee*·ta
washing machine *lavadora* ① la·va·*do*·ra
wasp *avispa* ① a·*vees*·pa
watch (clock) *reloj* ⓜ re·*lokh*
watch *observar* ob·ser·*var*
water *agua* ① *a*·gwa
water bottle *botella de agua* ①
bo·*te*·ya de *a*·gwa
water bottle (hot) *termo* ⓜ *ter*·mo
waterfall *catarata* ① ka·ta·*ra*·ta
watermelon *sandía* ① san·*dee*·a
waterproof *contra agua* *kon*·tra *a*·gwa
water-skiing *esquí acuático* ⓜ
es·*kee* a·*kwa*·tee·ko
wave (beach) *ola* ① *o*·la
way *camino* ⓜ ka·*mee*·no
we *nosotros/as* ⓜ/① pl no·*so*·tros/as
weak *débil* ⓜ&① *de*·beel
wealthy *rico/a* ⓜ/① *ree*·ko/a
wear *ponerse* po·*ner*·se
weather *tiempo* ⓜ *tyem*·po
wedding *boda* ① *bo*·da
wedding cake *queque de bodas* ⓜ
ke·ke de *bo*·das
wedding present *regalo de bodas* ⓜ
re·*ga*·lo de *bo*·das
Wednesday *miércoles* ⓜ *myer*·ko·les
week *semana* ① se·*ma*·na
weekend *fin de semana* ⓜ feen de se·*ma*·na
weigh *pesar* pe·*sar*
weight *peso* ⓜ *pe*·so
weights *pesas* ① pl *pe*·sas

welcome *dar la bienvenida*
  dar la byen·ve·*nee*·da
welfare *bienestar* ⓜ byen·es·*tar*
well *bien* byen
west *oeste* ⓜ o·es·te
wet *mojado/a* ⓜ/ⓕ mo·*kha*·do/a
what *qué* ke
wheel *rueda* ⓕ *rwe*·da
wheelchair *silla de ruedas* ⓕ
  see·ya de *rwe*·das
when *cuándo* *kwan*·do
where *dónde* *don*·de
which *cuál* kwal
white *blanco/a* ⓜ/ⓕ *blan*·ko/a
white wine *vino blanco* ⓜ *vee*·no *blan*·ko
who *quién* kyen
wholemeal bread *pan integral* ⓜ
  pan een·te·*gral*
why *por qué* por ke
wide *ancho/a* ⓜ/ⓕ *an*·cho/a
wife *esposa* ⓕ es·*po*·sa
wildlife *flora y fauna silvestre* ⓕ
  flo·ra ee *fow*·na seel·*ves*·tre
win *ganar* ga·*nar*
wind *viento* ⓜ *vyen*·to
window *ventana* ⓕ ven·*ta*·na
windscreen *parabrisas* ⓜ pa·ra·*bree*·sas
wine *vino* ⓜ *vee*·no
wings *alas* ⓕ pl *a*·las
winner *ganador/ganadora* ⓜ/ⓕ
  ga·na·*dor*/ga·na·*do*·ra
winter *invierno* ⓜ een·*vyer*·no
wire *alambre* ⓜ a·*lam*·bre
wish *desear* de·se·*ar*
with *con* kon
within (time) *dentro de* *den*·tro de
without *sin* seen
woman *mujer* ⓕ moo·*kher*
wonderful *maravilloso/a* ⓜ/ⓕ
  ma·ra·vee·*yo*·so/a
wood (food) *madera* ⓕ ma·*de*·ra
wool *lana* ⓕ *la*·na
word *palabra* ⓕ pa·*la*·bra
work *trabajo* ⓜ tra·*ba*·kho

work (function) *funcionar* foon·syo·*nar*
work (job) *trabajar* tra·ba·*khar*
work experience *experiencia laboral* ⓕ
  eks·pe·*ryen*·sya la·bo·*ral*
workout *sesión de ejercicios* ⓕ
  se·*syon* de e·kher·*see*·syos
work permit *permiso de trabajo* ⓜ
  per·*mee*·so de tra·*ba*·kho
workshop *taller* ⓜ ta·*yer*
world *mundo* ⓜ *moon*·do
World Cup *Mundial* ⓜ moon·*dyal*
worms (intestinal) *lombrices* ⓕ pl
  lom·*bree*·ses
worried *preocupado/a* ⓜ/ⓕ
  pre·o·koo·*pa*·do/a
worship *adorar* a·do·*rar*
wrist *muñeca* ⓕ moo·*nye*·ka
write *escribir* es·kree·*beer*
writer *autor* ⓜ ow·*tor*
wrong *equivocado/a* ⓜ/ⓕ e·kee·vo·*ka*·do/a

Y

year *año* ⓜ *a*·nyo
yellow *amarillo/a* ⓜ/ⓕ a·ma·*ree*·yo/a
yes *sí* see
yesterday *ayer* a·*yer*
(not) yet *todavía (no)* to·da·*vee*·a (no)
you sg inf *tú • vos* too • vos
you sg pol *usted* oos·*ted*
you pl *ustedes* oos·*te*·des
young *joven* ⓜ&ⓕ *kho*·ven
your sg inf *tu* too
your sg pol&pl *su* su
youth hostel *albergue juvenil* ⓜ
  al·*ber*·ge khoo·ve·*neel*

Z

zip(per) *zipper* ⓜ *see*·per
zodiac *zodíaco* ⓜ so·*dee*·a·ko
zoo *zoológico* ⓜ so·o·*lo*·khee·ko
zoom lens *lente zoom* ⓜ *len*·te soom

The words in this dictionary are listed in Spanish alphabetical order (see the box **spanish alphabet**, page 13). Spanish nouns have their gender indicated with ⓜ (masculine) and ① (feminine). If adjectives and nouns have just one form for both genders, it's marked as ⓜ&①. Where adjectives and nouns have separate masculine and feminine forms, the endings are divided by a slash (eg *bello/a* ⓜ/①). Where the letter *a* is added onto a masculine form to make a feminine form, the added ending is in brackets (eg *director(a)* ⓜ/①). See the **phrasebuilder** for more on gender. Words are also marked as n (noun), a (adjective), adv (adverb), v (verb), pl (plural), sg (singular), inf (informal) and pol (polite) where necessary. Verbs are given in the infinitive – for details on how to change verbs for use in a sentence, see the **phrasebuilder**, page 28.

A

a a *to*
— **bordo** bor·do *aboard*
— **menudo** me·noo·do *often*
— **tiempo** tyem·po *on time*
— **través** tra·ves *across*
— **veces** ve·ses *sometimes*
abajo a·ba·kho *down*
abeja ① a·be·kha *bee*
abierto/a ⓜ/① a·byer·to/a *open (business)*
abogado/a ⓜ/① a·bo·ga·do/a *lawyer*
abordar a·bor·dar *board (plane, ship)*
aborto ⓜ a·bor·to *abortion*
— **natural** na·too·ral *miscarriage*
abrazar a·bra·sar *hug*
abrelatas ⓜ a·bre·la·tas *can opener*
abridor ⓜ a·bree·dor *bottle opener*
abrigo ⓜ a·bree·go *coat*
abril ⓜ a·breel *April*
abrir a·breer *open* v
abuela ① a·bwe·la *grandmother*
abuelo ⓜ a·bwe·lo *grandfather*
aburrido/a ⓜ/① a·boo·ree·do/a *bored • boring*
acampar a·kam·par *camp* v
accidente ⓜ ak·see·den·te *accident*
aceite ⓜ a·say·te *oil (cooking)*
achaques ⓜ pl a·cha·kes *morning sickness*
ácido ⓜ a·see·do *acid*
acondicionador ⓜ a·kon·dee·syo·na·dor *hair conditioner*
acoso ⓜ a·ko·so *harassment*
acostarse a·kos·tar·se *lie (not stand)*
activista ⓜ&① ak·tee·vees·ta *activist*

actualidad ① ak·twa·lee·dad *current affairs*
acupuntura ① a·koo·poon·too·ra *acupuncture*
adaptador ⓜ a·dap·ta·dor *adaptor*
adelante a·de·lan·te *ahead*
adentro a·den·tro *indoor*
adicción ① a·deek·syon *addiction*
adiós a·dyos *goodbye*
adivinar a·dee·vee·nar *guess*
adivino/a ⓜ/① a·dee·vee·no/a *fortune teller*
administración ① ad·mee·nees·tra·syon *administration*
admisión ① ad·mee·syon *admission (price)*
admitir ad·mee·teer *admit*
adolorido/a ⓜ/① a·do·lo·ree·do/a *sore*
adorar a·do·rar *worship* v
aduana ① a·dwa·na *customs (immigration)*
adulto/a ⓜ/① a·dool·to/a *adult* n&a
advertir ad·ver·teer *warn*
aeróbicos ⓜ pl a·e·ro·bee·kos *aerobics*
aerolínea ① a·e·ro·lee·ne·a *airline*
aeropuerto ⓜ a·e·ro·pwer·to *airport*
aficionado/a ⓜ/① a·fee·syo·na·do/a *fan (sport, etc)*
afortunado/a ⓜ/① a·for·too·na·do/a *lucky*
afuera a·fwe·ra *outside*
agencia ① a·khen·sya *agency*
— **de noticias** de no·tee·syas *newsagency*
— **de viajes** de vya·khes *travel agency*
agenda ① a·khen·da *diary*
agente de bienes raíces ⓜ a·khen·te de bye·nes ra·ee·ses *real estate agent*
agosto ⓜ a·gos·to *August*
agradecer a·gra·de·ser *thank*

agradecido/a ⓜ/ⓕ a·gra·de·*see*·do/a
grateful

agricultura ⓕ a·gree·kool·*too*·ra *agriculture*

agua ⓕ *a*·gwa *water*

aguja ⓕ a·*goo*·kha *needle (sewing)*

ahí a·*ee* *there*

ahora a·*o*·ra *now*

aire ⓜ *ai*·re *air*
— **acondicionado** a·kon·de·syo·*na*·do
air conditioning

alas ⓕ pl *a*·las *wings*

albergue juvenil ⓜ al·*ber*·ge khoo·ve·*neel*
youth hostel

alcalde(sa) ⓜ/ⓕ al·*kal*·de/al·kal·de·sa *mayor*

alcohol ⓜ al·*kol alcohol*

alemán a·le·*man* German *(language)*

alergia ⓕ a·*ler*·khee·a *allergy*

alfarería ⓕ al·fa·re·*ree*·a *pottery*

alfombra ⓕ al·*fom*·bra *rug*

algo *al*·go *something*

algodón ⓜ al·go·*don cotton*

alguien *al*·gyen *someone*

algún/alguna ⓜ/ⓕ al·*goon*/al·*goo*·na *some*

almohada ⓕ al·mo·*a*·da *pillow*

almuerzo ⓜ al·*mwer*·so *lunch*

alojamiento ⓜ a·lo·kha·*myen*·to
accommodation

alquilar al·kee·*lar* rent v

alquiler de carros ⓜ al·kee·*ler* de *ka*·ros
car hire

altar ⓜ al·*tar altar*

alto/a ⓜ/ⓕ *al*·to/a *high • tall*

altura ⓕ al·*too*·ra *altitude*

amable ⓜ&ⓕ a·*ma*·ble *kind • nice*

amanecer a·ma·ne·*ser* dawn • *sunrise*

amante ⓜ&ⓕ a·*man*·te *lover*

amar a·*mar* love v

amargo/a ⓜ/ⓕ a·*mar*·go/a *bitter*

amarillo/a ⓜ/ⓕ a·ma·*ree*·yo/a *yellow*

ambos/as ⓜ/ⓕ pl *am*·bos/*am*·bas *both*

ambulancia ⓕ am·boo·*lan*·sya *ambulance*

amigo/a ⓜ/ⓕ a·*mee*·go/a *friend*

amor a·*mor* love

ampolla ⓕ am·*po*·ya *blister*

anaranjado/a ⓜ/ⓕ a·na·ran·*kha*·do/a
orange (colour)

anarquista ⓜ&ⓕ a·nar·*kees*·ta
anarchist n&a

ancho/a ⓜ/ⓕ *an*·cho/a *wide*

andar an·*dar* ride *(bike, horse)*
— **en bicicleta** en bee·see·*kle*·ta *cycle* v
— **en patineta** en pa·tee·*ne*·ta
skateboard v

anemia ⓕ a·*ne*·mya *anaemia*

anillo ⓜ a·*nee*·yo *ring (jewellery)*

animal ⓜ a·nee·*mal animal*

anotar a·no·*tar* score v

anteayer an·te·a·*yer* day before yesterday

anteojos ⓜ pl an·te·o·khos *glasses*
— **de sol** de sol *sunglasses*

anterior ⓜ&ⓕ an·te·*ryor* last *(previous)*

antes *an*·tes *before*

antibióticos ⓜ pl an·tee·byo·*tee*·kos
antibiotics

anticonceptivos ⓜ pl
an·tee·kon·sep·*tee*·vos *contraceptives*

antigüedad ⓕ an·tee·gwe·*dad antique*

antiguo/a ⓜ/ⓕ an·*tee*·gwo/a *ancient*

antiséptico ⓜ an·tee·*sep*·tee·ko *antiseptic*

anuncio ⓜ a·*noon*·syo *advertisement*

año ⓜ *a*·nyo *year*

Año Nuevo ⓜ *a*·nyo *nwe*·vo *New Year*

apagado/a ⓜ/ⓕ a·pa·*ga*·do/a *off (power)*

apartamento ⓜ a·par·ta·*men*·to
apartment • flat

apellido ⓜ a·pe·*yee*·do *surname*

apéndice ⓕ a·*pen*·dee·se *appendix (body)*

aplicadores ⓜ pl a·plee·ka·*do*·res
cotton buds (swabs)

apodo ⓜ a·*po*·do *nickname*

apostar a·pos·*tar* bet v

aprender a·pren·*der* learn

apuesta ⓕ a·*pwes*·ta *bet*

apurado/a ⓜ/ⓕ a·poo·ra·do/a *in a hurry*

aquí a·*kee* here

araña ⓕ a·*ra*·nya *spider*

árbitro ⓜ *ar*·bee·tro *referee*

árbol ⓜ *ar*·bol *tree*

área de acampar ⓕ *a*·re·a de a·kam·*par*
camping ground

arena ⓕ a·*re*·na *sand*

aretes ⓜ pl a·*re*·tes *earrings*

argumentar ar·goo·men·*tar* argue

armario ⓜ ar·*ma*·ryo *cupboard • wardrobe*

aromaterapia ⓕ a·ro·ma·te·*ra*·pya
aromatherapy

arqueológico/a ⓜ/ⓕ ar·ke·o·*lo*·khee·ko/a
archaeological

arquitecto/a ⓜ/ⓕ ar·kee·*tek*·to/a *architect*

arquitectura ⓕ ar·kee·tek·*too*·ra *architecture*

arrestar a·res·*tar* arrest v

arriba a·*ree*·ba *up*

arrollo ⓜ a·*ro*·yo *stream*

arte ⓜ *ar*·te *art*

artesanías ⓕ pl ar·te·sa·*nee*·as *handicraft*

artesano/a ⓜ/ⓕ ar·te·*sa*·no/a
craftsman/woman

artes marciales ⓕ pl *ar*·tes mar·*sya*·les
martial arts

artista ⓜ&ⓕ ar·*tees*·ta *artist*
— **callejero** ka·ye·*khe*·ro *busker*

asa m *a*-sa film speed
ascensor m a-sen-*sor* elevator (lift)
asesinar a-se-see-*nar* murder v
asesinato a-se-see-*na*-to murder
asiento m a-*syen*-to seat (place)
asistente de ventas m&f
a-sees-*ten*-te de ven-tas sales assistant
asma f *as*-ma asthma
aspirina f as-pee-*ree*-na aspirin
ataque al corazón m a-*ta*-ke al ko-ra-*son*
heart attack
atardecer m a-tar-de-*ser* sunset
atletismo m at-le-*tees*-mo athletics
atmósfera f at-*mos*-fe-ra atmosphere
atrás a-*tras* back (position)
atraso m a-*tra*-so delay
audífono m ow-*dee*-fo-no hearing aid
autopista f ow-to-*pees*-ta highway
autor m ow-*tor* writer
auto servicio m ow-to ser-*vee*-syo self-service
avenida f a-ve-*nee*-da avenue
aventón m a-ven-*ton* ride
avergonzado/a m/f a-ver-gon-*sa*-do/a
embarrassed
avión m a-*vyon* airplane
avispa f a-*vees*-pa wasp
ayer a-*yer* yesterday
ayuda f a-*yoo*-da help
ayudar a-yoo-*dar* help v
azúcar m a-*soo*-kar sugar
azul m&f a-*sool* blue

B

bailar bai-*lar* dance v
baile m *bai*-le dance
bajar ba-*khar* get off (bus, train)
bajo/a m/f ba-kho/a low • short (height)
balcón m bal-*kon* balcony
balde m *bal*-de bucket
balomano m ba-lo-*ma*-no handball
banco m *ban*-ko bank
bandera f ban-*de*-ra flag
baño m *ba*-nyo bath • bathroom • toilet
— **público** *poo*-blee-ko public toilet
bar m bar bar • pub
barato/a m/f ba-*ra*-to/a cheap
barbero m bar-*be*-ro barber
barco m *bar*-ko boat • ship
barra f *ba*-ra counter (at bar)
barro m *ba*-ro mud
básquetbol m *bas*-ket-bol basketball
basura f ba-*soo*-ra garbage
basurero m ba-soo-*re*-ro garbage can

batería f ba-te-*ree*-a battery • drums (kit)
bautismo m bow-*tees*-mo baptism
bebé m&f be-*be* baby
bebida f be-*bee*-da drink
béisbol m *bays*-bol baseball
bello/a m/f *be*-yo/a beautiful
besar be-*sar* kiss v
beso m *be*-so kiss
biblioteca f bee-blee-o-*te*-ka library
bibliotecario/a f bee-blee-o-te-*ka*-ryo/a
librarian
bicho m *bee*-cho bug
bicicleta f bee-see-*kle*-ta bicycle
— **de carreras** de ka-*re*-ras racing bike
— **montañera** mon-ta-*nye*-ra
mountain bike
bien byen fine • well
bienestar m byen-es-*tar* welfare
— **social** so-*syal* social welfare
billete de banco m bee-*ye*-te de *ban*-ko
banknote
binoculares m pl bee-no-koo-*la*-res
binoculars
blanco y negro *blan*-ko ee *ne*-gro
B&W (film) a
blanco/a m/f *blan*-ko/a white
bloqueado/a m/f blo-ke-*a*-do/a blocked
bloqueador m blo-ke-a-*dor* sunblock
boca f *bo*-ka mouth
boda f *bo*-da wedding
bola f *bo*-la ball (sport)
bolitas de algodón f pl
bo-*lee*-tas de al-go-*don* cotton balls
bollo de pan m *bo*-yo de pan bread roll
bolsa f *bol*-sa bag
bolsillo m bol-*see*-yo pocket
bolso m *bol*-so handbag
bomba f *bom*-ba gas station • petrol station
bombillo m bom-*bee*-yo light bulb
bonito/a m/f bo-*nee*-to/a pretty
borde m *bor*-de ledge
borracho/a m/f bo-*ra*-cho/a drunk
bosque m *bos*-ke forest
— **lluvioso** yoo-*vyo*-so rainforest
— **nuboso** noo-*bo*-so cloud forest
botas f pl *bo*-tas boots
— **para caminata** *pa*-ra ka-mee-*na*-ta
hiking boots
botella f bo-*te*-ya bottle
— **de agua** de *a*-gwa water bottle
botón m bo-*ton* button
boxeo m bok-*se*-o boxing
bóxer m *bok*-ser boxer shorts
bracier m bra-*syer* bra
brazo m *bra*-so arm (body)

brillo ⓜ *bree*-yo *lip balm*
bronceador ⓜ bron-se-a-*dor* *tanning lotion*
bronquitis ⓕ bron-*kee*-tees *bronchitis*
brújula ⓕ *broo*-khoo-la *compass*
buceo ⓜ boo-*se*-o *diving*
budista ⓜ&ⓕ boo-*dees*-ta *Buddhist* n&a
bueno/a ⓜ/ⓕ *bwe*-no/a *good • nice*
bufanda ⓕ boo-*fan*-da *scarf*
bulto ⓜ *bool*-to *lump*
bus ⓜ boos *bus • coach*
buscar boos-*kar* *look for*
buzón ⓜ boo-*son* *mailbox*

C

caballo ⓜ ka-*ba*-yo *horse*
cabeza ⓕ ka-*be*-sa *head*
cabra ⓕ *ka*-bra *goat*
cacao ⓜ ka-*kow* *cocoa*
cada ⓜ&ⓕ *ka*-da *each*
cadena ⓕ ka-*de*-na *chain • necklace*
— de bicicleta de bee-see-*kle*-ta *bike chain*
caer ka-*er* *fall* v
café ⓜ ka-*fe* *café • coffee • brown*
— internet een-ter-*net* *Internet café*
caja ⓕ *ka*-kha *box • cash register*
— de cambios de *kam*-byos *gearbox*
— fuerte *fwer*-te *safe (for valuables)*
cajero/a ⓜ/ⓕ ka-*khe*-ro/a *cashier*
cajero automático ⓜ
ka-*khe*-ro ow-to-ma-*tee*-ko *ATM*
calcetines ⓜ pl kal-se-*tee*-nes *stockings*
calculadora ⓕ kal-koo-la-*do*-ra *calculator*
calendario ⓜ ka-len-*da*-ryo *calendar*
calentado/a ⓜ/ⓕ ka-len-*ta*-do/a *heated*
calentador ⓜ ka-len-ta-*dor* *heater*
calentamiento ⓜ ka-len-ta-*myen*-to
heating
calidad ⓕ ka-lee-*dad* *quality*
caliente ⓜ&ⓕ ka-*lyen*-te *hot*
callado/a ⓜ/ⓕ ka-*ya*-do/a *quiet*
calle ⓕ *ka*-ye *road • street*
— principal preen-se-*pal* *main road*
calor ⓜ ka-*lor* *heat*
cama ⓕ *ka*-ma *bed*
— matrimonial ma-tree-mo-*nyal*
double bed
cámara ⓕ *ka*-ma-ra *camera*
— de video de ve-*de*-o *video camera*
camas sencillas ⓕ pl *ka*-mas sen-*see*-yas
twin beds
cambiar kam-*byar* *exchange (money)*
— un cheque oon *che*-ke *cash a cheque*
cambio ⓜ *kam*-byo *change • exchange*

— de moneda de mo-*ne*-da
currency exchange
caminar ka-mee-*nar* *hike • walk*
caminata ⓕ ka-mee-*na*-ta *hiking*
camino ⓜ ka-*mee*-no *path • track • trail*
— de montaña de mon-*ta*-nya
mountain path
camión ⓜ ka-*myon* *truck*
— de todo-terreno de to-do-te-*re*-no
all-terrain vehicle
camisa ⓕ ka-*mee*-sa *shirt*
camiseta ⓕ ka-mee-*se*-ta *T-shirt*
campeonatos ⓜ pl kam-pe-o-*na*-tos
championships
campo ⓜ *kam*-po *countryside • space (room)*
— de golf de golf *golf course*
canasta ⓕ ka-*nas*-ta *basket*
cancelar kan-se-*lar* *cancel*
cáncer ⓜ *kan*-ser *cancer*
cancha de tenis ⓕ *kan*-cha de te-*nees*
tennis court
canción ⓕ kan-*syon* *song*
candado ⓜ kan-*da*-do *lock • padlock*
— de bicicleta de bee-see-*kle*-ta *bike lock*
canoa ⓕ ka-*no*-a *canoe*
cansado/a ⓜ/ⓕ kan-*sa*-do/a *tired*
cantante ⓜ&ⓕ kan-*tan*-te *singer*
cantar kan-*tar* *sing*
capa ⓕ *ka*-pa *raincoat*
— de ozono de o-*so*-no *ozone layer*
cara ⓕ *ka*-ra *face*
caracol ⓜ ka-ra-*kol* *snail*
caravana ⓕ ka-ra-*va*-na *caravan*
cárcel ⓕ *kar*-sel *jail*
carne ⓕ *kar*-ne *meat*
carnicería ⓕ kar-nee-se-*ree*-a *butcher's shop*
carnicero ⓜ kar-nee-*se*-ro *butcher*
caro/a ⓜ/ⓕ *ka*-ro/a *expensive*
carpintero ⓜ kar-peen-*te*-ro *carpenter*
carrera ⓕ ka-*re*-ra *race (sport)*
carreras de caballo ⓕ pl
ka-*re*-ras de ka-*ba*-yo *horse racing*
carro ⓜ *ka*-ro *car*
carta ⓕ *kar*-ta *letter (mail)*
cartera ⓕ kar-*te*-ra *purse*
cartón ⓜ kar-*ton* *carton*
casa ⓕ *ka*-sa *house*
casado/a ⓜ/ⓕ ka-*sa*-do/a *married*
casarse ka-*sar*-se *marry*
casco ⓜ *kas*-ko *helmet*
casetilla de teléfono ⓕ
ka-se-*tee*-ya de te-*le*-fo-no *phone box*
casi ka-*see* *almost*
castellano kas-te-*ya*-no *Spanish (language)*
castillo ⓜ kas-*tee*-yo *castle*

catarata ① ka-ta-*ra*-ta *waterfall*
catedral ① ka-te-*dral* *cathedral*
católico/a ⓜ/① ka-to-lee-ko/a *Catholic* n&a
caza ① *ka*-sa *hunting*
cédula de identificación ① *se*-doo-la de ee-den-tee-fee-ka-*syon* *identification card*
celebración ① se-le-bra-*syon* *celebration*
celoso/a ⓜ/① se-*lo*-so/a *jealous*
cementerio ⓜ se-men-*te*-ryo *cemetery*
cena ① *se*-na *dinner*
cenicero ⓜ se-nee-*se*-ro *ashtray*
centavo ⓜ sen-*ta*-vo *cent*
centímetro ⓜ sen-*tee*-me-tro *centimetre*
central telefónica ① sen-*tral* te-le-fo-*nee*-ka *telephone centre*
centro ⓜ *sen*-tro *centre*
 — comercial ko-mer-*syal* *shopping centre*
 — de la ciudad de la syoo-*dad* *city centre*
cepillo ⓜ se-*pee*-yo *brush • hairbrush*
 — de dientes de *dyen*-tes *toothbrush*
cerámica ① se-*ra*-mee-ka *ceramics*
cerca ① *ser*-ka *fence*
cerca *ser*-ka *close • nearby*
cerdo ⓜ *ser*-do *pig • pork*
cerrado/a ⓜ/① se-*ra*-do/a *closed • shut*
 — con llave kon *ya*-ve *locked*
cerrar se-*rar* *close* v
 — con llave kon *ya*-ve *lock* v
certificado ⓜ ser-tee-fee-*ka*-do *certificate*
 — de nacimiento de na-see-*myen*-to *birth certificate*
cerveza ① ser-*ve*-sa *beer*
chaleco salvavidas ⓜ cha-*le*-ko sal-va-vee-das *life jacket*
champaña ① cham-*pa*-nya *champagne*
champú ⓜ cham-*poo* *shampoo*
chancho ⓜ *chan*-cho *pig • pork*
chancletas ① pl chan-*kle*-tas *sandals*
cheque ⓜ *che*-ke *check (banking) • cheque*
 — de viajero de vya-*khe*-ro *travellers cheque*
chequeo ⓜ *che*-ke-o *check-in (desk)*
chicle ⓜ *chee*-kle *chewing gum*
chica ① *chee*-ka *girl*
chico ⓜ *chee*-ko *boy*
chile ⓜ *chee*-le *chilli*
chineado/a ⓜ/① chee-ne-*a*-do/a *spoilt (person)*
chiquito/a ⓜ/① chee-*kee*-to/a *child*
chiste ⓜ *chees*-te *joke*
chivo ⓜ *chee*-vo *gig*
choque ⓜ *cho*-ke *crash*
chores ⓜ pl *cho*-res *shorts*
chupeta ① choo-*pe*-ta *dummy • pacifier*
ciclismo ⓜ see-*klees*-mo *cycling*

ciclista ⓜ&① see-*klees*-ta *cyclist*
ciclo ⓜ *see*-klo *bike shop*
ciego/a ⓜ/① *sye*-go/a *blind*
cielo ⓜ *sye*-lo *sky*
cien ⓜ syen *hundred*
ciencia ① *syen*-sya *science*
científico/a ⓜ/① syen-*tee*-fee-ko/a *scientist*
cigarrillo ⓜ see-ga-*ree*-yo *cigarette*
cigarro ⓜ see-*ga*-ro *cigar*
cilindro de gas ⓜ see-*leen*-dro de gas *gas cartridge*
cima ① *see*-ma *mountain peak*
cine ⓜ *see*-ne *cinema*
cinta de video ① *seen*-ta de vee-*de*-o *video tape*
cinturón ⓜ seen-too-*ron* *seatbelt*
circo ⓜ *seer*-ko *circus*
cistitis ① sees-*tee*-tees *cystitis*
cita ① *see*-ta *appointment*
ciudad ① syoo-*dad* *city*
ciudadanía ① syoo-da-da-*nee*-a *citizenship*
clarinete ⓜ kla-ree-*ne*-te *clarinet*
claro/a ⓜ/① *kla*-ro/a *light (colour)*
clase ① *kla*-se *class (category)*
 — económica e-ko-*no*-mee-ka *economy class*
 — ejecutiva e-khe-koo-*tee*-va *business class*
clásico/a ⓜ/① *kla*-see-ko/a *classical*
clavija ① kla-*vee*-kha *tent peg*
cliente ⓜ&① klee-*en*-te *client*
closh ⓜ klosh *clutch (car)*
club nocturno ⓜ kloob nok-*toor*-no *nightclub*
cobija ① ko-*bee*-kha *blanket*
cocaína ① ko-ka-*ee*-na *cocaine*
coche ⓜ *ko*-che *stroller*
cocina ① ko-*see*-na *cooking • kitchen • stove*
cocinar ko-see-*nar* *cook* v
cocinero/a ⓜ/① ko-see-*ne*-ro/a *cook*
coco ⓜ *ko*-ko *coconut*
coctel ⓜ kok-*tel* *cocktail*
código postal ⓜ *ko*-dee-go pos-*tal* *postcode*
cola ① *ko*-la *tail*
colchón ⓜ kol-*chon* *mattress*
colchoneta ① kol-cho-*ne*-ta *mat*
colector de tiquetes ⓜ ko-lek-*tor* de tee-*ke*-tes *ticket collector*
colega ⓜ&① ko-*le*-ga *colleague*
colegio ⓜ ko-*le*-khyo *high school*
color ⓜ ko-*lor* *colour*
comedia ① ko-*me*-dya *comedy*
comer ko-*mer* *eat*

comerciante ⓜ&ⓕ ko·mer·*syan*·te *tradesperson*

comercio ⓜ ko·*mer*·syo *trade*

comida ⓕ ko·*mee*·da *food • meal*
— **de bebé** de be·*be* *baby food*

cómo *ko*·mo *how*

cómodo/a ⓜ/ⓕ *ko*·mo·do/a *comfortable*

compañero/a ⓜ/ⓕ kom·pa·*nye*·ro/a *companion*

compañía ⓕ kom·pa·*nyee*·a *company (firm)*

compartir kom·*par*·teer *share* v

comprar kom·*prar* *buy*

compras ⓕ pl kom·pras *shopping*

comprometido/a ⓜ/ⓕ kom·pro·me·*tee*·do/a *engaged (to marry)*

compromiso ⓜ kom·pro·*mee*·so *engagement (to marry)*

computadora ⓕ kom·poo·ta·*do*·ra *computer*

comunicación ⓕ ko·moo·nee·ka·*syon* *communications (profession)*

comunión ⓕ ko·moo·*nyon* *communion*

comunista ⓜ&ⓕ ko·moo·*nees*·ta *communist* n&a

con kon *with*
— **aire acondicionado** *ai*·re a·kon·dee·syo·*na*·do *air-conditioned*

concierto ⓜ kon·*syer*·to *concert*

condición cardíaca ⓕ kon·dee·*syon* kar·dee·a·ka *heart condition*

conducir kon·doo·*seer* *drive* v

conejo ⓜ ko·*ne*·kho *rabbit*

conexión ⓕ ko·nek·*syon* *connection*

conferencia ⓕ kon·fe·*ren*·sya *conference (small)*

confesión ⓕ kon·fe·*syon* *confession (religious)*

confiar kon·*fyar* *trust* v

confirmar kon·feer·*mar* *confirm (a booking)*

confite ⓜ kon·*fee*·te *candy*

congelado/a ⓜ/ⓕ kon·khe·*la*·do/a *frozen*

congelar kon·khe·*lar* *freeze*

congreso ⓜ kon·*gre*·so *conference (big)*

conmoción ⓕ kon·mo·*syon* *commission*

conocer ko·no·*ser* *know (someone)*

conocerse ko·no·*ser*·se *meet (first time)*

consejo ⓜ kon·*se*·kho *advice*

conservador(a) ⓜ/ⓕ kon·ser·va·*dor*/kon·ser·va·*do*·ra *conservative* n&a

consigna ⓕ kon·*seeg*·na *left-luggage office*

constructor(a) ⓜ/ⓕ kons·trook·*tor*/kons·trook·*to*·ra *builder*

construir kons·troo·*eer* *build*

consulado ⓜ kon·soo·*la*·do *consulate*

contaminación ⓕ kon·ta·mee·na·*syon* *pollution*

contar kon·*tar* *count* v

contra agua *kon*·tra a·*gwa* *waterproof*

contratar kon·tra·*tar* *hire • rent* v

contrato ⓜ kon·*tra*·to *contract*

control remoto ⓜ kon·*trol* re·*mo*·to *remote control*

contusión ⓕ kon·too·*syon* *concussion*

convento ⓜ kon·*ven*·to *convent*

corazón ⓜ ko·ra·*son* *heart*

cordillera ⓕ kor·dee·*ye*·ra *mountain range*

cordón de zapato ⓜ kor·*don* de sa·*pa*·to *shoelace*

correcto/a ⓜ/ⓕ ko·*rek*·to/a *right (correct)*

correo ⓜ ko·*re*·o *mail • post office*

correr ko·*rer* *run* v

corriendo ko·*ryen*·do *running*

corriente ⓕ ko·*ryen*·te *current (electricity)*

corrupción ⓕ ko·roop·*syon* *corruption*

corrupto/a ⓜ/ⓕ ko·*roop*·to/a *corrupt*

cortada ⓕ kor·*ta*·da *cut*

cortar kor·*tar* *cut* v

cortauñas ⓜ kor·ta·oo·*nyas* *nail clippers*

corte ⓕ *kor*·te *court (legal)*

corte de pelo ⓜ *kor*·te de *pe*·lo *haircut*

coser ko·*ser* *sew*

costa ⓕ *kos*·ta *coast*

costar kos·*tar* *cost* v

costilla ⓕ kos·*tee*·ya *rib (body)*

costumbre ⓕ kos·*toom*·bre *custom*

cráneo ⓜ *kra*·ne·o *skull*

crecer kre·*ser* *grow*

crédito ⓜ *kre*·dee·to *credit*

crema ⓕ *kre*·ma *cream (food/lotion)*

cricket ⓜ *kree*·ket *cricket (sport)*

cristiano/a ⓜ/ⓕ krees·*tya*·no/a *Christian* n&a

crudo/a ⓜ/ⓕ *kroo*·do/a *raw*

cruz ⓕ kroos *cross (religious)*

cuaderno ⓜ kwa·*der*·no *notebook*

cuadrapléjico/a ⓜ/ⓕ kwa·dra·*ple*·khee·ko/a *quadriplegic*

cuál kwal *which*

cualidades ⓕ pl kwa·lee·*da*·des *qualifications*

cualquier(a) ⓜ/ⓕ kwal·*kyer*/kwal·*kye*·ra *any*

cuándo *kwan*·do *when*

cuánto *kwan*·to *how much*

cuarentena ⓕ kwa·ren·*te*·na *quarantine*

cuarto ⓜ *kwar*·to *bedroom • quarter*
— **doble** *do*·ble *double room*

cubiertos ⓜ pl koo·*byer*·tos *cutlery*

cucaracha ⓕ koo·ka·*ra*·cha *cockroach*

cuchara ⓕ koo·*cha*·ra *spoon*

cucharita ① koo-cha-*ree*-ta *teaspoon*
cuchilla ① koo-*chee*-ya *pocketknife*
cuchillo ⓜ koo-*chee*-yo *knife*
cuello ⓜ *kwe*-yo *neck*
cuenta ① *kwen*-ta *account • bill • cheque*
— **bancaria** ban-*ka*-rya *bank account*
cuento ⓜ *kwen*-to *story*
cuerda ① *kwer*-da *rope*
cuero ⓜ *kwe*-ro *leather*
— **cabelludo** ka-be-yoo-*do scalp*
cuerpo ⓜ *kwer*-po *body*
cuesta abajo *kwes*-ta a-*ba*-kho *downhill*
cuesta arriba *kwes*-ta a-*ree*-ba *uphill*
cueva ① *kwe*-va *cave*
cuidar de kwee-*dar* de *look after*
culebra ① koo-*le*-bra *snake*
culpa ① *kool*-pa *(someone's) fault*
culpable ⓜ&① kool-*pa*-ble *guilty*
cumpleaños ⓜ koom-ple-*a*-nyos *birthday*
cuna ① *koo*-na *crèche • child-minding centre*
cupón ⓜ koo-*pon coupon*
cura ⓜ *koo*-ra *priest*
curita ① koo-*ree*-ta *Band-Aid*
currículum ⓜ koo-*ree*-koo-loom *CV • résumé*

D

dar dar *give*
— **de comer** de ko-*mer feed* v
— **la bienvenida** la byen-ve-*nee*-da
welcome v
— **vuelta** *vwel*-ta *turn* v
de de *from*
debajo de de-*ba*-kho *below*
deber de-*ber owe*
débil ⓜ&① *de*-beel *weak*
decidir de-see-*deer decide*
decir de-*seer say • tell*
dedo ⓜ *de*-do *finger*
— **del pie** del pye *toe*
defectuoso/a ⓜ/① de-fek-*two*-so/a *faulty*
deforestación ① de-fo-res-ta-*syon*
deforestation
delgado/a ⓜ/① del-*ga*-do/a *thin*
demasiado de-ma-*sya*-do *too (much)*
democracia ① de-mo-*kra*-sya *democracy*
demostración ① de-mos-tra-*syon*
demonstration (display)
dentista ⓜ&① den-*tees*-ta *dentist*
dentro *den*-tro *inside*
— **de** within *(time)*
deporte ⓜ de-*por*-te *sport*
deportista ⓜ&① de-por-*tees*-ta
sportsperson
depósito ⓜ de-*po*-see-to *deposit (bank)*

derecha ① de-*re*-cha *right (direction)*
derechista ⓜ&① de-re-*chees*-ta *right-wing*
derecho ⓜ de-*re*-cho *law (profession)*
derechos civiles ⓜ pl
de-*re*-chos see-*vee*-les *civil rights*
derechos humanos ⓜ pl
de-*re*-chos oo-*ma*-nos *human rights*
derrame ① de-*ra*-me *stroke (health)*
descansar des-kan-*sar rest* v
descendiente ⓜ de-sen-*dyen*-te *descendent*
descompuesto/a ⓜ/① des-kom-*pwes*-to/a
broken down (car, etc)
desconocido/a ⓜ/① des-ko-no-*see*-do/a
stranger
descuento ⓜ des-*kwen*-to *discount*
desde *des*-de *from • since*
desear de-se-*ar wish* v
desechos nucleares ⓜ pl
de-*se*-chos noo-kle-*a*-res *nuclear waste*
desecho tóxico ⓜ de-*se*-cho *tok*-see-ko
toxic waste
desempleado/a ⓜ/① de-sem-ple-*a*-do/a
unemployed
desfase de horario ⓜ des-*fa*-se de o-*ra*-ryo
jet lag
desierto ⓜ de-*syer*-to *desert*
desodorante ⓜ de-so-do-*ran*-te *deodorant*
despacio des-*pa*-syo *slowly*
despertar des-per-*tar* wake (someone) up
después des-*pwes* after
destino ⓜ des-*tee*-no *destination*
detallado/a ⓜ/① de-ta-*ya*-do/a *itemised*
detalles ⓜ pl de-*ta*-yes *details*
detrás de-*tras* behind
día ⓜ *dee*-a *day*
diabetes ① dee-a-*be*-tes *diabetes*
diafragma ⓜ dya-*frag*-ma
diaphragm (contraceptive)
diapositivas ① pl dya-po-see-*tee*-vas
slide (film)
diarrea ① dee-a-*re*-a *diarrhoea*
diccionario ⓜ deek-syo-*na*-ryo *dictionary*
diciembre ⓜ dee-*syem*-bre *December*
diente ⓜ *dyen*-te *tooth*
dientes ⓜ pl *dyen*-tes *teeth*
dieta ① *dye*-ta *diet*
diferencia de hora ① dee-fe-*ren*-sya de o-ra
time difference
diferente ⓜ&① dee-fe-*ren*-te *different*
difícil ⓜ&① dee-*fee*-seel *difficult*
digital ⓜ&① dee-khee-*tal digital*
diminuto/a ⓜ/① dee-mee-*noo*-to/a *tiny*
dinero ⓜ dee-*ne*-ro *money*
dios ⓜ *dee*-os *god*

dirección ① dee-rek-syon *address • direction*

directo/a ⑩/① dee-rek-to/a *direct • express*

director(a) ⑩/① dee-rek-tor/dee-rek-to-ra *director • manager (sport)*

discapacitado/a ⑩/① dees-ka-pa-see-ta-do/a *disabled*
— **visual** vee-swal *visually impaired*

discriminación ① dees-kree-mee-na-syon *discrimination*

diseño ⑩ dee-se-nyo *design*

disfrutar dees-froo-tar *enjoy (oneself)*

disparar dees-pa-rar *shoot* v

disponible ⑩&① dees-po-nee-ble *free (available)*

disquete ⑩ dees-ke-te *disk (floppy)*

DIU ⑩ de ee oo *IUD*

divertido/a ⑩/① dee-ver-tee-do/a *fun*

divertirse dee-ver-teer-se *have fun*

divorciado/a ⑩/① dee-vor-sya-do/a *divorced*

doble ⑩&① do-ble *double*

docena ① do-se-na *dozen*

doctor(a) ⑩/① dok-tor/dok-to-ra *doctor*

documental ⑩ do-koo-men-tal *documentary*

dólar ⑩ do-lar *dollar*

doler do-ler *hurt (be painful)*

dolor ⑩ do-lor *pain*
— **de cabeza** de ka-be-sa *headache*
— **de diente** de dyen-te *toothache*
— **de estómago** de es-to-ma-go *stomachache*

dolores menstruales ⑩ pl do-lo-res mens-trwa-les *period pain*

doloroso/a ⑩/① do-lo-ro-so/a *painful*

domingo ⑩ do-meen-go *Sunday*

dónde don-de *where*

dormir dor-meer *sleep* v

dos dos *two*
— **veces** ve-ses *twice*

drama ⑩ dra-ma *drama*

droga ① dro-ga *drug (illicit)*

drogadicción ① dro-ga-deek-syon *drug addiction*

drogadicto/a ⑩/① dro-ga-deek-to/a *drug user*

ducha ① doo-cha *shower (bath)*

dueño/a ⑩/① dwe-nyo/a *landlord/lady • owner*

dulce ⑩&① dool-se *sweet* a

dulces ⑩ pl dool-ses *sweets* n

duro/a ⑩/① doo-ro/a *hard (not soft) • hard-boiled (egg) • loud*

E

eczema ① ek-se-ma *eczema*

edad ① e-dad *age*

edificio ⑩ e-dee-fee-syo *building*

educación ① e-doo-ka-syon *education*

efectivo ⑩ e-fek-tee-vo *cash*

egoísta ⑩&① e-go-ees-ta *selfish*

ejemplo ⑩ e-khem-plo *example*

ejército ⑩ e-kher-see-to *military*

él el *he • him*

elección ① e-lek-syon *election*

electricidad ① e-lek-tree-see-dad *electricity*

electricista ⑩&① e-lek-tree-sees-ta *electrician*

ella e-ya *her • she*

ellos/as ⑩/① pl e-yos/as *them • they*

embajada ① em-ba-kha-da *embassy*

embajador(a) ⑩/① em-ba-kha-dor/ em-ba-kha-do-ra *ambassador*

embarazada ① em-ba-ra-sa-da *pregnant*

emergencia ① e-mer-khen-sya *emergency*

emocional ⑩&① e-mo-syo-nal *emotional*

empezar em-pe-sar *start* v

empinado/a ⑩/① em-pee-na-do/a *steep*

empleado/a ⑩/① em-ple-a-do/a *employee*

empleador(a) ⑩/① em-ple-a-dor/em-ple-a-do-ra *employer*

empujar em-poo-khar *push* v

en at • in
— **frente de** fren-te de *in front of • opposite*

enagua ① en-a-gwa *skirt*

encantador(a) ⑩/① en-kan-ta-dor/en-kan-ta-do-ra *charming*

encendedor ⑩ en-sen-de-dor *cigarette lighter*

encendido/a ⑩/① en-sen-dee-do/a *on (power)*

enchufe ⑩ en-choo-fe *plug (electricity)*

encías ① pl en-see-as *gums (mouth)*

encontrar en-kon-trar *find*

encontrarse en-kon-trar-se *meet (get together)*

energía nuclear ① e-ner-khee-a noo-kle-ar *nuclear energy*

enero ⑩ e-ne-ro *January*

enfadado/a ⑩/① en-fa-da-do/a *angry*

enfermedad ① en-fer-me-dad *disease*
— **del viajero** del vya-khe-ro *travel sickness*
— **venérea** ve-ne-re-a *venereal disease*

enfermero/a ⑩/① en-fer-me-ro/a *nurse*

enfermo/a ⑩/① en-fer-mo/a *ill*

enorme ⑩&① e-nor-me *huge*

ensalada ① en-sa-*la*-da *salad*
enseñar en-se-*nyar* v • *teach*
entender en-ten-*der* *understand*
entrada ① en-*tra*-da *cover charge* • *entry*
entrar en-*trar* *enter*
entre *en*-tre *between*
entrenador(a) ⑩/① en-tre-na-*dor*/en-tre-na-*do*-ra *coach*
entrenar en-tre-*nar* *coach* v
entrevista ① en-tre-*vees*-ta *interview*
enviar en-*vyar* *deliver* • *mail* • *send*
equipaje ⑩ e-kee-*pa*-khe *luggage*
equipo ⑩ e-*kee*-po *equipment* • *team*
— **de buceo** de boo-*se*-o *diving equipment*
— **de sonido** de so-*nee*-do *stereo*
equitación ① e-kee-ta-*syon* *horse riding*
equivocado/a ⑩/① e-kee-vo-*ka*-do/a *wrong*
error ⑩ e-*ror* *mistake*
escalada ① es-ka-*la*-da *rock climbing*
escalar es-ka-*lar* *climb* v
escalas sociales ① es-*ka*-las so-*sya*-les *class system*
escaleras ① pl es-ka-*le*-ras *stairway*
escape ⑩ es-*ka*-pe *exhaust (car)*
escarcha ① es-*kar*-cha *frost*
escasez ① es-ka-*ses* *shortage*
escoger es-ko-*kher* *choose*
escribir es-kree-*beer* *write*
escuchar es-koo-*char* *listen*
escuela ① es-*kwe*-la *school*
escultura ① es-kool-*too*-ra *sculpture*
ese/a ⑩/① *e*-se/a *that a*
esgrima ① es-*gree*-ma *fencing (sport)*
esguince ⑩ es-*geen*-se *sprain*
esnorclear es-nor-kle-*ar* *snorkelling*
espacio disponible ⑩ es-*pa*-syo dees-po-*nee*-ble *vacancy*
espalda ① es-*pal*-da *back (body)*
España ① es-*pa*-nya *Spain*
español es-pa-*nyol* *Spanish (language)*
especial ⑩&① es-pe-*syal* *special*
especialista ⑩&① es-pe-sya-*lees*-ta *specialist* n&a
espectáculo ⑩ es-pek-*ta*-koo-lo *show*
espejo ⑩ es-*pe*-kho *mirror*
esperar es-pe-*rar* *wait* v
espiral para mosquitos ① es-pee-*ral* *pa*-ra mos-*kee*-tos *mosquito coil*
esposa ① es-*po*-sa *wife*
esposo ⑩ es-*po*-so *husband*
espuma de afeitar ① es-*poo*-ma de a-fay-*tar* *shaving cream*
esquí ⑩ es-*kee* *skiing*
— **acuático** a-*kwa*-tee-ko *water-skiing*

esquiar es-*kyar* *ski*
esquina ① es-*kee*-na *corner*
esta noche *es*-ta *no*-che *tonight*
estación ① es-ta-*syon* *station*
— **de bus** de boos *bus station*
— **de policía** de po-lee-*see*-a *police station*
— **de tren** de tren *railway station*
estadio ⑩ es-*ta*-dyo *stadium*
estado civil ⑩ es-*ta*-do see-*veel* *marital status*
Estados Unidos ⑩ pl es-*ta*-dos oo-*nee*-dos *USA*
estallar es-ta-*yar* *puncture*
estampilla ① es-tam-*pee*-ya *stamp (postage)*
estar es-*tar* *be (temporary)*
— **de acuerdo** de a-*kwer*-do *agree*
— **resfriado** res-free-*a*-do *have a cold*
estatua ① es-*ta*-twa *statue*
este/a ⑩/① *es*-te/a *this a*
este ⑩ *es*-te *east*
estilista ⑩&① es-tee-*lees*-ta *beautician*
estilo ⑩ es-*tee*-lo *style*
estómago ⑩ es-*to*-ma-go *stomach*
estrella ① es-*tre*-ya *star*
estreñimiento ⑩ es-tre-nyee-*myen*-to *constipation*
estuario ⑩ es-*twa*-ryo *estuary*
estudiante ⑩&① es-too-*dyan*-te *student*
estudio ⑩ es-*too*-dyo *studio*
estúpido/a ⑩/① es-*too*-pee-do/a *stupid*
etiqueta del equipaje ① e-tee-*ke*-ta del e-kee-*pa*-khe *luggage tag*
eutanasia ① e-oo-ta-*na*-sya *euthanasia*
exactamente ek-sak-ta-*men*-te *exactly*
excelente ⑩&① ek-se-*len*-te *excellent*
exceso de equipaje ⑩ ek-*se*-so de e-kee-*pa*-khe *excess baggage*
excluido/a ⑩/① eks-kloo-*ee*-do/a *excluded*
exhibición ① ek-see-bee-*syon* *exhibition*
experiencia ① eks-pe-*ryen*-sya *experience*
— **laboral** la-bo-*ral* *work experience*
explotación ① eks-plo-ta-*syon* *exploitation*
éxtasis ⑩ *eks*-ta-sees *ecstasy (drug)*
extensión ① eks-ten-*syon* *extension (visa)*
extranjero/a ⑩/① eks-tran-*khe*-ro/a *foreign*
extrañar eks-tra-*nyar* *miss (feel absence of)*

F

fábrica ① *fa*-bree-ka *factory*
fácil ⑩&① *fa*-seel *easy*
faja del abanico ① *fa*-kha del a-ba-*nee*-ko *fanbelt*
familia ① fa-*mee*-lya *family*
famoso/a ⑩/① fa-*mo*-so/a *famous*

fantástico fan-*tas*-tee-ko *great • fantastic*
farmacéutico/a ⓜ/① far-ma-se-oo-tee-ko/a *chemist • pharmacist*
farmacia ① far-*ma*-sya *pharmacy*
faul ⓜ *fa*-ool *foul (soccer)*
fax ⓜ faks *fax machine*
febrero ⓜ fe-*bre*-ro *February*
fecha ① *fe*-cha *date (day)*
— **de nacimiento** de na-see-*myen*-to *date of birth*
felicidades fe-lee-see-*da*-des *congratulations*
feliz ⓜ&① fe-*lees* *happy*
feriado ⓜ fe-ree-*a*-do *holiday*
ferretería ① fe-re-te-*ree*-a *hardware store*
ficción ① feek-*syon* *fiction*
fiebre ① *fye*-bre *fever*
— **del heno** del *e*-no *hay fever*
fiesta ① *fyes*-ta *festival • party (night out)*
fila ① *fee*-la *queue*
filtrado/a ⓜ/① feel-*tra*-do/a *filtered*
fin ⓜ feen *end*
— **de semana** de se-*ma*-na *weekend*
finca ① *feen*-ka *farm*
finquero/a ⓜ/① feen-*ke*-ro/a *farmer*
firma ① *feer*-ma *signature*
firmar feer-*mar* *sign (one's name)*
flash ⓜ flash *flash (camera)*
flauta ① *flow*-ta *flute*
flojo/a ⓜ/① flo-*kho*/a *loose*
flor ① flor *flower*
flora y fauna ① *flo*-ra ee *fow*-na *wildlife*
floristería ① flo-rees-te-*ree*-a *florist (shop)*
foco ⓜ *fo*-ko *flashlight • torch*
focos ⓜ pl *fo*-kos *headlights*
fondo ⓜ *fon*-do *bottom (position)*
forma ① *for*-ma *shape • manner*
fósforos ⓜ pl *fos*-fo-ros *matches (lighting)*
foto ① *fo*-to *photo*
fotografía ① fo-to-gra-*fee*-a *photography*
fotografiar fo-to-gra-*fyar* *photograph*
fotógrafo/a ⓜ/① fo-*to*-gra-fo/a *photographer*
frágil ⓜ&① *fra*-kheel *fragile*
francés fran-*ses* *French (language)*
franela ① fra-*ne*-la *flannel (face cloth)*
franqueo ⓜ fran-*ke*-o *postage*
frasco ⓜ *fras*-ko *jar*
freír fre-*eer* *fry*
frenos ⓜ pl *fre*-nos *brakes*
fresco/a ⓜ/① *fres*-ko/a *cool • fresh*
frío/a ⓜ/① *free*-o/a *cold*
frito/a ⓜ/① *free*-to/a *fried*
frontera ① fron-*te*-ra *border (geographic)*
fruta ① *froo*-ta *fruit*
frutas secas ① pl *froo*-tas *se*-kas *dried fruit*

fuego ⓜ *fwe*-go *fire*
fuera de servicio *fwe*-ra de ser-*vee*-syo *out of order*
fuerte ⓜ&① *fwer*-te *strong*
fumar foo-*mar* *smoke* v
funcionar foon-syo-*nar* *work (function)*
funda ① *foon*-da *pillowcase*
funeral ⓜ foo-ne-*ral* *funeral*
fútbol ⓜ *foot*-bol *football • soccer*
futuro ⓜ foo-*too*-ro *future*

G

galería ① ga-le-*ree*-a *gallery*
galleta ① ga-*ye*-ta *biscuit (sweet) • cookie*
— **salada** sa-*la*-da *cracker*
ganador(a) ⓜ/① ga-na-*dor*/ga-na-*do*-ra *winner*
ganar ga-*nar* *earn • win*
garaje ⓜ ga-*ra*-khe *garage*
garantizado/a ⓜ/① ga-ran-tee-*sa*-do/a *guaranteed*
garganta ① gar-*gan*-ta *throat*
gas ⓜ gas *gas (cooking)*
gasa ① *ga*-sa *gauze*
gasolina ① ga-so-*lee*-na *gas • petrol*
gastritis ① gas-*tree*-tees *gastroenteritis*
gato/a ⓜ/① *ga*-to/a *cat*
gay ⓜ&① gay *gay* n&a
gemelos/as ⓜ/① pl khe-*me*-los/as *twins*
gente ① *khen*-te *people*
gerente ⓜ&① khe-*ren*-te *manager (business)*
gimnasia ① kheem-*na*-sya *gymnastics*
gimnasio ⓜ kheem-*na*-syo *gym (place)*
ginebra ① khe-*ne*-bra *gin*
ginecólogo/a ⓜ/① khee-ne-*ko*-lo-go/a *gynaecologist*
gobierno ⓜ go-*byer*-no *government*
gol ⓜ gol *goal (sport)*
golpe ⓜ *gol*-pe *strike (hit)*
gordo/a ⓜ/① *gor*-do/a *fat*
gotas para los ojos ① pl *go*-tas *pa*-ra los o-*khos* *eye drops*
grabación ① gra-ba-*syon* *recording*
grabar gra-*bar* *record* v
grada ① *gra*-da *step*
gradas ① pl *gra*-das *escalator*
grados ⓜ pl *gra*-dos *degrees (temperature)*
gramo ⓜ *gra*-mo *gram*
grande ⓜ&① *gran*-de *big*
granola ① gra-*no*-la *muesli*
gratis ⓜ&① *gra*-tees *complimentary (free)*
gripe ① *gree*-pe *influenza*
gris ⓜ&① grees *grey*

234

gritar gree-*tar* shout
grueso/a ⓜ/ⓕ *grwe*-so/a thick
grupo ⓜ *groo*-po group
— **de rock** de rok rock group
— **musical** moo-see-*kal* band (music)
— **sanguíneo** san-*gee*-ne-o blood group
guantes ⓜ pl *gwan*-tes gloves
guapo/a ⓜ/ⓕ *gwa*-po/a handsome
guardaropa ⓜ gwar-da-*ro*-pa cloakroom
guarda rural ⓜ&ⓕ *gwar*-da roo-*ral*
  police officer (country)
guerra ⓕ *ge*-ra war
guía ⓕ *gee*-a audio guide
— **de entretenimiento**
  de en-tre-te-nee-*myen*-to
  entertainment guide
— **telefónica** te-le-fo-nee-ka phone book
— **turística** too-*rees*-tee-ka guidebook
guía ⓜ&ⓕ *gee*-a guide (person)
guitarra ⓕ gee-*ta*-ra guitar
gustar goos-*tar* like v

H

habitación ⓕ a-bee-ta-*syon* room
— **sencilla** sen-*see*-ya single room
hablar ab-*lar* speak • talk
hace (tres días) a-se (tres *dee*-as)
  (three days) ago
hacer a-*ser* do • make
hachís ⓜ a-*chees* hashish
hacia a-see-a towards
halal ⓜ&ⓕ a-*lal* halal
halar a-*lar* pull
hamaca ⓕ a-*ma*-ka hammock
hambriento/a ⓜ/ⓕ am-bree-*yen*-to/a
  hungry
hasta as-ta until
hecho/a a mano ⓜ/ⓕ *e*-cho/a a *ma*-no
  handmade
heladería ⓕ e-la-de-*ree*-a ice-cream parlour
helado ⓜ e-*la*-do ice cream
hembra ⓕ *em*-bra female
hepatitis ⓕ e-pa-*tee*-tees hepatitis
herida ⓕ e-*ree*-da injury
hermana ⓕ er-*ma*-na sister
hermano ⓜ er-*ma*-no brother
heroína ⓕ e-ro-*ee*-na heroin
herpes ⓜ *er*-pes shingles (illness)
hervido/a ⓜ/ⓕ er-*vee*-do/a boiled
hielo ⓜ *ye*-lo ice
hierba ⓕ *yer*-ba dope (drugs) • herb
hierbero/a ⓜ/ⓕ yer-*be*-ro/a herbalist
hija ⓕ *ee*-kha daughter
hijo ⓜ *ee*-kho son

hilo ⓜ *ee*-lo string • thread
— **dental** den-*tal* dental floss
hinchazón ⓕ een-cha-*son* swelling
hindú ⓜ&ⓕ een-*doo* Hindu n&a
historia ⓕ ees-*to*-rya history
histórico/a ⓜ/ⓕ ees-*to*-ree-ko/a historical
hogar ⓜ o-*gar* home
hoja ⓕ *o*-kha leaf
hombre ⓜ *om*-bre man
— **de negocios** de ne-*go*-syos
  businessman
hombro ⓜ *om*-bro shoulder
homeopatía ⓕ o-me-o-pa-*tee*-a
  homeopathy
homosexual ⓜ&ⓕ o-mo-*sek*-swal
  homosexual n&a
hondo/a ⓜ/ⓕ *on*-do/a deep
hora ⓕ *o*-ra hour
horario ⓜ o-*ra*-ryo opening hours
hormiga ⓕ or-*mee*-ga ant
horno ⓜ *or*-no oven
— **microondas** mee-kro-*on*-das
  microwave oven
horóscopo ⓜ o-*ros*-ko-po horoscope
horrible ⓜ&ⓕ o-*ree*-ble awful
hospital ⓜ os-pee-*tal* hospital
hospitalidad ⓕ os-pee-ta-lee-*dad* hospitality
hotel ⓜ o-*tel* hotel
hoy oy today
huelga ⓕ *wel*-ga strike (stoppage)
hueso ⓜ *we*-so bone
huevo ⓜ *we*-vo egg
humanidades ⓕ pl oo-ma-nee-*da*-des
  humanities
humectante ⓜ oo-mek-*tan*-te moisturiser

I

identificación ⓕ ee-den-tee-fee-ka-*syon*
  identification
idioma ⓜ ee-*dyo*-ma language
idiota ⓜ&ⓕ ee-*dyo*-ta idiot
iglesia ⓕ ee-*gle*-sya church
igualdad ⓕ ee-gwal-*dad* equality
— **de oportunidades**
  de o-por-too-nee-*da*-des equal opportunity
importante ⓜ&ⓕ eem-por-*tan*-te
  important
imposible ⓜ&ⓕ eem-po-*see*-ble impossible
impresora ⓕ eem-pre-*so*-ra
  printer (computer)
impuesto ⓜ eem-*pwes*-to tax
— **de salida** de sa-*lee*-da airport tax
— **de ventas** de *ven*-tas sales tax
incluido/a ⓜ/ⓕ een-kloo-*ee*-do/a included

incómodo/a ⓜ/ⓕ een·ko·mo·do/a *uncomfortable*
indicador ⓜ een·dee·ka·*dor* *indicator*
indigente ⓜ&ⓕ een·dee·*khen*·te *homeless* n&a
indigestión ⓕ een·dee·khes·*tyon* *indigestion*
industria ⓕ een·*doos*·tree·a *industry*
infección ⓕ een·fek·*syon* *infection*
— **urinaria** oo·ree·na·rya *urinary infection*
inflamación ⓕ een·fla·ma·*syon* *inflammation*
información ⓕ een·for·ma·*syon* *information*
informática ⓕ een·for·ma·tee·ka *IT*
ingeniería ⓕ een·khe·nye·ree·a *engineering*
ingeniero/a ⓜ/ⓕ een·khe·nye·ro/a *engineer*
Inglaterra ⓕ een·gla·*te*·ra *England*
inglés een·*gles* *English (language)*
ingrediente ⓜ een·gre·*dyen*·te *ingredient*
inicio ⓜ ee·*nee*·syo *start*
injusto/a ⓜ/ⓕ een·*khoos*·to/a *unfair*
inocente ⓜ&ⓕ e·no·*sen*·te *innocent*
insecto ⓜ een·*sek*·to *insect*
inseguro/a ⓜ/ⓕ een·se·*goo*·ro/a *unsafe*
insolación ⓕ een·so·la·*syon* *sunstroke*
instructor(a) ⓜ/ⓕ eens·trook·*tor*/eens·trook·*to*·ra *instructor*
interesante ⓜ&ⓕ een·te·re·*san*·te *interesting*
intermedio ⓜ een·ter·*me*·dyo *intermission*
internacional ⓜ&ⓕ een·ter·na·syo·*nal* *international*
intérprete ⓜ&ⓕ een·*ter*·pre·te *interpreter*
inundación ⓕ ee·noon·da·*syon* *flood*
invierno ⓜ een·*vyer*·no *winter*
invitar een·vee·*tar* *invite* v
inyección ⓕ een·yek·*syon* *injection*
inyectar een·yek·*tar* *inject*
ir eer *go*
— **de compras** de *kom*·pras *go shopping*
isla ⓕ *ees*·la *island*
itinerario ⓜ ee·tee·ne·*ra*·ryo *timetable*
izquierda ⓕ ees·*kyer*·da *left (direction)*
izquierdista ⓜ&ⓕ ees·kyer·*dees*·ta *left-wing*

J

jabón ⓜ kha·*bon* *soap*
jarabe para la tos ⓜ kha·*ra*·be *pa*·ra la tos *cough medicine*
jardín ⓜ khar·*deen* *garden*
— **botánico** bo·*ta*·nee·ko *botanic garden*
jardinería ⓕ khar·dee·ne·*ree*·a *gardening*
jardinero/a ⓜ/ⓕ khar·dee·*ne*·ro/a *gardener*
jardines públicos ⓜ pl khar·*dee*·nes poo·blee·kos *public gardens*
jeringa ⓕ khe·*reen*·ga *syringe*
joven ⓜ&ⓕ *kho*·ven *young*
joyas ⓕ pl *kho*·yas *jewellery*
judío/a ⓜ/ⓕ khoo·*dee*·o/a *Jewish*
juego de computadora ⓜ *khwe*·go de kom·poo·ta·*do*·ra *computer game*
Juegos Olímpicos ⓜ pl *khwe*·gos o·*leem*·pee·kos *Olympic Games*
jueves ⓜ *khwe*·ves *Thursday*
juez(a) ⓜ/ⓕ khwes/*khwe*·sa *judge*
jugar khoo·*gar* *play (cards, etc)*
jugo ⓜ *khoo*·go *juice*
juguetería ⓕ khoo·ge·te·*ree*·a *toy shop*
julio ⓜ *khoo*·lyo *July*
junio ⓜ *khoo*·nyo *June*
junto a *khoon*·to a *beside • next to*
juntos/as ⓜ/ⓕ pl *khoon*·tos/as *together*

K

kilogramo ⓜ kee·lo·*gra*·mo *kilogram*
kilómetro ⓜ kee·*lo*·me·tro *kilometre*
kínder ⓜ *keen*·der *kindergarten*
klínex ⓜ *klee*·neks *tissues*
kosher ⓜ&ⓕ ko·*sher* *kosher*

L

labios ⓜ pl *la*·byos *lips*
lado ⓜ *la*·do *side*
ladrón(a) ⓜ/ⓕ la·*dron*/la·*dro*·na *thief*
lagartija ⓕ la·gar·*tee*·kha *lizard*
lago ⓜ *la*·go *lake*
lana ⓕ *la*·na *wool*
lancha ⓕ *lan*·cha *motorboat*
lapicero ⓜ la·pee·*se*·ro *ballpoint pen*
lápiz ⓜ *la*·pees *pencil*
largo/a ⓜ/ⓕ *lar*·go/a *long*
lastimado/a ⓜ/ⓕ las·tee·*ma*·do/a *injured*
lastimar las·tee·*mar* *hurt (cause pain)*
lata ⓕ *la*·ta *can • tin*
lavadora ⓕ la·va·*do*·ra *washing machine*
lavandería ⓕ la·van·de·*ree*·a *launderette • laundry (place)*
lavar la·*var* *wash (something)*
lavarse la·*var*·se *wash (oneself)*
laxante ⓜ lak·*san*·te *laxative*
leche ⓕ *le*·che *milk*
lectura ⓕ lek·*too*·ra *reading*
leer le·*er* *read*
legal ⓜ&ⓕ le·*gal* *legal*
legislación ⓕ le·khees·la·*syon* *legislation*

lejos *le*-khos *far (away)*
lentes de contacto ⓜ pl *len*-tes de kon-*tak*-to *contact lenses*
lente zoom ⓜ *len*-te soom *zoom lens*
lento/a ⓜ/ⓕ *len*-to/a *slow*
leña ⓕ *le*-nya *firewood*
lesbiana ⓕ les-*bya*-na *lesbian* n&a
ley ⓕ lay *law (legislation)*
libra ⓕ *lee*-bra *pound (currency/weight)*
libre ⓜ&ⓕ *lee*-bre *free (not bound)*
librería ⓕ lee-bre-*ree*-a *book shop • stationer*
libro ⓜ *lee*-bro *book*
— **de frases** de *fra*-ses *phrasebook*
— **de oraciones** de o-ra-*syo*-nes *prayer book*
licencia ⓕ lee-*sen*-sya *licence*
— **de conductor** de kon-*dook*-tor *driving licence*
licorera ⓕ lee-ko-*re*-ra *bottle shop • liquor store*
líder ⓜ/ⓕ *lee*-der *leader*
ligar lee-*gar* *chat up (flirt)*
límite de equipaje ⓜ *lee*-mee-te de e-kee-*pa*-khe *baggage allowance*
límite de velocidad ⓜ *lee*-mee-te de ve-lo-see-*dad* *speed limit*
limonada ⓕ lee-mo-*na*-da *lemonade*
limpiar leem-*pyar* *clean* v
limpieza ⓕ leem-*pye*-sa *cleaning*
limpio/a ⓜ/ⓕ leem-*pyo*/a *clean*
lino ⓜ *lee*-no *linen (material)*
listo/a ⓜ/ⓕ *lees*-to/a *ready*
litera ⓕ lee-*te*-ra *sleeping berth*
liviano/a ⓜ/ⓕ lee-*vya*-no/a *light (weight)*
llamada a cobrar ⓕ ya-*ma*-da a ko-*brar* *collect call*
llamar ya-*mar* *call* v • *telephone* v
llanta ⓕ *yan*-ta *tire • tyre*
llanuras ⓕ pl ya-*noo*-ras *tropical plains*
llave ⓕ *ya*-ve *key (door etc)*
llegadas ⓕ pl ye-*ga*-das *arrivals (airport)*
llegar ye-*gar* *arrive*
llenar ye-*nar* *fill*
lleno/a ⓜ/ⓕ *ye*-no/a *full*
— **de gente** de *khen*-te *crowded*
llevar ye-*var* *carry • take*
lluvia ⓕ *yoo*-vya *rain*
local ⓜ&ⓕ lo-*kal* *local*
loco/a ⓜ/ⓕ *lo*-ko/a *crazy*
loma ⓕ *lo*-ma *hill*
lombrices ⓕ pl lom-*bree*-ses *intestinal worms*
loro/a ⓜ/ⓕ *lo*-ro/a *parrot*
lubricante ⓜ loo-bree-*kan*-te *lubricant*
lucrar loo-*krar* *profit* v

lugar ⓜ loo-*gar* *place • venue*
— **de nacimiento** de na-see-*myen*-to *place of birth*
lujoso/a ⓜ/ⓕ loo-*kho*-so/a *luxury*
luna ⓕ *loo*-na *moon*
— **de miel** de myel *honeymoon*
lunes ⓜ *loo*-nes *Monday*
luz ⓕ lus *light*

M

macrobiótica ⓕ ma-kro-*byo*-tee-ka *health-food store*
madera ⓕ ma-*de*-ra *wood*
madre ⓕ *ma*-dre *mother*
maestro/a ⓜ/ⓕ ma-*es*-tro/a *teacher*
malaria ⓕ ma-*la*-rya *malaria*
maleta ⓕ ma-*le*-ta *suitcase*
malo/a ⓜ/ⓕ *ma*-lo/a *bad • off (spoilt)*
mamografía ⓕ ma-mo-gra-*fee*-a *mammogram*
mandar man-*dar* *send*
mandíbula ⓕ man-*dee*-boo-la *jaw*
manglar man-*glar* *mangrove*
manifestación ⓕ ma-nee-fes-ta-*syon* *demonstration (rally)*
manillar ⓜ ma-nee-*yar* *handlebars*
mano ⓕ *ma*-no *hand*
mantel ⓜ man-*tel* *tablecloth*
mañana ⓕ ma-*nya*-na *morning*
mañana ma-*nya*-na *tomorrow*
mapa ⓜ *ma*-pa *map*
— **de calles** de *ka*-yes *road map*
maquillaje ⓜ ma-kee-*ya*-khe *make-up*
máquina ⓕ *ma*-kee-na *machine*
— **de tiquetes** de tee-*ke*-tes *ticket machine*
mar ⓜ mar *sea*
maravilloso/a ⓜ/ⓕ ma-ra-vee-*yo*-so/a *wonderful*
marcación directa ⓕ mar-ka-*syon* dee-*rek*-ta *direct-dial*
marcador ⓜ mar-ka-*dor* *scoreboard*
marcapasos ⓜ mar-ka-*pa*-sos *pacemaker*
Mar Caribe ⓜ mar ka-*ree*-be *Caribbean Sea*
marea ⓕ ma-*re*-a *tide*
mareado/a ⓜ/ⓕ ma-re-*a*-do/a *dizzy • seasick*
margarina ⓕ mar-ga-*ree*-na *margarine*
marihuana ⓕ ma-ree-*wa*-na *marijuana*
mariposa ⓕ ma-ree-*po*-sa *butterfly*
martes ⓜ *mar*-tes *Tuesday*
martillo ⓜ mar-*tee*-yo *hammer*
marzo ⓜ *mar*-so *March*

más mas *more*
— **cerca** *ser*·ka *closer*
— **grande** ⓜ&ⓕ *gran*·de *bigger*
— **pequeño/a** ⓜ/ⓕ pe·ke·nyo/a *smaller*
— **tarde** *tar*·de *later*
masaje ⓜ ma·*sa*·khe *massage*
masajeador ⓜ ma·sa·khe·a·*dor masseur*
masajeadora ⓕ ma·sa·khe·a·*do*·ra *masseuse*
mascara ⓕ mas·*ka*·ra *goggles (diving)*
mascarilla ⓕ mas·ka·*ree*·ya
  goggles (swimming)
mata ⓕ *ma*·ta *plant*
matrimonio ⓜ ma·tree·mo·nyo *marriage*
mayo ⓜ *ma*·yo *May*
mecánico/a ⓜ/ⓕ me·ka·nee·ko/a *mechanic*
medianoche ⓕ me·dya·no·che *midnight*
medias ⓕ pl me·dyas *socks*
medicamento ⓜ me·dee·ka·*men*·to
  medication
medicina ⓕ me·de·*see*·na
  medicine (profession)
medidor de luz ⓜ me·dee·*dor* de lus
  light meter
medio ⓜ *me*·dyo *half*
— **ambiente** am·*byen*·te *environment*
mediodía ⓜ me·dyo·*dee*·a *midday • noon*
medios ⓜ pl *me*·dyos *media*
meditación ⓕ me·de·ta·*syon meditation*
mejor me·*khor better*
melodía ⓕ me·lo·*dee*·a *tune*
mendigo/a ⓜ/ⓕ men·*dee*·go/a *beggar*
menos *me*·nos *less*
mensaje ⓜ men·*sa*·khe *message*
mentir men·*teer lie (not tell the truth)*
mentiroso/a ⓜ/ⓕ men·tee·ro·so/a *liar*
menú ⓜ me·*noo menu*
menudo ⓜ me·*noo*·do *loose change*
mercado ⓜ mer·*ka*·do *market*
— **callejero** ka·ye·*khe*·ro *street market*
— **de pulgas** de *pool*·gas *fleamarket*
— **negro** *ne*·gro *black market*
merienda ⓕ me·*ryen*·da *snack*
mes ⓜ mes *month*
mesa ⓕ *me*·sa *table*
mesero/a ⓜ/ⓕ me·se·ro/a *waiter*
meseta ⓕ me·*se*·ta *plateau*
meta ⓕ *me*·ta *finish*
metal ⓜ me·*tal metal*
metro ⓜ *me*·tro *metre*
mezclar mes·*klar mix*
mezquita ⓕ mes·*kee*·ta *mosque*
mi mee *my*
mí mee *me*
miembro/a ⓜ/ⓕ myem·bro/a *member*
miércoles ⓜ *myer*·ko·les *Wednesday*

migración ⓕ mee·gra·*syon immigration*
migraña ⓕ mee·*gra*·nya *migraine*
milímetro ⓜ mee·*lee*·me·tro *millimetre*
millón ⓜ mee·*yon million*
minuto ⓜ mee·*noo*·to *minute*
mirador ⓜ mee·ra·*dor lookout*
misa ⓕ *mee*·sa *mass (Catholic)*
mismo/a ⓜ/ⓕ *mees*·mo/a *same*
mitad ⓕ mee·*tad half*
mochila ⓕ mo·*chee*·la *backpack*
moda ⓕ *mo*·da *fashion*
módem ⓜ *mo*·dem *modem*
moderno/a ⓜ/ⓕ mo·*der*·no/a *modern*
mojado/a ⓜ/ⓕ mo·*kha*·do/a *wet*
monasterio ⓜ mo·nas·*te*·ryo *monastery*
monedas ⓕ pl mo·*ne*·das *coins*
monja ⓕ *mon*·kha *nun*
monje ⓜ *mon*·khe *monk*
mono ⓜ *mo*·no *monkey*
mononucleosis ⓕ mo·no·noo·kle·o·sees
  glandular fever
montaña ⓕ mon·*ta*·nya *mountain*
montañismo ⓜ mon·ta·*nyees*·mo
  mountaineering
montura ⓕ mon·*too*·ra *saddle*
monumento ⓜ mo·noo·*men*·to *monument*
moquera ⓕ mo·*ke*·ra *runny nose*
morado/a ⓜ/ⓕ mo·*ra*·do/a *purple*
mordida ⓕ mor·*dee*·da *bite (dog)*
moretón ⓜ mo·re·*ton bruise*
morir mo·*reer die*
mosca ⓕ *mos*·ka *fly*
mosquitero ⓜ mos·kee·*te*·ro *mosquito net*
mota ⓕ *mo*·ta *dope (drugs)*
motel ⓜ mo·*tel motel*
moto ⓕ *mo*·to *motorbike*
motor ⓜ mo·*tor engine*
mucho/a ⓜ/ⓕ *moo*·cho/a *(a) lot • much*
muchos/as ⓜ/ⓕ pl *moo*·chos/as *many*
mudo/a ⓜ/ⓕ *moo*·do/a *mute*
muebles ⓜ pl *mwe*·bles *furniture*
muerto/a ⓜ/ⓕ *mwer*·to/a *dead*
mujer ⓕ moo·*kher woman*
— **de negocios** de ne·*go*·syos
  businesswoman
multa ⓕ *mool*·ta *fine (payment)*
Mundial ⓜ moon·*dyal World Cup*
mundo ⓜ *moon*·do *world*
muñeca ⓕ moo·*nye*·ka *doll • wrist*
músculo ⓜ *moos*·koo·lo *muscle*
museo ⓜ moo·*se*·o *museum*
música ⓕ *moo*·see·ka *music*
músico/a ⓜ/ⓕ *moo*·see·ko/a *musician*

musulmán/musulmana ⓜ/ⓕ moo-sool-*man*/moo-sool-*ma*-na *Muslim* n&a

muy mooy *very*

N

nacionalidad ⓕ na-syo-na-lee-*dad* *nationality*

nada *na*-da *nothing*

nadar na-*dar* *swim*

nado ⓜ *na*-do *swimming*

naipes ⓜ pl *nai*-pes *cards (playing)*

narcotraficante ⓜ&ⓕ nar-ko-tra-fee-*kan*-te *drug dealer*

narcotráfico ⓜ nar-ko-*tra*-fee-ko *drug trafficking*

nariz ⓕ na-*rees* *nose*

naturaleza ⓕ na-too-ra-*le*-sa *nature*

náuseas ⓕ pl *now*-se-as *nausea*

navaja ⓕ na-*va*-kha *penknife*

navajilla ⓕ na-va-*khee*-ya *razor blade*

Navidad ⓕ na-vee-*dad* *Christmas*

necesario/a ⓜ/ⓕ ne-se-*sa*-ryo/a *necessary*

necesitar ne-se-see-*tar* *need* v

negar ne-*gar* *refuse* v

negativo/a ⓜ/ⓕ ne-ga-*tee*-vo/a *negative*

negativos ⓜ pl ne-ga-*tee*-vos *negatives (photos)*

negocio ⓜ ne-*go*-syo *business*

negro/a ⓜ/ⓕ *ne*-gro/a *black*

neumático ⓜ ne-oo-*ma*-tee-ko *tube (tyre)*

neuropatía ⓕ ne-oo-ro-pa-*tee*-a *naturopathy*

nieto/a ⓜ/ⓕ *nye*-to/a *grandchild*

nieve ⓕ *nye*-ve *snow*

ninguno/a ⓜ/ⓕ neen-*goo*-no/a *neither • none*

niñera ⓕ nee-*nye*-ra *babysitter*

niño/a ⓜ/ⓕ *nee*-nyo/a *child*

niños/as ⓜ/ⓕ pl *nee*-nyos/as *children*

no no *no • not*

— **fumado** foo-*ma*-do *nonsmoking*

noche ⓕ *no*-che *evening • night*

nombre ⓜ *nom*-bre *name*

— **cristiano** krees-*tya*-no *given name*

norte ⓜ *nor*-te *north*

nosotros/as ⓜ/ⓕ pl no-*so*-tros/as *we*

nostálgico/a ⓜ/ⓕ nos-*tal*-khee-ko/a *homesick*

noticias ⓕ pl no-*tee*-syas *news*

novela ⓕ no-*ve*-la *soap opera*

novia ⓕ *no*-vya *girlfriend*

noviembre ⓜ no-*vyem*-bre *November*

novio ⓜ *no*-vyo *boyfriend*

nube ⓕ *noo*-be *cloud*

nublado/a ⓜ/ⓕ noo-*bla*-do/a *cloudy*

nuestro/a ⓜ/ⓕ *nwes*-tro/a *our*

nuevo/a ⓜ/ⓕ *nwe*-vo/a *new*

número ⓜ *noo*-me-ro *number*

— **de habitación** de a-bee-ta-*syon* *room number*

— **de pasaporte** de pa-sa-*por*-te *passport number*

— **de placa** de *pla*-ka *license plate number*

nunca *noon*-ka *never*

O

o o *or*

objetivo ⓜ ob-khe-*tee*-vo *lens (camera)*

obra de teatro ⓕ *o*-bra de te-*a*-tro *play (theatre)*

observar ob-ser-*var* *watch* v

obtener ob-te-*ner* *get*

océano ⓜ o-se-*a*-no *ocean*

Océano Atlántico ⓜ o-se-*a*-no at-*lan*-tee-ko *Atlantic Ocean*

Océano Pacífico ⓜ o-se-*a*-no pa-*see*-fee-ko *Pacific Ocean*

octubre ⓜ ok-*too*-bre *October*

ocupado/a ⓜ/ⓕ o-koo-*pa*-do/a *busy • engaged (phone)*

oeste ⓜ o-*es*-te *west*

oficina ⓕ o-fee-*see*-na *office*

— **de objetos perdidos** de ob-*khe*-tos per-*dee*-dos *lost-property office*

— **de turismo** de too-*rees*-mo *tourist office*

oír o-*eer* *hear*

ojos ⓜ pl *o*-khos *eyes*

ola ⓕ *o*-la *wave (beach)*

olla ⓕ *o*-ya *pot • saucepan*

olor ⓜ o-*lor* *smell*

olvidar ol-vee-*dar* *forget*

operación ⓕ o-pe-ra-*syon* *operation (medical)*

operador(a) ⓜ/ⓕ o-pe-ra-*dor*/o-pe-ra-*do*-ra *telephone operator*

opinión ⓕ o-pee-*nyon* *opinion*

oportunidad ⓕ o-por-too-nee-*dad* *chance*

optometrista ⓜ&ⓕ op-to-me-*trees*-ta *optometrist*

opuesto o-*pwes*-to *opposite*

oración ⓕ o-ra-*syon* *prayer*

orden ⓕ *or*-den *command • order*

ordenar or-de-*nar* *order* v

ordinario/a ⓜ/ⓕ or-dee-*na*-ryo/a *ordinary*

oreja ⓕ o-*re*-kha *ear*

orgasmo ⓜ or-*gas*-mo *orgasm*

original ⓜ&ⓕ o-ree-khee-*nal* *original*

oro ⓜ *o*-ro *gold*

orquesta ① or-kes-ta *orchestra*
oscuro/a ⓜ/① os-koo-ro/a *dark (colour/night)*
otoño ⓜ o-to-nyo *autumn • fall*
otra vez o-tra ves *again*
otro/a ⓜ/① o-tro/a *another • other*
ovario ⓜ o-va-ryo *ovary*
oveja ① o-ve-kha *sheep*
oxígeno ⓜ ok-see-khe-no *oxygen*

P

padre ⓜ pa-dre *father*
pagar pa-gar *pay*
página ① pa-khee-na *page*
pago ⓜ pa-go *payment*
país ⓜ pa-ees *country*
pájaro ⓜ pa-kha-ro *bird*
palabra ① pa-la-bra *word*
palacio ⓜ pa-la-syo *palace*
palillo de dientes ⓜ pa-lee-yo de dyen-tes *toothpick*
palillos chinos ⓜ pl pa-lee-yos chee-nos *chopsticks*
pan ⓜ pan *bread*
panadería ① pa-na-de-ree-a *bakery*
pancito ⓜ pan-see-to *biscuit (savoury)*
panfleto ⓜ pan-fle-to *brochure*
pantalones ⓜ pl pan-ta-lo-nes *trousers*
pañal ⓜ pa-nyal *diaper • nappy*
paño ⓜ pa-nyo *towel*
— para la cara pa-ra la ka-ra *face cloth*
pañuelo ⓜ pa-nywe-lo *handkerchief*
papá ⓜ pa-pa *dad*
papanicolau ⓜ pa-pa-nee-ko-low *pap smear*
papás ⓜ pl pa-pas *parents*
papel ⓜ pa-pel *paper*
— higiénico ee-khye-nee-ko *toilet paper*
papeleo ⓜ pa-pe-le-o *paperwork*
paperas ① pl pa-pe-ras *mumps*
paquete ⓜ pa-ke-te *package • packet*
para pa-ra *for*
— siempre syem-pre *forever*
parabrisas ⓜ pa-ra-bree-sas *windscreen*
parada ① pa-ra-da *stop (bus, tram)*
— de bus de boos *bus stop*
— de taxis de tak-sees *taxi stand*
parapléjico/a ⓜ/① pa-ra-ple-khee-ko/a *paraplegic*
parar pa-rar *stop (cease)*
parcela ① par-se-la *parcel*
pared ① pa-red *wall*
pareja ① pa-re-kha *couple • pair*
parlamento ⓜ par-la-men-to *parliament*
parque ⓜ par-ke *park*
— nacional na-syo-nal *national park*

parquear par-ke-ar *park (vehicle)* v
parqueo ⓜ par-ke-o *car park*
parte ① par-te *part (component)*
partidario/a ⓜ/① par-tee-da-ryo/a *supporter (sport)*
partido ⓜ par-tee-do *game (sport) • match • party (politics)*
partir par-teer *depart*
pasado ⓜ pa-sa-do *past*
— mañana ma-nya-na *day after tomorrow*
pasado/a ⓜ/① pa-sa-do/a *last (previous)*
pasajero/a ⓜ/① pa-sa-khe-ro/a *passenger*
pasaporte ⓜ pa-sa-por-te *passport*
pasar pa-sar *pass* v
Pascua ① pas-kwa *Easter*
pasillo ⓜ pa-see-yo *aisle (on plane)*
pasta de dientes ① pas-ta de dyen-tes *toothpaste*
pastel ⓜ pas-tel *pastry • pie*
pastelería ① pas-te-le-ree-a *cake shop*
pastilla ① pas-tee-ya *pill*
— anticonceptiva an-tee-kon-sep-tee-va *the pill (contraceptive)*
— para el dolor pa-ra el do-lor *painkiller*
pastillas para dormir ① pl pas-tee-yas pa-ra dor-meer *sleeping pills*
patear pa-te-ar *kick* v
patinar pa-tee-nar *skate* v
paz ① pas *peace*
peatón ⓜ pe-a-ton *pedestrian*
pecho ⓜ pe-cho *breast • chest*
pedal ⓜ pe-dal *pedal*
pedazo ⓜ pe-da-so *piece*
pedido ⓜ pe-dee-do *order (food)*
pedir pe-deer *ask (for something)*
— prestado pres-ta-do *borrow*
— un aventón oon a-ven-ton *hitchhike*
pegamento ⓜ pe-ga-men-to *glue*
peine ⓜ pay-ne *comb*
pelea ① pe-le-a *fight*
película ① pe-lee-koo-la *film (cinema)*
peligroso/a ⓜ/① pe-lee-gro-so/a *dangerous*
pelo ⓜ pe-lo *hair*
peluquero/a ⓜ/① pe-loo-ke-ro/a *hairdresser*
pene ⓜ pe-ne *penis*
pensar pen-sar *think*
pensión ① pen-syon *guesthouse*
pensionado/a ⓜ/① pen-syo-na-do/a *pensioner*
pequeño/a ⓜ/① pe-ke-nyo/a *small*
perder per-der *lose • miss*
perdido/a ⓜ/① per-dee-do/a *lost*
perdonar per-do-nar *forgive*
perezoso/a ⓜ/① pe-re-so-so/a *lazy*
perfecto/a ⓜ/① per-fek-to/a *perfect*

perfume ⓜ per-*foo*-me *perfume*
periódico ⓜ pe-*ryo*-dee-ko *newspaper*
periodista ⓜ&ⓕ pe-ree-o-*dees*-ta *journalist*
permiso ⓜ per-*mee*-so *permission • permit*
　— **de trabajo** de tra-*ba*-kho *work permit*
pero *pe*-ro *but*
perro/a ⓜ/ⓕ *pe*-ro/a *dog*
　— **guía** *gee*-a *guide dog*
persona ⓕ per-*so*-na *person*
pesado/a ⓜ/ⓕ pe-*sa*-do/a *heavy*
pesar pe-*sar* *weigh*
pesas ⓕ pl *pe*-sas *weights*
pesca ⓕ *pes*-ka *fishing*
pescado ⓜ pes-*ka*-do *fish (meat)*
peso ⓜ *pe*-so *weight*
petición ⓕ pe-tee-*syon* *petition*
petróleo ⓜ pe-*tro*-le-o *oil (petrol)*
pez ⓜ pes *fish (animal)*
picada ⓕ pee-*ka*-da *bite (insect)*
picadillo ⓜ pee-ka-*dee*-yo *mince*
picazón ⓕ pee-ka-*son* *itch*
pico ⓜ *pee*-ko *pickaxe*
pie ⓜ pye *foot*
piedra ⓕ *pye*-dra *rock • stone*
piel ⓕ pyel *skin*
pierna ⓕ *pyer*-na *leg (body)*
pijiado/a ⓜ/ⓕ pee-*khya*-do/a
　stoned (drugged)
pimienta ⓕ pee-*myen*-ta *pepper (spice)*
pintor(a) ⓜ/ⓕ peen-*tor*/peen-*to*-ra *painter*
pintura ⓕ peen-*too*-ra *painting*
　— **de labios** de *la*-byos *lipstick*
pinzas ⓕ pl *peen*-sas *tweezers*
piojos ⓜ pl *pyo*-khos *lice*
piscina ⓕ pee-*see*-na *swimming pool*
piso ⓜ *pee*-so *floor (storey)*
pista ⓕ *pees*-ta *racetrack*
pistola ⓕ pees-*to*-la *gun*
placa ⓕ *pla*-ka *numberplate*
plancha ⓕ *plan*-cha *iron (for clothes)*
planeta ⓜ pla-*ne*-ta *planet*
plano/a ⓜ/ⓕ *pla*-no/a *flat*
plástico ⓜ *plas*-tee-ko *plastic*
plata ⓕ *pla*-ta *silver*
plataforma ⓕ pla-ta-*for*-ma *platform*
plato ⓜ *pla*-to *dish (food) • plate*
　— **hondo** *on*-do *bowl*
playa ⓕ *pla*-ya *beach*
plaza ⓕ *pla*-sa *square (town)*
plomero ⓜ plo-*me*-ro *plumber*
pobre ⓜ&ⓕ *po*-bre *poor*
pobreza ⓕ po-*bre*-sa *poverty*
poco/a ⓜ/ⓕ *po*-ko/a *few • little (quantity)*
poder po-*der* *power*
poder po-*der* *can (be able/have permission)*

podrido/a ⓜ/ⓕ po-*dree*-do/a *spoilt (food)*
poesía ⓕ po-e-*see*-a *poetry*
polen ⓜ *po*-len *pollen*
policía ⓕ po-lee-*see*-a *police*
policía ⓜ&ⓕ po-lee-*see*-a *police officer (city)*
política ⓕ po-*lee*-tee-ka *policy • politics*
político ⓜ po-*lee*-tee-ko *politician*
político/a ⓜ/ⓕ po-*lee*-tee-ko/a *political*
polvo ⓜ *pol*-vo *powder*
poner po-*ner* *put*
ponerse po-*ner*-se *wear*
popular ⓜ&ⓕ po-poo-*lar* *popular*
por por *for*
　— **a noche** a *no*-che *overnight*
　— **qué** ke *why*
porcentaje ⓜ por-sen-*ta*-khe *per cent*
porque *por*-ke *because*
portero ⓜ por-*te*-ro *goalkeeper*
posible ⓜ&ⓕ po-*see*-ble *possible*
positivo/a ⓜ/ⓕ po-see-*tee*-vo/a *positive*
postal ⓕ pos-*tal* *postcard*
póster ⓜ *pos*-ter *poster*
postre ⓜ *pos*-tre *dessert*
precio ⓜ *pre*-syo *price*
precipicio ⓜ pre-see-*pee*-syo *cliff*
preferir pre-fe-*reer* *prefer*
pregunta ⓕ pre-*goon*-ta *question*
preguntar pre-goon-*tar* *ask (a question)*
preocupado/a ⓜ/ⓕ pre-o-koo-*pa*-do/a
　worried
preparar pre-pa-*rar* *prepare*
presentación ⓕ pre-sen-ta-*syon*
　performance
presente ⓜ pre-*sen*-te *present (time)*
preservativo ⓜ pre-ser-va-*tee*-vo *condom*
presidente ⓜ&ⓕ pre-see-*den*-te *president*
presión ⓕ pre-*syon* *pressure (tyre)*
　— **sanguínea** san-*gee*-ne-a *blood pressure*
presupuesto ⓜ pre-soo-*pwes*-to *budget*
prevenir pre-ve-*neer* *stop (prevent)*
primavera ⓕ pree-ma-*ve*-ra *spring (season)*
primera clase ⓕ pree-*me*-ra *kla*-se *first class*
primer(a) ministro/a ⓜ/ⓕ pree-*mer*
　mee-*nees*-tro/pree-*me*-ra mee-*nees*-tra
　prime minister
primero/a ⓜ/ⓕ pree-*me*-ro/a *first*
primeros auxilios ⓜ pl
　pree-*me*-ros owk-*see*-lyos *first-aid kit*
principal ⓜ&ⓕ preen-see-*pal* *main*
privado/a ⓜ/ⓕ pree-*va*-do/a *private*
producir pro-doo-*seer* *produce* v
programa ⓜ pro-*gra*-ma *program* v
prometer pro-me-*ter* *promise*
prometido/a ⓜ/ⓕ pro-me-*tee*-do/a
　fiancé/fiancée

promoción ① pro·mo·*syon* *sale*
pronto ⓜ *pron*·to *soon*
propina ① pro·*pee*·na *tip (gratuity)*
prostituto/a ⓜ/① pros·tee·*too*·to/a
    prostitute
protectores ⓜ pl pro·tek·*to*·res *panty liners*
proteger pro·te·*kher* *protect*
protegido/a ⓜ/① pro·te·*khee*·do/a
    protected
protesta ① pro·*tes*·ta *protest*
protestar pro·tes·*tar* *protest* v
provisiones ① pl pro·vee·*syo*·nes *provisions*
próximo/a ⓜ/① *prok*·see·mo/a
    following · next
proyector ⓜ pro·yek·*tor* *projector*
prueba ① *prwe*·ba *test*
    — **de embarazo** de em·ba·*ra*·so
        pregnancy test kit
    — **de sangre** de *san*·gre *blood test*
pruebas nucleares ① pl
    prwe·bas noo·kle·*a*·res *nuclear testing*
pueblo ⓜ *pwe*·blo *village*
puente ⓜ *pwen*·te *bridge (structure)*
puerta ① *pwer*·ta *door · gate (airport, etc)*
    — **de salida** de sa·*lee*·da *departure gate*
puerto ⓜ *pwer*·to *harbour · port*
pulga ① *pool*·ga *flea*
pulmón ⓜ pool·*mon* *lung*
punto de control ⓜ *poon*·to de kon·*trol*
    checkpoint (border)
puro/a ⓜ/① *poo*·ro/a *pure*

Q

qiropráctico ⓜ kee·ro·*prak*·tee·ko
    chiropractor
qué ke *what*
quebrado/a ⓜ/① ke·*bra*·do/a *broken*
quebrar ke·*brar* *break (in general)* v
quedarse ke·*dar*·se *stay*
    — **varado** va·*ra*·do *break down (car)*
queja ① *ke*·kha *complaint*
quejarse ke·*khar*·se *complain*
quemado/a ⓜ/① ke·*ma*·do/a *burnt*
quemadura ① ke·ma·*doo*·ra *burn*
    — **de sol** de sol *sunburn*
queque ⓜ *ke*·ke *cake*
querer ke·*rer* *want*
quién kyen *who*
quincena ① keen·*se*·na *fortnight*
quiosco ⓜ *kyos*·ko *kiosk*
quiste en los ovarios ⓜ
    kees·te en los o·*va*·ryos *ovarian cyst*

R

rabia ① *ra*·bya *rabies*
racismo ⓜ ra·*sees*·mo *racism*
radiador ⓜ ra·dya·*dor* *radiator*
radio ⓜ *ra*·dyo *spoke (wheel)*
radio ① *ra*·dyo *radio*
rancio/a ⓜ/① *ran*·syo/a *stale*
rápido/a ⓜ/① *ra*·pee·do/a *fast*
raqueta ① ra·*ke*·ta *racquet*
raro/a ⓜ/① *ra*·ro/a *rare · strange · unusual*
rasuradora ① ra·soo·da·*do*·ra *razor*
rasurar ra·soo·*rar* *shave* v
rata ① *ra*·ta *rat*
ratón ⓜ ra·*ton* *mouse (animal)*
razón ① ra·*son* *reason*
realista ⓜ&① re·a·*lees*·ta *realistic*
receta ① re·*se*·ta *prescription (medical)*
recibo ⓜ re·*see*·bo *receipt*
reciclable ⓜ&① re·see·*kla*·ble *recyclable*
reciclar re·see·*klar* *recycle*
recientemente re·syen·te·*men*·te *recently*
reclamo de equipaje ⓜ
    re·*kla*·mo de e·kee·*pa*·khe *baggage claim*
recomendar re·ko·men·*dar* *recommend*
recto/a ⓜ/① *rek*·to/a *straight*
recuerdo ⓜ re·*kwer*·do *souvenir*
recursos humanos ⓜ pl
    re·*koor*·sos oo·*ma*·nos *human resources*
red ① red *net · network (phone/Internet)*
redondo/a ⓜ/① re·*don*·do/a *round*
referencia ① re·fe·*ren*·sya *reference*
reflexología ① re·flek·so·lo·*khee*·a
    reflexology
refresco ⓜ re·*fres*·ko *soft drink*
refri ⓜ re·*free* *refrigerator*
refugiado/a ⓜ/① re·foo·*khya*·do/a *refugee*
regalo ⓜ re·*ga*·lo *gift*
    — **de bodas** de *bo*·das *wedding present*
regional ⓜ&① re·khyo·*nal* *regional*
registro del carro ⓜ re·*khees*·tro del *ka*·ro
    car registration
regla ① *re*·gla *menstruation · rule*
reina ① *ray*·na *queen*
reintegro ⓜ re·een·*te*·gro *refund*
reír re·*eer* *laugh* v
relación ① re·la·*syon* *relationship*
relaciones públicas ① pl
    re·la·*syo*·nes *poo*·blee·kas *public relations*
relajarse re·la·*khar*·se *relax*
religión ① re·lee·*khyon* *religion*
religioso/a ⓜ/① re·lee·*khyo*·so/a *religious*
reliquia ① re·*lee*·kya *relic*
reloj ⓜ re·*lokh* *clock · watch*
    — **despertador** des·per·ta·*dor* *alarm clock*

remo ⓜ *re·mo rowing*
remoto/a ⓜ/ⓕ *re·mo·to/a remote*
reo/a ⓜ/ⓕ *re·o/a prisoner*
reparar re·pa·*rar repair*
repelente ⓜ re·pe·*len·te insect repellent*
repisa ⓕ re·*pee·sa shelf*
república ⓕ re·*poo·blee·ka republic*
reservación ⓕ re·ser·va·*syon*
 reservation (booking)
reservar re·ser·*var book (make a booking)*
resorte ⓜ re·*sor·te spring (coil)*
responder res·pon·*der answer* v
respuesta ⓕ res·*pwes·ta answer*
restaurante ⓜ res·tow·*ran·te restaurant*
retirado/a ⓜ/ⓕ re·tee·*ra·do/a retired*
revisar re·vee·*sar check* v
revisión ⓕ re·vee·*syon review*
revista ⓕ re·*vees·ta magazine*
revuelto/a ⓜ/ⓕ re·*vwel·to/a*
 scrambled (eggs)
rey ⓜ *ray king*
rico/a ⓜ/ⓕ *ree·ko/a rich · tasty · wealthy*
riesgo ⓜ *ryes·go risk*
riñón ⓜ ree·*nyon kidney*
río ⓜ *ree·o river*
ritmo ⓜ *reet·mo rhythm*
robado/a ⓜ/ⓕ ro·*ba·do/a stolen*
robar ro·*bar steal*
robo ⓜ *ro·bo rip-off*
rodilla ⓕ ro·*dee·ya knee*
rojo/a ⓜ/ⓕ *ro·kho/a red*
rollo ⓜ *ro·yo film (for camera)*
romántico/a ⓜ/ⓕ ro·*man·tee·ko/a*
 romantic n&a
romper rom·*per break (smash)*
ron ⓜ *ron rum*
ronda ⓕ *ron·da round (drinks)*
ropa ⓕ *ro·pa clothing · laundry*
 — de cama de *ka·ma bedding*
 — interior een·te·*ryor underwear*
rosado/a ⓜ/ⓕ ro·*sa·do/a pink*
rotonda ⓕ ro·*ton·da roundabout*
rubéola ⓕ roo·*be·o·la rubella*
rueda ⓕ *rwe·da wheel*
ruidoso/a ⓜ/ⓕ rwee·*do·so/a noisy*
ruinas ⓕ pl *rwee·nas ruins*
ruta ⓕ *roo·ta route*

S

sábado ⓜ *sa·ba·do Saturday*
sábana ⓕ *sa·ba·na sheet (bed)*
sábanas ⓕ pl *sa·ba·nas linen (sheets)*
saber sa·*ber know (something)*
sacacorchos ⓜ sa·ka·*kor·chos corkscrew*

saco de dormir ⓜ *sa·ko de dor·meer*
 sleeping bag
sal ⓕ *sal salt*
sala de espera ⓕ *sa·la de es·pe·ra*
 waiting room
salario ⓜ sa·*la·ryo salary*
saldo ⓜ *sal·do balance (account)*
salida ⓕ sa·*lee·da departure · exit*
 — de noche de *no·che night out*
salir sa·*leer go out*
 — con kon *go out with (date)*
salón de belleza ⓜ sa·*lon de be·ye·sa*
 beauty salon
salpullido ⓜ sal·poo·*yee·do nappy rash*
salsa ⓕ *sal·sa sauce*
saltar sal·*tar jump* v
salud ⓕ sa·*lood health*
sangre ⓕ *san·gre blood*
santo/a ⓜ/ⓕ *san·to/a saint*
santuario ⓜ san·too·a·*ryo shrine*
sarampión ⓜ sa·ram·*pyon measles*
sartén ⓜ sar·*ten frying pan*
sastre ⓜ *sas·tre tailor*
secar se·*kar dry (clothes, etc)* v
secarse se·*kar·se dry (oneself)* v
seco/a ⓜ/ⓕ *se·ko/a dried · dry*
secretario/a ⓜ/ⓕ se·kre·ta·*ryo/a secretary*
seda ⓕ *se·da silk*
seguir se·*geer follow*
segunda clase ⓕ se·*goon·da kla·se*
 second class
segundo ⓜ se·*goon·do second (time unit)*
segundo/a ⓜ/ⓕ se·*goon·do/a*
 second (number)
seguro ⓜ se·*goo·ro insurance*
seguro/a ⓜ/ⓕ se·*goo·ro/a safe*
semáforo ⓜ se·*ma·fo·ro traffic light*
semana ⓕ se·*ma·na week*
sencillo/a ⓜ/ⓕ sen·*see·yo/a simple*
sendero ⓜ sen·*de·ro footpath · hiking route*
 — de bicicleta de bee·see·*kle·ta bike trail*
senos ⓜ pl *se·nos breasts (body)*
sensible ⓜ&ⓕ sen·*see·ble sensible*
sensual ⓜ&ⓕ sen·*swal sensual*
sentarse sen·*tar·se sit*
sentimientos ⓜ pl seen·tee·*myen·tos*
 feelings
sentir sen·*teer feel (emotions)*
señal ⓕ se·*nyal sign*
señalar se·nya·*lar point* v
separado/a ⓜ/ⓕ se·pa·*ra·do/a separate*
septiembre ⓜ sep·*tyem·bre September*
ser ser *be (permanent)*
serio/a ⓜ/ⓕ *se·ryo/a serious*
servicio ⓜ ser·*vee·syo service · service charge*
 — militar mee·lee·*tar military service*

T

servilleta ① ser·vee·ye·ta *serviette*
sesión de ejercicios ①
  se·syon de e·kher·see·syos *workout*
sexismo ⓜ sek·sees·mo *sexism*
sexo ⓜ sek·so *sex*
  — seguro se·goo·ro *safe sex*
si see *if*
sí see *yes*
SIDA ⓜ see·da *AIDS*
siempre syem·pre *always*
silla ① see·ya *chair*
  — de comer para niños
  de ko·mer pa·ra nee·nyos *highchair*
  — de ruedas de rwe·das *wheelchair*
  — para niños pa·ra nee·nyos *child seat*
similar ⓜ&① see·mee·lar *similar*
sin seen *without*
  — espacio es·pa·syo *booked out*
  — plomo plo·mo *unleaded (petrol)*
sinagoga ① see·na·go·ga *synagogue*
sintético/a ⓜ/① seen·te·tee·ko/a *synthetic*
sobornar so·bor·nar *bribe* v
soborno ⓜ so·bor·no *bribe*
sobre so·bre *about • above • on*
sobre ⓜ so·bre *envelope*
sobredosis ① so·bre·do·sees *overdose*
socado/a ⓜ/① so·ka·do/a *tight*
socialista ⓜ&① so·sya·lees·ta *socialist* n&a
sol ⓜ sol *sun*
solamente so·la·men·te *only*
soldado sol·da·do *soldier*
soleado/a ⓜ/① so·le·a·do/a *sunny*
sólo so·lo *only*
solo/a ⓜ/① so·lo/a *alone*
soltero/a ⓜ/① sol·te·ro/a *single (person)*
sombra ① som·bra *shade • shadow*
sombrero ⓜ som·bre·ro *hat*
sombrilla ① som·bree·ya *umbrella*
sonreír son·re·eer *smile* v
sopa ① so·pa *soup*
sordo/a ⓜ/① sor·do/a *deaf*
sorpresa ① sor·pre·sa *surprise*
su soo *her • his • their • your* sg pol&pl
subtítulos ⓜ pl soob·tee·too·los *subtitles*
suburbio soo·boor·byo *suburb*
sucio/a ⓜ/① soo·syo/a *dirty*
suegra ① swe·gra *mother-in-law*
suegro ⓜ swe·gro *father-in-law*
suelo ⓜ swe·lo *floor (ground)*
sueño ⓜ swe·nyo *dream • sleep*
suerte ① swer·te *luck*
suéter ⓜ swe·ter *jumper • sweater*
suficiente soo·fee·syen·te *enough*
súper ⓜ soo·per *convenience store*
supermercado ⓜ soo·per·mer·ka·do *supermarket*

superstición ① soo·per·stee·syon *superstition*
sur ⓜ soor *south*
surf ⓜ soorf *surfing*
surfear soor·fe·ar *surf* v

T

tabaco ⓜ ta·ba·ko *tobacco*
tabaquería ① ta·ba·ke·ree·a *tobacconist*
tabla de surf ① ta·bla de soorf *surfboard*
tabla para picar ① ta·bla pa·ra pee·kar *chopping board*
tajada ① ta·kha·da *slice*
talcos ⓜ pl tal·kos *baby powder*
taller ⓜ ta·yer *workshop*
tal vez tal ves *maybe*
tamaño ⓜ ta·ma·nyo *size (general)*
también tam·byen *also • too*
tambor ⓜ tam·bor *drum (instrument)*
tampón ⓜ tam·pon *tampon*
tapón ⓜ ta·pon *plug (bath)*
tapones para los oídos ⓜ pl
  ta·po·nes pa·ra los o·ee·dos *earplugs*
tarde ① tar·de *afternoon*
tarde tar·de *late*
tarifa ① ta·ree·fa *fare*
tarjeta ① tar·khe·ta *card*
  — de crédito de kre·dee·to *credit card*
  — de memoria de me·mo·rya *memory card*
  — de teléfono de te·le·fo·no *phone card*
  — SIM seem *SIM card*
taxi ⓜ tak·see *taxi*
taza ① ta·sa *cup*
té ⓜ te *tea*
teatro ⓜ te·a·tro *theatre*
teclado ⓜ te·kla·do *keyboard*
técnica ① tek·nee·ka *technique*
tela ① te·la *fabric*
teleférico ⓜ te·le·fe·ree·ko *cable car*
teléfono ⓜ te·le·fo·no *telephone*
  — celular se·loo·lar *cell/mobile phone*
  — público poo·blee·ko *public phone*
telegrama ⓜ te·le·gra·ma *telegram*
telescopio ⓜ te·les·ko·pyo *telescope*
televisión ① te·le·vee·syon *television*
televisor ⓜ te·le·vee·sor *TV*
temperatura ① tem·pe·ra·too·ra *temperature (weather)*
templo ⓜ tem·plo *temple (building)*
temporada ① tem·po·ra·da *season*
temprano tem·pra·no *early* adv
tendedero ⓜ ten·de·de·ro *clothesline*
tenedor ⓜ te·ne·dor *fork*
tener te·ner *have*
  — sed sed *be thirsty*
  — sueño swe·nyo *be sleepy*

244

tenis ⓜ *te-nees* tennis
— **de mesa** de *me*-sa table tennis
tensión premenstrual ⓕ *ten-syon pre-mens-trwal* premenstrual tension
tercero/a ⓜ/ⓕ *ter-se-ro/a* third
terco/a ⓜ/ⓕ *ter-ko/a* stubborn
terminar *ter-mee-nar* finish v
termo ⓜ *ter-mo* hot water bottle
ternera ⓕ *ter-ne-ra* veal
terremoto ⓜ *te-re-mo-to* earthquake
terrible ⓜ&ⓕ *te-ree-ble* terrible
terrorismo ⓜ *te-ro-rees-mo* terrorism
ti tee *you* sg inf
tía ⓕ *tee-a* aunt
tibio/a ⓜ/ⓕ *tee-byo/a* warm
tiempo ⓜ *tyem-po* time • weather
— **completo** kom-*ple*-to full-time
— **parcial** par-*syal* part-time
tienda ⓕ *tyen-da* shop
— **de artículos usados** de ar-*tee*-koo-los oo-*sa*-dos secondhand shop
— **de cámaras** de *ka*-ma-ras camera shop
— **de campaña** de kam-*pa*-nya tent
— **de electrónicos** de e-lek-*tro*-nee-kos electrical store
— **de música** de *moo*-see-ka music shop
— **de recuerdos** de re-*kwer*-dos souvenir shop
— **de ropa** de *ro*-pa clothing store
— **deportiva** de-por-*tee*-va sports store
— **por departamentos** por de-par-ta-*men*-tos department store
tierno/a ⓜ/ⓕ *tyer*-no/a soft-boiled (eggs)
tierra ⓕ *tye*-ra Earth • land
tifoidea ⓕ *tee-foy*-de-a typhoid
tijeras ⓕ pl tee-*khe*-ras scissors
timbre ⓜ *teem*-bre ring (phone)
tímido/a ⓜ/ⓕ *tee*-mee-do/a shy
tío ⓜ *tee*-o uncle
típico/a ⓜ/ⓕ *tee*-pee-ko/a typical
tipo ⓜ *tee*-po type
— **de cambio** de *kam*-byo exchange rate
tiquete ⓜ tee-*ke*-te ticket
— **de abordaje** de a-bor-*da*-khe boarding pass
— **de ida** de *ee*-da one-way ticket
— **de ida y vuelta** de *ee*-da ee *vwel*-ta return ticket
— **de stand-by** de stan-*bai* stand-by ticket
título de propiedad ⓜ *tee*-too-lo de pro-*pye*-dad car owner's title
toalla sanitaria ⓕ to-a-ya sa-nee-*ta*-rya sanitary napkin
toallita ⓕ to-a-*yee*-ta wash cloth (flannel)
tobillo ⓜ to-*bee*-yo ankle
tocar to-*kar* touch • play (instrument)

todavía (no) to-da-*vee*-a (no) (not) yet
todo *to*-do everything
todo/a ⓜ/ⓕ *to*-do/a all • every
todos/as ⓜ/ⓕ pl *to*-dos/as everyone
todos los días *to*-dos los *dee*-as every day
tomar to-*mar* take • drink
— **una foto** *oo*-na *fo*-to take a photo
tono ⓜ *to*-no dial tone
tormenta ⓕ tor-*men*-ta storm
— **eléctrica** e-*lek*-tree-ka thunderstorm
torre ⓕ *to*-re tower
tos ⓕ tos cough
toser to-*ser* cough v
tostada ⓕ tos-*ta*-da toast (food)
tostador ⓜ tos-ta-*dor* toaster
tour ⓜ toor tour
— **con guía** kon *gee*-a guided tour
trabajador(a) ⓜ/ⓕ tra-ba-*kha*-dor/ tra-ba-*kha*-do-ra labourer • worker
trabajar tra-ba-*khar* work v
trabajo ⓜ tra-*ba*-kho work
— **temporal** tem-po-*ral* casual work
traducir tra-doo-*seer* translate
traductor(a) ⓜ/ⓕ tra-dook-*tor*/tra-dook-*to*-ra translator
traer tra-*er* bring
trago ⓜ *tra*-go alcoholic drink
tramposo/a ⓜ/ⓕ tram-*po*-so/a cheat
tránsito ⓜ *tran*-see-to traffic
transporte ⓜ trans-*por*-te transport
tranvía ⓕ tran-*vee*-a tram
trasero ⓜ tra-*se*-ro bottom (body)
tratar tra-*tar* try (attempt)
tren ⓜ tren train
triste ⓜ&ⓕ *trees*-te sad
trompeta ⓕ trom-*pe*-ta trumpet
trotar ⓜ tro-*tar* jogging
tu too *your* sg inf
tú too *you* sg inf
tubo ⓜ *too*-bo faucet • tap
— **interno** een-*ter*-no inner tube (tyre)
tumba ⓕ *toom*-ba grave
tumor ⓜ too-*mor* tumour
turista ⓜ&ⓕ too-*rees*-ta tourist

U

último/a ⓜ/ⓕ *ool*-tee-mo/a last (final)
ultrasonido ⓜ *ool*-tra-so-nee-do ultrasound
una vez *oo*-na ves once
uniforme ⓜ oo-nee-*for*-me uniform
universidad ⓕ oo-nee-ver-see-*dad* university
universo ⓜ oo-nee-*ver*-so universe
uno/a ⓜ/ⓕ *oo*-no/a one n&a
urgente ⓜ&ⓕ oor-*khen*-te urgent

usado/a ⓜ/ⓕ oo-*sa*-do/a *secondhand*
usted oos-*ted* *you* sg pol
ustedes oos-*te*-des *you* pl
útil ⓜ&ⓕ *oo*-teel *useful*

V

vaca ⓕ *va*-ka *cow*
vacación ⓕ va-ka-*syon* *holidays • vacation*
vacilón/vacilona ⓜ/ⓕ
  va-see-*lon*/va-see-*lo*-na *funny*
vacío/a ⓜ/ⓕ va-*see*-o/a *empty*
vacunación ⓕ va-koo-na-*syon* *vaccination*
vagina ⓕ va-*khee*-na *vagina*
validar va-lee-*dar* *validate*
valiente ⓜ&ⓕ va-*lyen*-te *brave*
valija ⓕ va-*lee*-kha *briefcase*
valioso/a ⓜ/ⓕ va-*lyo*-so/a *valuable*
valle ⓜ *va*-ye *valley*
valor ⓜ va-*lor* *value (price)*
van ⓜ *van*
varicela ⓕ va-ree-*se*-la *chicken pox*
varios/as ⓜ/ⓕ pl *va*-ryos/as *several*
vasija ⓕ va-*see*-kha *pot (ceramics)*
vaso ⓜ *va*-so *glass (drinking)*
vegetal ⓜ ve-khe-*tal* *vegetable*
vegetariano/a ⓜ/ⓕ ve-khe-ta-*rya*-no/a
  vegetarian n&a
vejiga ⓕ ve-*khee*-ga *bladder*
vela ⓕ *ve*-la *candle*
velocidad ⓕ ve-lo-see-*dad* *speed (travel)*
velocímetro ⓜ ve-lo-*see*-me-tro
  speedometer
vena ⓕ *ve*-na *vein*
vendaje ⓜ ven-*da*-khe *bandage*
vendedor de pescado ⓜ
  ven-de-*dor* de pes-*ka*-do *fishmonger*
vender ven-*der* *sell*
venenoso/a ⓜ/ⓕ ve-ne-*no*-so/a *poisonous*
venir ve-*neer* *come*
venta de periódicos ⓕ
  ven-ta de pe-*ryo*-dee-kos *newsstand*
ventana ⓕ ven-*ta*-na *window*
ventanilla ⓕ ven-ta-*nee*-ya *ticket office*
ventilador ⓜ ven-tee-la-*dor* *fan (machine)*
ver ver *look • see*
verano ⓜ ve-*ra*-no *summer*
verde ⓜ&ⓕ *ver*-de *green*
verdurería ⓕ ver-doo-re-*ree*-a *greengrocer*
vestíbulo ⓜ ves-*tee*-boo-lo *foyer*
vestido ⓜ ves-*tee*-do *dress*
  — de baño de *ba*-nyo *bathing suit*

vestidores ⓜ pl ves-tee-*do*-res
  changing room
viajar vya-*khar* *travel*
viaje ⓜ *vya*-khe *journey*
vid ⓕ *veed* *vine*
vida ⓕ *vee*-da *life*
viejo/a ⓜ/ⓕ *vye*-kho/a *old (age)*
viento ⓜ *vyen*-to *wind*
viernes ⓜ *vyer*-nes *Friday*
VIH ⓜ ve ee *a*-che *HIV*
vinagre ⓜ vee-*na*-gre *vinegar*
vino ⓜ *vee*-no *wine*
viñedo ⓜ vee-*nye*-do *vineyard*
violación ⓕ vyo-la-*syon* *rape*
violar vyo-*lar* *rape* v
violín ⓜ vee-o-*leen* *violin*
virus ⓜ *vee*-roos *virus*
visa ⓕ *vee*-sa *visa*
visita ⓕ vee-*see*-ta *visit*
vista ⓕ *vees*-ta *view*
vitaminas ⓕ pl vee-ta-*mee*-nas *vitamins*
vivir vee-*veer* *live*
volar vo-*lar* *fly* v
volcán ⓜ vol-*kan* *volcano*
volibol ⓜ vo-lee-*bol* *volleyball*
  — de playa de *pla*-ya *beach volleyball*
volumen ⓜ vo-*loo*-men *volume*
volver vol-*ver* *return*
vos vos *you* sg inf
votar vo-*tar* *vote* v
voz ⓕ vos *voice*
vuelo ⓜ *vwe*-lo *flight*
vuelto ⓜ *vwel*-to *change (coins)*

Y

y ee *and*
ya ya *already*
yo yo *I*

Z

zacate ⓜ sa-*ka*-te *grass (lawn)*
zancudo ⓜ san-*koo*-do *mosquito*
zapatería ⓕ sa-pa-te-*ree*-a *shoe shop*
zapato ⓜ sa-*pa*-to *shoe*
zodíaco ⓜ so-*dee*-a-ko *zodiac*
zoológico ⓜ so-o-*lo*-khee-ko *zoo*
zorzal ⓜ sor-*sal* *thrush (health)*

The topics covered in this book are listed below in Spanish. Show this page to your Costa Rican friends if you're having trouble understanding them.

KEY PATTERNS

When's (the next bus)?	¿A qué hora sale (el próximo bus)?	a ke o·ra sa·le (el prok·see·mo boos)
Where's (the bank)?	¿Dónde está (el banco)?	don·de es·ta (el ban·ko)
Where can I (buy a ticket)?	¿Dónde puedo (comprar un tiquete)?	don·de pwe·do (kom·prar oon tee·ke·te)
How much is (a room)?	¿Cuánto cuesta (una habitación)?	kwan·to kwes·ta (oo·na a·bee·ta·syon)
I'm looking for (a cabin).	Estoy buscando (una cabina).	es·toy boos·kan·do (oo·na ka·bee·na)
Do you have (a map)?	¿Tiene (un mapa)?	tye·ne (oon ma·pa)
Is there (a toilet)?	¿Hay (un baño)?	ai (oon ba·nyo)
I'd like (a coffee).	Quisiera (un café).	kee·sye·ra (oon ka·fe)
I'd like (to hire a car).	Quisiera (alquilar un carro).	kee·sye·ra (al·kee·lar oon ka·ro)
Can I (park here)?	¿Puedo (parquear aquí)?	pwe·do (par·ke·ar a·kee)
Could you please (help me)?	¿Podría (ayudarme), por favor?	po·dree·a (a·yoo·dar·me) por fa·vor
Do I have to (get a visa)?	¿Necesito (obtener una visa)?	ne·se·see·to (ob·te·ner oo·na vee·sa)